MEATY, BEATY, BIG & BOUNCY

THE WHO

CLASSIC **ROCK** ALBUMS
Series Editor: Clinton Heylin

MEATY, BEATY, BIG & BOUNCY

THE WHO

John Perry

SCHIRMER BOOKS
New York

Schirmer Books
1633 Broadway
New York, New York 10019

Library of Congress Catalog Number:

Printed in the United States of America

Printing number
1 2 3 4 5 6 7 8 9 10

Library of Congress Cataloging-in-Publication Data

Perry, John
    Meaty, beaty, big & bouncy : The Who / John Perry.
        p. cm. — (classic rock albums)
    Discography: p.
    ISBN 0-02-864773-4 (alk. paper)
    1. Who (Musical group). Meaty, beaty, big, and bouncy.   2. Rock music — History and ciriticism.
    I. Title.   II. Series.
    ML421.W5P47   1998
    782.42166'2—dc21
    [B]   97-50604
                                                                       CIP
                                                                       MN

For
Hilarie Dawes
&
John McCormack

CONTENTS

ACKNOWLEDGMENTS

Of those whose help was freely and generously given during the writing of this book, along with the loan of tapes, records, books, papers and memories, I'd like to thank Sue Armstrong, Dr. Gordon Atkinson, Svante Börjesson, Chris Charlesworth, Barry Fantoni, Mick Green, Ed Hanel, Clinton Heylin, Klem Jäger, Max Ker-Seymer, Andrew Neil, Brian O'Reilly, Richard Weiner, Paul Williams—and everyone else whose name escapes me.

For technical assistance, Richard Carlin, Greg Jackmann, Dave Petrucci, Andrew Muir, and the staff of the British Newspaper Library at Colindale.

Trade advertisements courtesy of the Ed Hanel collection.

Writing about the noisiest band on the planet seemed more fun in quiet places—

> *Clunton and Clunbury,*
> *Clungunford and Clun,*
> *Are the quietest places*
> *Under the sun.*

Trad. arr. Housman

—So my thanks to all those who provided me with the peace to write in their houses—Nicholas of Ludlow, Ada of Leintwardine, Larry & Manice Stabbins of Helford, Lord Parmoor of Frieth, the Cistercian Brothers of Caldey Island, E.H. of Porlock. Finally, thanks to Maria, without whose constant and heroic assistance the book might well have been completed considerably sooner.

INTRODUCTION

"... THE GREATEST OF WHO ALBUMS."

Peter Townshend

***Rolling Stone* Magazine (No. 97, Dec. 9, 1971)**

Meaty, Beaty, Big & Bouncy is a collection of singles recorded in the 1960s, which form the basis of The Who's reputation in England. From 1965 to '67 the band's status grew with each successive single, and their live shows—widely, indisputably, and accurately acknowledged as the most exciting gigs in town—further enhanced their standing. In America, however, the singles hardly sold at all with the result that when they *finally* made the breakthrough at the end of the decade, many among their audience knew nothing about the band's roots. Among The Who's growing American audience since 1969, an entire section was completely unaware of the existence of Life before *Tommy.* While many English fans had always regarded the singles as The Who's major work, an album was needed to familiarize U.S. fans with the band's previous existence as makers of two- and three-minute pop songs—marvels of succinct excitement that represent The Who's essence. That album was *Meaty, Beaty, Big & Bouncy.*

The first eight singles, all top-10 hits, selected themselves. Then, in addition to the "genuine" (Who-approved) singles, there are two tracks which owe their existence as 45s to the 1966 contractual battle between the band and their first producer, Shel Talmy—a man who believed he turned groups who were "nothing" into stars. These tracks are "A Legal Matter" and "The Kids Are Alright." At Townshend's instigation the John Entwistle song "Boris the Spider" was included since, according to Townshend, only "politics or my own shaky vanity"[1] had precluded its release as a single. A notably different version of "I'm a Boy" was selected—an entirely separate take—softer, featuring more harmonies; and different edits of "Magic Bus" appeared (longer on the LP, shorter on the CD). Some of the earlier singles appeared in different versions in specific territories—"Substitute," for instance, will sound very different to American listeners familiar with the Atco single, and "Anyway, Anyhow, Anywhere" may sound different to French EP buyers—but generally the versions included are the standard issue.

The fourteen songs span a period from January 1965 to May 1970, years in which popular music, and the scene it reflected, changed beyond recognition. When The Who's first single was recorded, The Beatles were still loveable mop-tops and the pop era was at its height. By the time "I Can See for Miles" came out, little more than two and a half years later, "pop" had become "rock" and ceased to be seen as simple entertainment. Entering the political arena, it became the rallying cry of a postwar generation eager to confront their elders and betters, parents and governments—or so they said at the time; many were equally eager just to crash about making a lot of noise, attract the maximum media attention, and screw anything that moved. As above, so below.

In the years before pop music split into factions, success was measured in 7" singles. Artists were expected to come up with a minimum of three hits per annum—or make way for someone else. As Keith Richards observed, "Singles were all important then. You put yourself on the line every three months and therefore it had better be distinctive, or else. . ." Singles *were* the market. Looking back at the mid-'60s in his own 1971 *Rolling Stone* review of *Meaty, Beaty, Big & Bouncy*, Pete Townshend wrote, "In England albums were what you got for Christmas, singles were what you bought for prestige. We believed only in singles. In the Top 10 records and pirate radio. We, I repeat, believed only in singles."

The relationship between singles and albums was perceived entirely differently by English and American record companies. In England, singles were singles; items in their own right, and very rarely included on LPs, but in America it was more or less taken for granted that albums were built around—and often named after—successful singles. While

English companies tended to release U.S. albums unchanged, American companies generally tinkered with track lists to include hit singles, frequently altering the titles of albums. Thus the English LP *A Quick One* became *Happy Jack* in the U.S. (with the addition of the "Happy Jack" single). This wasn't a peculiarity of Decca, but rather was standard practice. No major U.S. company would have done any differently. It's on this account that so much confusion reigned when English and American fans tried to discuss their favorite Stones or Beatles albums from the years prior to 1967. Most of the works bore completely different titles and contained totally different tracks; not just confusing the fans but interfering too with that sense of a group's development which comes with proper, chronological release.

It's helpful when listening to *Meaty, Beaty, Big & Bouncy* to know the true order in which the "genuine," Who-approved singles were released, because it's by no means clear from the album. These songs, which represent the heart of The Who, form an unbroken row of hits between 1965 and 1967 running:

"I Can't Explain"
"Anyway, Anyhow, Anywhere"
"My Generation"
"Substitute"
"I'm a Boy"
"Happy Jack"
"Pictures of Lily"
"I Can See for Miles"

at which point Pete exhausted his first batch of songs, or, not to put too fine a point on it, ran out of suitable material. Though he reckoned to have demoed as many as "300 songs" in this period, none (of those that we know) quite fit into the style of the eight above. Pete was looking to write material of more "substance," and as *The Who Sell Out* album (which includes "I Can See for Miles") demonstrates, he was writing more ballads based around an increasingly complicated acoustic guitar style and his newly learned piano skills.

It was a wonderful run, in its day equaled only by The Beatles and The Stones, though at the time, Pete—characteristically—seems to have expressed doubts about its worth: "I can't write this shit anymore. I'd got to come up with something of substance." Subsequently, of course it became the one area of his work he afforded unconditional recognition, as time, distance, and historical context revealed its quality. The central irony of Townshend's career is that his most durable work emerges from the most "disposable" period of the band's history. Throughout, it's clear that he writes best when unencumbered by notions of "High Art." With his sights firmly set on "Low Pop" he produced timeless work; when he consciously set out to achieve something momentous, the work was often overwrought.

*   *   *

Changes are easy to catalog in retrospect, but notoriously difficult to define while they're happening. Demographics show 1968 as the year in which albums first outsold singles, but the shift had been coming for a while. As anyone who was alive and even half awake at the time will confirm, the key year was 1966. Month by month, as new songs came over the radio, the music gathered strength. Where it was leading, and ultimately what it meant, was anybody's guess, but it felt good at the time—and it sounded wonderful. Albums like The Beatles' *Revolver* and Bob Dylan's *Blonde on Blonde* signalled a qualitative change. Something new was afoot, and somewhere between the moment when The Beatles exchanged live performance for the calm of the studio, and the passing of The Marine Offences Broadcasting Act which drove pirate radio from the seas in August 1967, the broad musical consensus fragmented forever.

At first the scene divided into two distinct markets: broadly, a pop audience who continued to buy singles, and an increasingly self-conscious youth culture who bought albums. With The Beatles gone from the live stage, and Bob Dylan's neck broken, the torch passed to The Stones and The Who. The Stones, like Dylan, were far too cool and too self-possessed to ever commit themselves to any agenda other than their own, but Pete Townshend was a natural. Pete was a believer. He was passionate about things, even if the objects of his passion changed rapidly, or were mutually contradictory. As a young man he believed in Youth, and as a rock 'n' roller he believed in Rock itself, investing the latter with an almost mystical power, capable of transforming lives and transcending the mundane; it had worked for him, and onstage he put his all into attempting to make it work for his audience.

For all Townshend's identification with new underground youth culture, The Who's roots lay firmly in the first camp—the pop singles market—a fact amply demonstrated by comparing their album output with that of their peers. Both the quantity and the nature of The Who's pre-*Tommy* albums indicate that all their real instincts were toward the single—you only have to look at the figures. During the '60s, the Rolling Stones issued eight LPs and The Beatles ten. Admittedly, both groups had a couple of years' head start on The Who. Nonetheless, in their first five years, The Who managed to record only four albums: *My Generation, A Quick One, The Who Sell Out,* and *Tommy.* Of these, the second was effectively a wheeze to collect publishing advances for all four band members, and only made album length by cobbling together a bunch of Townshend snippets into the ten-minute title track. It's an album that many Who fans regard with great affection, but there's no covering up the fact that it contains some pretty moderate filler material. The third, *The Who Sell Out,* dates from late '67, the heyday of concept albums; but, at the time of its release, it was widely misunderstood, seeming to fall between two stools. Was it psychedelic? Was it pop? What was it? Today it is clearly work of the highest quality, yet at the time of its release I remember taking a couple of listens, then buying *Axis Bold as Love* instead. The tracks—on side one at least—are linked by parody commercials and jingles from the recently silenced pirate station Radio London. Townshend's friend, the writer Nik Cohn, noted

> What this album should've been is a total ad-explosion, incredibly fast, loud, brash and vulgar, stuffed full of the wildest jingles, insane commercials . . . a holocaust, an utter wipe-out, a monster rotor whirl of everything that pop and advertising really are.

That's fine, but when you go back and listen to the record, it's surprisingly pastoral. Featuring some of Pete's best acoustic guitar playing, lovely melodies, and lots of harmonies, the nature of the songs sits ill with the concept of a brash, pop-art explosion. With the exception of the first LP, the Shel Talmy–produced *My Generation,* which is a magnificent debut album packed with catchy Townshend songs—and paradoxically the closest in conception to a modern album—The Who's pre-*Tommy* albums were decidedly makeshift.

Tommy itself needs little explanation here. Recorded cheaply on 8 track—all the band could afford—it represented something of a last-ditch gamble, a make-or-break effort to keep the band alive. As Townshend put it, "We were going down the drain . . . after making corny singles like 'Dogs' and 'Magic Bus' . . . making *Tommy* united the group." The gamble succeeded; *Tommy*'s commercial success not only ensured The Who's survival, it brought prosperity on a scale previously unimagined. The album marks the point at which the band evolved from a singles group into the million-selling album outfit who conquered America and in the process created a blueprint for the modern touring rock band.

Not that American success came easily. Despite regular U.S. touring from 1967 onward, Who records wouldn't sell. "Happy Jack" reached number 24; "I Can See For Miles" would be their first—and only—single to enter the U.S. Top 10, and yet all around them lesser English acts were cleaning up. Once the mass American market warmed to The Beatles it couldn't get enough of the English. The Stones and then The Kinks broke through, as did a mixture of well-marketed but essentially second-rate bands and washed-up cabaret "artistes." Records that could hardly be given away in England topped the American charts. Recycled music-hall favorites like "I'm Henry the VIIIth I Am" were swept from the shops by U.S. fans eager for anything English, while more "difficult" acts like The Who were lost in the shuffle. As successive English bands—Cream, Hendrix, Led Zeppelin—appeared and promptly overtook them, The Who must've despaired. Eventually, in 1969, *Tommy* turned the tide, and The Who received their due, but thereafter they were a different band from the one which recorded the series of singles—neither pop nor underground— that constitute *Meaty, Beaty, Big & Bouncy*. Townshend once said, "I got a much bigger buzz out of 'I'm a Boy' reaching No. 1 than out of all the success of *Tommy*." Sadly, the "number 1" was not on the recognized chart, but the point is the same: it's the singles that represent The Who in their purest form.

Because Who 45s had appeared on a variety of labels on both sides of the Atlantic, the (roughly) concurrent U.K. and U.S. release in late 1971 of a complete singles compilation—*Meaty, Beaty, Big & Bouncy*— filled an obvious gap in the market. By the end of '71, The Who were nearing their ninth year as a performing band, and their audience now included a generation that wasn't around when the singles were original- ly issued; nearly seven years had passed since the release of "I Can't Explain." There had been two previous attempts to round up The Who's scattered output, but both were flawed: *Direct Hits* on Track (U.K.) was only a partial collection and (U.S.) Decca's *Magic Bus: The Who on Tour* bordered on fraud.

In common with most of The Who's 1968 output, *Direct Hits* (November 1968) was a stopgap, something to put in the shops when it became obvious that the long-awaited *Tommy* album wasn't going to be ready for Christmas. In England, everybody already knew the singles, so the need for a complete collection was less pressing. Unable to use The Who's earliest work—the Shel Talmy productions "I Can't Explain," "Anyway, Anyhow, Anywhere," and "My Generation"—Track assembled all the singles they controlled ("Substitute" onward) and added material from the *Ready Steady Who* EP.

In America, the position was simpler, because fewer labels were involved. The Who had originally been signed to Talmy, who leased his productions to the American company Decca (the English releases then appeared on one of Decca's U.K. outlets, Brunswick). After the break with Talmy, Chris Stamp placed one single with Atlantic, but then re-signed the band directly to Decca. Thus in September 1968, Decca controlled the U.S. rights to almost all The Who's material. They were now free to assem- ble a complete, accurate, chronological collection of the singles. Perhaps so much freedom overawed them, because when The Who proposed just such an album, putatively titled *The Who's Greatest Flops,* Decca demurred. Instead, they eventually assembled a curious collection of B- sides, album cuts, and EP tracks, often using rejected mixes and low-gen- eration masters, even managing to duplicate a track they'd already issued on the previous *Happy Jack* album and omitting half a dozen of the most powerful songs available to them. "Run, Run, Run" is a good song, but you wouldn't play it to a new Who listener who didn't know "I Can't Explain"; likewise "Doctor, Doctor" is fun, but nowhere near as much fun as "I'm a Boy."

It was a commonly held view among English musicians that, as a record company, Decca made pretty good radar. As if to confirm this opin- ion, the American company compounded the mess they'd made of track selection by naming their new collection *Magic Bus: The Who on Tour*, hoping presumably, that it might pass as a live album if nobody looked too closely. Were these people mad? Their faculties impaired? Tragic as such handicaps are at a personal level, they should not be allowed to affect the workings of a "major label," even one whose sole intention is to satisfy the shareholders by cashing in quickly on a trend before the Next Big Thing comes along. Even then, one wonders why a *badly* assembled record should be thought more likely to cash in than a well-assembled one? *Magic Bus: The Who on Tour* was roasted by the hipper elements of the American press—Paul Williams in *The San Francisco Express Times* and Greil Marcus in *Rolling Stone*—and Townshend himself called it a "bummer."

Three years later *Meaty, Beaty, Big & Bouncy* was released, and at last the correct material was compiled—though that's about as much as you can say in the record's favor. Few would contend that *Meaty, Beaty, Big & Bouncy* is a beautiful object to look at. Little effort seems to have been wasted in finding original masters or sequencing the tracks, and the packaging is refreshingly free of unsightly information.

In the end though, the power of the songs cuts through all the vagaries of presentation. Given the relationship between stage and studio, it's one more paradox among many, that a group which was unquestionably the most exciting live band of their—and possibly of any—era, are best represented by their singles. As Paul Williams writes in his book *Rock and Roll—The 100 Best Singles*, of "I Can't Explain":

> There's a sweet ringing quality to the guitar and wondrous snap to the drums that isn't quite the same on LP or even CD, you have to hear the Who on seven-inch vinyl to really appreciate them fully. . . . Worth going to an antique store and buying a phonograph just for the experience.

MEATY, BEATY, BIG & BOUNCY

THE WHO

THE OBSERVER

MARCH 20

THE WHO

The prediction business (2)

I CAN'T EXPLAIN

"HERE'S A GROUP I LIKE IMMENSELY —AND THEIR ABSORBING SOUND MATCHES THE GIMMICK NAME, THE WHO. 'I CAN'T EXPLAIN' IS A POUNDING SHUFFLE-SHAKER WITH SURF-LIKE COUNTER-HARMONIES BEHIND THE MAIN LYRIC. IT'S INSIDIOUS AND INSISTENT—A SORT OF BLEND OF MERSEY BEAT AND SURFING!"

—**Derek Johnson**, *New Musical Express*, **January 15, 1965**

The Who's first record, "I Can't Explain," was released in mid-January 1965 onto a U.K. chart containing The Beatles' "I Feel Fine," Georgie Fame's "Yeh-Yeh," and The Moody Blues' "Go Now." Merseybeat was still going strong, and pop music was just hanging on to its innocence. A totting up of chart positions by the *NME* showed the previous year's most successful artists to have been, in order: The Beatles, The Bachelors (an Irish vocal trio), The Rolling Stones, Jim Reeves, and Roy Orbison—three tenors, two groups, one counter-tenor, and an easy-listening country and western baritone. Every week, record companies bought advertising space alongside the *NME* chart; the January 15, 1965, issue has a sidebar listing sixteen new single releases from Decca Records. If you scan down the list, past Paul Anka and The Kingston Trio, past Peter, Paul and Mary, and James Brown's "Have Mercy," past the names of artists who mean nothing today, right at the foot of the column, second-to-the-last,

1

you find the bare details of a first single by a new band: "I Can't Explain"—The Who—Brunswick 05926.

Clocking in at a few seconds over two minutes, that first single sounds, as much today as it did in 1965, like a declaration of intent. With hindsight we know it's the start of a glorious run of singles, but the whole enterprise could easily have been stillborn; The Who becoming just one more amid the hundreds of groups who came and went, and "I Can't Explain" an isolated, intriguing one-off. The record's progress was jerky and its eventual number 8 position on the U.K. chart was only achieved through skillful hustling and exceptional good luck. As Nik Cohn noted, "if 'I Can't Explain' had flopped, the entire Who crusade would very likely have collapsed before it had even got properly started."

Most artists need several attempts to define their sound—The Stones, for instance, didn't really hit their stride until their third single, "Not Fade Away"—but from the opening notes of "I Can't Explain," The Who are *there*. All the characteristic elements and musical relationships are in place: ringing 12-string Rickenbacker guitar, heavily attacked and full of overtones; aggressive vocals sweetened by an engaging melody and background harmonies; an unprecedented drum battery, played as though nobody had ever told the drummer he wasn't the lead instrument; the entire sound tied up tight with cool, precise bass playing—just listen to Entwistle's entry, a slide up to the opening E.

Few groups set out their stall so concisely on a first record. There had of course been prior sessions by the band's earlier incarnations as The Detours and The High Numbers; Townshend's earliest completed composition, "It Was You," was recorded by The (pre-Keith Moon) Detours at a home studio belonging to a friend of Pete's father but never released, though the song was subsequently covered by The Fourmost and The Naturals. More substantially, The High Numbers recorded several numbers for Fontana in June 1964 from which "I'm the Face" and "Zoot Suit" were released (though only 1,000 copies were pressed, which gives a clue as to the extent of Fontana's commitment). Neither are Townshend songs, but speedy knockoffs by the band's acting manager, Pete Meaden—novelty-single "mod" lyrics thrown on top of a Slim Harpo tune. Pete Townshend once described prolonged exposure to the record as likely to "banish Who mystique for ever." The trail really begins with their first release as The Who, "I Can't Explain," the song which Pete says "came out of the top of my head when I was eighteen and a half."

The musicians who went into Pye Studios[1] at Marble Arch to record "I Can't Explain" were all extremely young men: Entwistle was twenty, Roger and Pete were nineteen, and Keith was seventeen[2]. Though their influence would be recognized in time as comparable to that of The Beatles and The Stones, they belonged to a different generation—at nineteen, age differences of a couple of years mean a lot. The Who members were born between 1944 and 1947, only a few years later than The Stones and The Beatles (who were mostly born between 1939-43) but in pop terms they were a new, younger generation. Pete, for instance, was a major Stones fan. While all three groups looked to American blues, James Brown, and Tamla-Motown, The Who—spectators rather than participants in the first wave of the beat boom—also looked to their English counterparts. This distinction, so apparent in the early years, faded with time and success until they came to be seen as completing the English Trinity. From wildly different perspectives, both Christopher Booker in *The Neophiliacs* and Nik Cohn in *Pop From the Beginning*, agreed that The Who represented the end of an era. As Booker looked up, "a last meteor flashed across the sky," while to Cohn they were "the last great fling of Superpop." Both descriptions are apt; The Who were the last of the Great Sixties bands to emerge from a less self-conscious age of pop, but they were also forerunners of a more self-referential form, rock. Essentially, they made a synthesis of English pop as it stood at mid-decade—and then trashed it.

*   *   *

From 1964 until the mid-'70s, The Who were managed by a duo every bit as mutable and mercurial as themselves. Kit Lambert and Chris Stamp met each other knocking round the edges of the English film industry. Coming from opposite ends of the class spectrum, they must initially have seemed an unlikely pair in a country where every aspect of life is permeated by class (never more so than during the "classless" '60s) but they quickly became adept at playing off each other in a manner that exploited the advantages of both backgrounds. Lambert was a typical product of his class, a privately educated upper-middle-class gentleman who had attended Lancing and Trinity College, Oxford; Stamp (Plaistow Grammar School), from the East End of London, was the son of a Thames tugboatman, an archetypal tough, working-class kid. Both were bright, quick-witted, and sharp-tongued, and in Nik Cohn's phrase "shared a taste for hard flashy living."

Helpfully, in a culture as essentially dynastic as England's, both men had interesting family connections. Kit's father, Constant Lambert, was a noted composer and conductor, who at the age of twenty-one had been commissioned by dance impressario Sergei Diaghilev to write for the *Ballets Russes*. But for an early death at the age of forty-six (the same age that Kit reached) he would almost certainly today be as celebrated a composer as Michael Tippett, Benjamin Britten, or Kit's godfather, William Walton. Chris's brother, Terence Stamp, was already a successful film actor and a key figure in the iconography of "Swinging London." He and Julie Christie (another archetypal '60s London face) are immortalized in Ray Davies's lovely ballad "Waterloo Sunset": "Terry meets Julie, Waterloo station, every Friday night . . ."

Deciding there might be money to be made by putting together a short film about a Beat group, the pair noted groups, dates, and venues from posters and drove all over town attending gigs and checking out talent. Kit told Tony Palmer, "I used to drive around looking for pubs and clubs with the largest number of motor scooters outside." If you travel northwest from The Who's adopted home of Shepherds Bush, through Acton where Pete, John, and Roger attended grammar school, past Wembley where Keith grew up, you reach the outer suburb of Harrow and Wealdstone. Just where the road-bridge crosses the tracks stands The Railway Tavern, known in 1964 as The Railway Hotel, a thriving venue for live music. It was here that Kit Lambert found his band:

> I paid my few shillings and went into the back. On a stage made entirely of beer crates . . . were The High Numbers, ugly in the extreme. Roger with his teeth crossed at the front, moving from foot to foot like a zombie. John immobile, looking like a stationary blob. Townshend like a lanky beanpole. Behind them Keith Moon sitting on a bicycle saddle, with his ridiculous eyes in his round moon face, bashing away for dear life, sending them all up and

Miming "I Can't Explain" on *Ready, Steady, Go!* **Early 1965.**
COURTESY MICHAEL OCHS ARCHIVES/VENICE, CA

I CAN'T EXPLAIN

ogling the audience. They were all quarrelling among themselves between numbers. Yet there was an evil excitement about it all and instantly I knew they could become world superstars.

A short film was all well and good (and some 16mm footage was eventually shot at The Railway), but Lambert and Stamp swiftly saw greater opportunities in managing the band. At the time of Lambert's arrival, however, the group had already signed a contract of dubious validity with a local businessman, Helmut Gorden—a man whose total ignorance of the music business in no way impeded his dream of becoming a second Brian Epstein. More financial backer than manager, he allowed responsibility for the group's musical and visual direction to devolve to an altogether different type—an experienced though eccentric freelance publicist named Pete Meaden—who was currently 'resting' after a spell doing Stones promo for Andrew Loog Oldham. Though technically only a temporary employee, Meaden immediately saw the new band as a vehicle for his own obsessive vision of "Mod," and set to work transforming them. It was Meaden who introduced the Mod terminology, clothing, and dances. He wrote Mod lyrics to go with the Mod name he chose for the group (The High Numbers), and arranged a residency at *the* Mod venue: Ronan O'Rahilly's Scene Club in Soho (where the DJ was another seminal figure in English rock, Guy Stevens). Meaden also introduced another essential Mod commodity—one whose effect on The Who would be felt long after the clothes and dance steps had been dispensed with—amphetamine.

Meaden was a serious pillhead. The initial speed cults had grown up in and around the towns where the pills were made—Drinamyl was manufactured under license by Smith Kline & French at Welwyn, just north of London, where they disappeared off the production line in such numbers it's a miracle the company survived—but spread to all the major cities as skinny little Mods everywhere found doctors ready to treat their "appetite disorders." By the mid-'60s, pharmaceutical speed was so widely available, under so many brand names and in such volume, consumers scarcely thought of it as illegal. Mick Green of The Pirates recalls the band's driver stopping to ask a policeman directions to a gig, as Green sat in the car's front seat counting out one hundred blues from a plastic bag; the policeman's only comment was "Would that be the stage-door you wanted, sir?"

Dex, Bombers, and Blues, all could be bought at sixpence a time, though the pills most favored by Mods were undoubtedly Drinamyl, better known as "purple hearts." A pale, powder-blue, uncoated, scored tablet in the shape of an irregular ellipse, wider at one end of the score mark than at the other, thus looking shield-shaped (which is where the idea of a "purple heart" came in), Drinamyl contained 5mg dexamphetamine sulphate and 32mg amylobarbitone (a downer), which gave a smoother ride, better traction, and also acted as an accelerant. The two drugs had quite a different half-life (the barbiturate lasting probably twelve to fourteen hours and the amphetamine four to six hours), so the barbiturate eased the rough edges when the dexedrine wore off. Licensed for use in cases of mild temporary neurosis, the recommended dose was one tablet two or three times daily; Mods typically consumed anywhere up to one hundred or more in the course of a long weekend. Townshend speaks of playing The Marquee, a twenty-five minute tube ride from his parents' home beside Ealing Common, a perfect time span to drop his purple hearts, hop on the underground, and arrive at the gig as the speed began to cut in, "just about ready to play . . ."

Meaden's was an essentially mystical attitude toward Mod, whose outward and visible form was the Purple Heart. His devotion was such that, like certain Pentecostal prophets, he tended on occasions to foam at the mouth and speak in tongues. As Stamp talked and Meaden foamed, Lambert realized that even with their minimal show-biz experience, they'd have little difficulty taking over the band. Gorden's contract was worthless (his signatories were all minors), and despite all Meaden's enthusiasm—which must have been considerable in its day—he had no consistent plan of action. As an established Wardour Street hustler, Meaden probably recognized that he was outclassed by Lambert, and ceded control to the newcomers without much of a struggle. A payoff of £500 was suggested and, of course, never paid.

The group had been through several names in the preceding years. The Detours begat The Who, who became The High Numbers; then on Lambert's advice, The High Numbers reverted to The Who. As Pete Townshend explained, "We chose the name The Who a little bit prematurely, it was too weird for a long time. So we used The High Numbers for a bit and then the time came when we were able to use The Who again."

Though the band's potential was clear enough onstage, the industry A&R men proved as short sighted and recalcitrant as ever. Unable to find a record company willing to sign the band directly, Lambert approached an independent producer, Shel Talmy, an American resident in London who'd recently had hits with The Kinks. Talmy listened to a demo of "I Can't Explain," came to see The Who, and liked them. Pete readily acknowledges "I Can't Explain"'s debt to "You Really Got Me"—"it can't be beat for straightforward Kink copying"—but has never, as far as I know, indicated whether it was written as an intentional appeal to Talmy's vanity (though given the band's ambition and their level of frustration, I think the inference is clear enough). Talmy went for it, and the inexperienced team of Lambert and Stamp signed the band to a production deal with him. Initially this seemed an excellent move, but too little attention was paid to the details of the contract, resulting in a conflict which remains unresolved at the time of writing.

Tightened up by steady gigging, confident that "I Can't Explain" was a strong, potentially commercial song, and excited to be working with a proven hit-maker in Talmy, The Who went into the studio to record their debut single in December 1964, augmented by a male vocal trio, The Ivy League (Townshend likes to credit "The Beverley Sisters"), and Jimmy Page on second guitar. In 1964 there weren't very many capable rock 'n' roll guitarists in England—within three years the country would be crawling with them—but at this stage there were few players with any studio experience who could rock. Between them, Big Jim Sullivan, Mick Green from the Pirates, and James Page Esq. (plus two or three others whose names mean little outside of studio circles) had the session market cornered. Countless singles from this period feature Big Jim or another of the gang; never in the field of recording have so many groups owed so much to so few.

It was standard practice for producers to keep reliable musicians on call when taking unknown groups into the studio. Dummers were thought to be especially suspect, as Ringo Starr discovered on the "Love Me Do" session, when George Martin replaced him with Andy White. Talmy retained the great Clem Cattini (ex-Johnny Kidd and The Pirates), a drummer of whom it was said, "he swung like a donkey's dick." Talmy would've had Moon off the kit in a second given the chance, and legend has it that Jimmy Page was slotted to play the solo on "I Can't Explain" until, in a shrewd piece of Realpolitik, Townshend refused to allow him to use his 12-string Rickenbacker, the only instrument that would produce those ringing overtones. Score one to Townshend. The fixture ended in a draw though, since the B-side called for a fuzz-box. Such devices were virtually unknown in England at this date, but Page owned one (possibly a Gibson Maestro; more probably an early construction by Roger Mayer, a guitar-playing technical wizard, who after attending the same school as Jeff Beck and Page, worked on classified defence equipment at the Admiralty—a job which provided a first-rate source of Class-A electronic components). It was Mayer who made (or modified) Hendrix's fuzz-boxes, wah wah pedals, octavia, and other equipment.

As another authentic survivor from this era, Ritchie Blackmore has pointed out (with considerable glee), Page makes a point of talking about his session work—always including the early Kinks and Who singles—but does little to discourage the notion that it's his lead guitar heard on classic sides like "You Really Got Me" and "I Can't Explain." Not so; they are the work of Dave Davies and Pete Townshend, respectively. In both cases, Page plays lead on the B-side, but the A-sides only feature him playing second guitar, doubling the rhythm guitar part to fatten out the sound, in a primitive form of ADT (automatic double-tracking).

Of this disputed solo, Townshend is self-deprecatory, saying, "It was so simple even I could play it." He's underselling himself. While it's not a complex piece technically, it's full of well-placed rhythmic ideas—listen to the way the staccato licks are played off against the handclaps—and nicely suited to the requirements of the song. Moreover, it sounds like a solo that came easily; it flows in a way which suggests a first take rather than hours of labored overdubbing. Simple it may be, but not, as Pete implies, simplistic.

The song actually has two guitar breaks. The first, only four bars long, is so short that Pete probably doesn't count it as a solo at all, though it's among the crispest, most compact breaks he's ever recorded. It comes after the second chorus, fifty-nine seconds into the song, and is gone again before you fully have time to catch it. The main solo is twice as long and comes right at the end. Though they're played on a 12-string Rickenbacker, there's nothing of Roger McGuinn's trademark "Byrds" sound, nor of the distinctive tone that George Harrison gets from the same instrument on "Day Tripper" and many other Beatles records. Less folky than McGuinn and with far more attack than Harrison, even at this formative stage Pete's tone was all his own.

Both breaks are sharp, but the first is something special, possessing real rhythmic imagination. Whether the result of skill or just a happy accident doesn't really matter: it's perfect. No wonder Page fancies it. A model of tight, understated chord-based soloing, much more to do with rhythm and nuance than with melody, it has a quality that one doesn't always associate with The Who: it's extremely danceable.

A remarkably confident solo for a debut record, with a lot of ideas crammed into just four bars, it sounds quite unlike anything anyone else was playing at the time. Though we can sense Pete's taste for Mick Green and Steve Cropper's spare guitar sounds, neither would have taken the solo quite like this. There's something oblique about the angle at which Pete comes in, owing more perhaps to his banjo-playing background than to any notion of blues guitar. Townshend told Steve Rosen:

> I played banjo for about two years and . . . a lot of that was a layover from the fact that I developed a lot of those techniques when I was learning the banjo. Those trad banjo solos always used a lot of syncopation and I took that over to guitar. I got a mandolin banjo and then I got a small tenor banjo and I started to play in a trad group and that was when I first worked with John Entwistle. He played trumpet and I played banjo in this small Dixieland band.

Here, and for several years after, Townshend was alone, working territory quite alien to the mainstream English players. Parallels are hard to find; it's not until Richard Thompson begins to find his own voice early in the '70s that anyone else gets close. Compare Thompson's first solo on "Hokey-Pokey." Though Thompson ranges further melodically, there's something of the same syncopation about his phrasing. (His taste for The Who is demonstrated by his choice of "Substitute" as the opening number for his solo shows in the late '80s.)

Pete's ideas from the first solo are restated and extended in the second, though the perfect poise of the first break is never quite equaled, and at the end he abandons the attempt altogether, inserting a stock run in the style Joe Moretti used on the original Johnny Kidd and The Pirates' "Shakin' All Over." Before that, the morse-like phrasing reappears, expanded into eleven staccato hits in triplet time against the handclaps (1'36" to 1'39"). In this case the notes are played, although Pete often created this sort of sound using the pickup selector. It's a simple enough idea. Most guitars with two or more pickups (the exception being Fenders) have a separate volume control for each pickup. Turn one full on and the other full off, then rapidly toggle the selector switch—thereby switching abruptly between top volume and silence. Strike a chord and hold it, toggle to and fro, and you have an effect which sounds like morse code. This rapidly became a Townshend trademark, used on "Anyway, Anyhow, Anywhere" and "My Generation." Pete explains:

> I'm still a very crude player and on a recording session one of the nice things is I can drink half a bottle of brandy and spend a couple of hours experimenting. Often the best things I do are accidents, complete accidents. I just go for it and see what happens. If I play a safe guitar solo, if I set out to do something safe, I can't pull it off. Because I haven't actually got any formal approach to it.

*　*　*

On release, "I Can't Explain" entered the bottom of the top 50, eventually reaching the mid-20s before starting to fade. Pirate radio played the disc, but reception was limited mainly to London and the southeast; what the record needed was national exposure. Sales were falling and the record looked to have had its day, when two television appearances helped resurrect it: ITV's *Ready, Steady, Go!* and the BBC's *Top of the Pops.*

Of the two, *RSG* was altogether the hipper proposition. Recorded at studios in Kingsway (home turf for The Who), it featured a sharp London audience, and even sharper directors in Michael Lindsay-Hogg and Mike Mansfield. Predicated not so much on the charts as on the tastes of its staff, producer Vicki Wickham always booked the best of the English acts—Stones, Animals, Dusty, Kinks, The Jimi Hendrix Experience—and made a point of including as many American R&B acts as possible— James Brown, Ike and Tina Turner, and specials where the whole program was turned over to visiting troupes like The Otis Redding Show or The Tamla-Motown package tour. *Top of the Pops* was entertaining, but *RSG* was the show you rushed home from school to catch. As "I Can't Explain" started to drop down the chart, Lambert and Stamp invited the *RSG* crew down to see the band play The Marquee; *RSG* reciprocated by inviting the band to appear on their January 29th show. When the filming took place, Lambert packed the audience with Who fans to ensure the band a noisy reception. The record reappeared in the top 50.

Broadcast live, originally from a converted church in Manchester, BBC's *Top of the Pops* was an entirely different type of show. Built around a simple, mainstream top-10 format, it was the single most important music show on television because of its large viewing figures and broad demographic base. What it lacked in kudos it made up for in clout: it sold a lot of records. A single exposure on *TOTP* could make a record, and for over four decades it has remained the prime target for pluggers and record company marketing men. The Who scraped onto the show—much less their natural habitat than *RSG*—filling the "Tip for the Top" slot when another group canceled at short notice. The relative sales power of the two shows is demonstrated by what happened next: "I Can't Explain" promptly bashed back up the chart to number 8.

Brunswick didn't organize much in the way of a media campaign. With so many singles released every week, only the surest bets would have received full promotion. Press response was generally good, though not all the music papers noticed the single. The *NME*'s review of January 15 is rather spoiled when the normally perceptive Derek Johnson continues, "Even better is the B-side, 'Bald Headed Woman,' which starts with a bluesy solo vocal with gospel-type chanting." Oh dear.

Subtlety doesn't appear to have been a major component of Talmy's business plan. If you turn over his production of "I Can't Explain" and then examine the first Kinks LP, you will discover the same song—"Bald Headed Woman"—on both records. What is a song as slight as this doing on two debut records in the same year? The answer, of course, is simple: it's one of those traditional numbers which can be credited as "Trad. Arr. x," where x = anybody who wants to pocket the composing royalties without the tiresome business of actually writing a song. Placed on the B-side of a single, it would earn its composer the same amount of money as the writer of the A-side. Who is the listed composer? The label credits "S. Talmy."

As "I Can't Explain" revived on the charts, the music press started to show more interest, running features and interviews on the band. Below a picture in which all four members are wrongly identified, an *NME* feature of April 23, 1965, was captioned "ONE HIT BUT FOUR FILMS!," a reference to the Lambert/Stamp adventures in celluloid. The piece informs us that the "bass player John Entwistle prefers to be known as John Browne." Entwistle appears to have had as many surnames as he has basses; in The High Numbers, he'd already experimented with the surname Allison. The boys apparently do not see themselves as all-round entertainers. An already doomy-sounding Pete discusses longevity: "I figure we will probably have about a year as a popular group." Then, a moment of high melodrama: "We want to make the most of the time we have. . . . We would also like to get to number 1." Though they lasted considerably longer than a year, they never did get that number 1.

On April 2, The Who made their first BBC radio appearance, as guests on the long-running *Joe Loss Show*. The veteran bandleader, with featured vocalist Ross McManus (father of Elvis Costello) broadcast live every Friday at lunchtime from the Playhouse Theatre on Northumberland Avenue, in the center of London's West End, with guest acts appearing in between his own numbers. Starting with a show in Wembley on April 1, The Who played a total of twenty-six gigs that month, including a Saturday night double, first doing an evening show at Borehamwood Lynx Club, to the north of London, then dashing over to Tottenham to play an All Nite Rave at Club Noreik, one of the original midnight-to-six clubs where they'd have been lucky to finish up much before 4 A.M. (Noreik and clubs like it were vital staging posts in the ritual Mod weekend, which consisted of taking enough pills to stay up from the time *Ready, Steady, Go!* began on Friday evening until Sunday night.) The majority of these shows were in the south of England, within reasonable distance of London, but it was still a frantically busy month—one television appearance, one radio show, and twenty-six gigs—into which studio time had to be fitted to record a follow-up single.

Based on the success of the "I Can't Explain" single, in mid-April Kit was able to sign the Who to the Malcolm Rose Agency, and immediately they started playing further afield. Their May itinerary shows them in Leicester, Nottingham, and Newcastle, before crossing the border for three dates in Scotland. In between the gigs, came television appearances in Manchester, Southampton, Birmingham, Bristol, and the celebrated May 21 live *Ready, Steady, Go!* performance of "Anyway, Anyhow, Anywhere" (featured in *The Kids Are Alright*). A May 24 daytime studio session for BBC radio—recording "Just You and Me," "Good Lovin'," "Anyway, Anyhow, Anywhere," and "Leaving Here" for the *Saturday Club* program—was followed by an evening gig in Reading and a Marquee show the next night. With further dates at Worthing, Windsor, Buxton, and Sheffield, the group had only five days off in the whole month. A direct result of such intensive live work is the tight ensemble playing you hear on the next single, "Anyway, Anyhow, Anywhere."

As a debut, "I Can't Explain" proved a complete success. Commercially, it pitched an unknown group straight in the top 10 (the record remained a total of 6 weeks on the chart) and sold a respectable number of copies. Artistically, there's no discussion. The record sounds as good today as it did in January 1965. As Chris Charlesworth writes in his *Complete Guide*: "Perhaps the best testament to 'Explain' is that throughout their career, The Who have almost always opened their live shows with this song, occasionally alternating it with 'Substitute.' Is there any other band in the entire history of rock whose first single was so good, so timeless that they could continue to use it as their opening number on stage for 25 years?"

ANYWAY, ANYHOW, ANYWHERE

"WE WERE TRYING TO ACHIEVE THE SOUND WHICH WE GET ON THE STAGE AT PRESENT. 'CAN'T EXPLAIN' WAS WRITTEN AS A COMMERCIAL NUMBER TO INTRODUCE US TO THE CHARTS AND WE JUST WANNA GET RID OF ALL THAT . . ."

—Pete Townshend speaking to Brian Matthew on *BBC Light Programme*.

Most musicians would have been delighted with a single as tough and focused as "I Can't Explain." To reach number 8 with a debut single, especially after the record initially appeared to have foundered, is a considerable achievement. Yet even at this early stage, Townshend was already expressing disgust with himself and displeasure with the process. Dismissing "I Can't Explain" as a Kinks copy and a blatant piece of commercialism, he set out to write a follow-up that would deliver on vinyl all the excitement and aggression that The Who were generating nightly on stage. He came up with "Anyway, Anyhow, Anywhere."

Released on May 21, 1965, a couple of days after Pete's twentieth birthday, the record charted in mid-June, without any of the erratic stops and starts that marked the progress of "I Can't Explain," and peaked at number 10, spending a total of six weeks on the chart. With a top-10 record behind them, the follow-up single was automatically granted a degree of status by television shows like *Top of the Pops*. Closer to home,

"Anyway, Anyhow, Anywhere"'s cause was helped considerably when *Ready, Steady, Go!* adopted the song as an unofficial theme. Every Friday as the opening titles rolled and the weekend formally began, the record went out straight to its ideal target audience.

The band was no longer a complete unknown to the media. "I Can't Explain" had been reviewed by some of the music papers, but "Anyway, Anyhow, Anywhere" was noticed by them all—even those whom the record obviously baffled. *Melody Maker* is the longest established of the English music papers, and as befits so venerable an organ, generally the most conservative. Other magazines went in and out of favor, but *MM* was always read, not least because its classified section was never seriously challenged as the place where musicians advertised and looked for work. Not always the quickest to detect new trends, once it did get hold of an idea, it clung on tenaciously. Having, for instance, discovered that "BEAT-LEMANIA" made a good headline, it ran variants—"Now it's Kinks-Mania," "America gripped by Hermits-Mania," etc.—for a good decade.

One institution in its pages was the "Blind Date" column, where celebrity reviewers were asked to comment on a selection of the week's new releases without being told the identity of the artist. A good idea, which occasionally succeeded in eliciting some genuinely indiscreet comments, the system was on the whole rigged, at least in part so that friends could comment on friends. Although The Who were beginning to be accepted, they were not yet insiders, and the celebrity in whose lap the second Who single landed (*MM*, May 29, 1965) was a ballad singer by the name of Jackie Trent. Forgotten now as a singing star, she went on to become the reigning Queen of Soap Opera themes. With husband Tony Hatch, she cowrote hits like Petula Clark's "Don't Sleep in the Subway" and "I Couldn't Live Without Your Love"—top-10 on both sides of the Atlantic—but the couple's finest hour came when, having written for several U.K. soaps, they moved down under and created the theme for the Australian soap *Neighbours*, whose countless daily showings on channels all around the world must generate performance income beyond the dreams of Croesus. Speaking from her "Forest Hill mansion," Jackie listened to "Anyway, Anyhow, Anywhere," then opined:

> Sounds very like Jan and Dean. I don't like it at all, it sounds as
> though everybody is trying to solo at once. I don't know whether it's

Keith Moon (right) confers with Terence Stamp at a New York press party, March 1967.
Photo © Don Paulsen

supposed to be an instrumental or a vocal. Who is it? The Who? I'm surprised. They probably do it very well onstage . . . but it's bound to be an enormous hit.

Ms. Trent obviously had ears. Despite her distaste, or perhaps because of it, she hits a number of nails squarely on the head: surf music; monstrous disregard for etiquette, "everybody soloing at once" rather than dutifully supporting the vocalist for 2'33" and only letting rip for seven seconds on the fade, as was customary at the time. Querying "instrumental or a vocal," she identified the song's odd asymmetry; though it wasn't "an enormous hit," the record sold respectably enough to give The Who their second top-10 single.

Over at the *NME*, Derek Johnson could also hear the sound of surf:

After a startling guitar opening The Who's "Anyway, Anyhow, Anywhere" bursts into a wild raver, with just about every conceivable gimmick—the leader [!] semi-shouts in r-and-b style, with high-pitched surf-like chanting support, rumbling piano, cymbal crashes and violent tempo changes. Midway through it erupts into a veritable explosion of sound. You can't ignore this disc—it commands attention and should do well.

Alongside the reviews came interviews and general features. In the July 23 *NME*, the band was featured in the "Lifelines" series, a sort of questionnaire involving the usual nonsense about favorite foods and colors. While Pete reworked his favorite themes, wishing to "die young" and "be a recognised composer," the best joke is Keith's favorite food, which he lists as "French Blues." (In the same series, Keith Richards's culinary taste had run more to opium.) Moon also mentioned his ambition to "smash 100 drumkits."

Things were also stirring on the business front. Half of the *NME*'s May 28 cover was an advertisement announcing the formation of "The Independent Recording Company of Arthur Howes and Shel Talmy: The Orbit Universal Music Company." Among his new productions Talmy listed "Set Me Free" by The Kinks and "Anyway, Anyhow, Anywhere" by The Who, while a sidebar boasted "Artists Shel Talmy has recorded with include The Kinks, The Bachelors, The Who, Chad & Jeremy, Goldie & The Gingerbreads," etc. The full list contains a certain amount of padding, but the Kinks hits were solid enough, and with The Who starting to look decidedly promising, Talmy appears to have been planning an Empire. With The Who under contract directly to him, there's every reason to suppose he'd have pulled it off, too, if they'd been the sort of outfit happy to stand still for it. They weren't, of course—any more than Lambert and Stamp were the sort of managers likely to cede control of their only act to an ambitious freelance producer. The Who's short infatuation with Talmy was over.

*   *   *

Structurally, "Anyway, Anyhow, Anywhere" is *highly* eccentric, owing nothing to any formal notion of the way songs are ordered. The 8- or 16-bar conventions of verse/chorus/bridge songwriting simply don't apply. In fact, the closer one looks, the odder it gets. Clocking in at a snappy 2'40," the song consists of a number of irregular length segments which act—suitably, given the stated aim "to achieve the sound which we get on the stage"—as showcases for Roger and Pete. Everything about the structure is irregular. The verse is three time longer than the chorus, yet verse and chorus combined are less than half as long as the bridge.

Like most rock 'n' roll, the song is in common time (4/4), yet Pete's opening guitar fanfare is in 6/4. There are six beats on each chord, bashed out in what was already becoming a recognizable trademark, a rapidly strummed flourish with fierce attack—what flamenco guitarists call *rasgueado*. As on the first single, the initial sound you hear is Pete. The song opens with a solo guitar figure, then the whole band enters; an arrangement found throughout The Who's work. Everything suggests it's an instinctive part of the way Pete hears things, rather than a conscious device; exactly half of the songs on *MBBB* start with unaccompanied guitar.

The chorus is so short—just the title, plus the words "I choose"—it might as well be part of the verse. It's more catchphrase than chorus. The actual verses—"I can go anywhere," etc.—are an unusual six bars long, though the first verse is broken for Roger to sing the opening line *a cappella*. (A brief, unaccompanied vocal passage introducing the first verse is another very common feature of Townshend's songs; listen to "The Kids Are Alright" or "I Can't Explain"). "Anyway, Anyhow, Anywhere"'s combined verse/chorus segments act as "sweeteners," conventional melodic pop counterweights to the long bridge sections—"Nothin' gets in my way"—where Roger stretches out in R&B style, and to the "noise break" in which Pete runs through his repertoire of guitar stunts.

Unlike some horrible, contrived piece of early-'70s "progressive rock," similarly designed to showcase (alleged) virtuosity, the structural oddities don't intrude on the song. It's perfectly possible to be familiar with the song and never notice the asymmetry. The distinction is between songs written to impress by their cleverness and songs that just happen to be a bit skewed. "Anyway, Anyhow, Anywhere" flows; the segments never sound isolated, not least because session pianist Nicky Hopkins is always there, smoothing the path, covering the potentially awkward moments, and vamping through the transitions. Hopkins is superb: melodic, inventive, yet unobtrusive. He reads the song perfectly, emerging in the gaps to play barrelhouse trills in the right hand, then sitting out and just adding weight, presence, and attack to the guitar chords, with octaves in the left hand. As Pete commented, "On the first album we had Nicky Hopkins in there with us. There's something about recording that diminishes the power of a three-man group and you have to have the extra harmonic element."

Hopkins provides that extra element, although a guitar-led three piece with The Who's attack—at times more like three lead instruments than a trio—is *far* from natural piano territory, and there are any number of ways a keyboard could mess up a song like "Anyway, Anyhow, Anywhere"—texturally, tonally, or melodically. With very little to go on in the way of an arrangement, Hopkins negotiates the oddities of the structure without a slip. If he bothered to write anything down, his notation for this session must have been a riot.

Once the backing track was put down, the smash-and-grab sound of the live show was reproduced. Pete's Fender amps were set up on the studio floor, and a number of passes were recorded while he recreated the violent electric storm of the live experience: Cadenza for Rickenbacker and Pickup Selector! Certainly a "noise break" was an ambitious inclusion by prevailing standards. Mainstream pop music in 1965 tended to be sparing in its use of dissonance and atonality. Quickest off the mark was U.S. Decca, who took one listen and returned the tape on the grounds that it must be faulty. Surely, they reasoned, nobody could *intend* a record to sound like that?

The noise break opens with a single introductory powerchord, timed to produce that most characteristic of all Townshend effects: the moment of calm before the storm; a brief equilibrium before all hell breaks loose. Typically, the single chord would be held for four or even eight beats—drawing out the tension—before the onslaught began. As choreography, his *slow* windmill was the precise visual analogue; the same sense of power about to uncoil, expressed as gesture. After the opening chord—and some gallant vamping from Hopkins—the first effect you hear is the selector-switch morse code,[1] punctuated by string glissandi and Fender amp vibrato. String glissandi, or plectrum scrape, is produced by running the edge of the pick down a string—usually the bottom string—starting high up on the neck and scraping right down to the nut. The sound reproduces the effects of dive-bombing or of jets passing low overhead according to how it is timed.

A standard effect on most Fender amps of the period was vibrato. Intended by the makers to add a pleasing light "wobble"—especially nice on waltzes—it can be heard in conventional mode all over West Coast albums of the period. For example, Neil Young's *Everybody Knows This Is Nowhere* is dripping with the stuff.)

The effect had two controls: one to govern the speed or rate of the "wobble," the other to control how deeply the effect bit into the chord. By turning both the controls up full, it's possible to produce a sound that resembles a chord being physically shaken to pieces at high speed. Along with feedback, these same three ingredients—powerchord, vibrato, and string-gliss—constitute the chaotic solo on the following single, "My Generation," although as individual components they can be heard with far greater clarity on the studio take of "Man With Money," available on the extended *A Quick One* CD.[2] This flat-out use of amp vibrato—and some slightly more controlled derivatives, including setting the wobble-rate to match the tempo of the track—quickly entered common usage and were employed to great effect on contemporary records like The Smoke's "My Friend Jack," a good, early-1967 piece of pop-psychedelia, similar in mood to much of The Creation's output (another Talmy-produced group).

Townshend links these various effects with feedback. The wonderful thing about feedback is how much it will cover. Accidental wrong notes, little slips in pitching, or errors in timing? Slam some feedback across the top and your problem is gone. Dull moment on the track? Nothing much happening? Jam the neck of the guitar firmly into the speaker cabinet, flick the volume up full, and there you are. You don't even have to move if you don't feel like it; whether you stand still or chuck the guitar around the studio, something exciting is bound to happen. It is surprising that more musicians don't make greater use of it. True, there's a certain skill to controlling the range and register, but on the whole you can count on a note feeding back either as itself (the fundamental), at an octave above the fundamental, or an octave plus a fifth above—nothing which might strain the brain of even the most addled guitarist. Properly controlled, feedback renders an entire range of devices redundant, if you know how to control a guitar and work the space in front of the speaker cabinets. The whole weight of manufacturing industry—makers of pedals and processors—however, have a vested interest in leading people to believe that buying their product is preferable to learning to control one guitar, one amp, and a lead.

There are many refinements, but the concept of feedback is simple enough. When the sound coming out of the speakers is loud enough to start the guitar strings vibrating of their own accord, a loop is created. Instead of fading in the normal manner, a note sustains indefinitely. The guitarist no longer needs to *pick* strings; the instrument will howl by itself. The most effective method of control is to move about the area immediately in front of the loudspeakers, where surprisingly small adjustments of distance and angle will cause radically different notes to feed back. Pete Townshend explains:

> First I got into feedback. Jim Marshall started manufacturing amplifiers and somebody in his store came up with the idea of building a 4 x 12 cabinet for bass. And John Entwistle bought one and I looked at it and suddenly John Entwistle doubled in volume. And so I bought one and then later on I bought another one and I stacked it on top of the other one. I was using a Rickenbacker at the time and because the pickup was right in line with the speakers I was instantly troubled by feedback. But I really used to like to hear the sound in my ears. And I started to get quite interested in feedback, but I was very frustrated at first. So I just started getting into feedback and expressed myself physically.

Arguments about who "invented" feedback still break out periodically, though the issue is unlikely ever to be resolved because nobody really invented it. Essentially an accidental noise, it's no different from the electronic squawk that occurs when a microphone is brought too close to a loudspeaker. The dispute concerns which guitar player discovered that *controlled* feedback could be used as a device to sustain notes and create new effects. Among the principal contenders are Townshend, Jeff Beck, Dave Davies—and even John Lennon. Pete told *Sound International* magazine:

> To tell the truth, Dave Davies, Jeff [Beck] and me have got a tacit agreement that we will all squabble 'til the day we die that we invented it. I think possibly the truth is that it was happening in a lot of places at once. As the level went up, as people started to use bigger amps, and we were all still using semi-acoustic instruments, it started to happen quite naturally. I think the word was around the street and then Lennon used it at the beginning of that record "I Feel Fine" and then it became quite common and a lot of people started to use it.

Shel Talmy likes to claim "Anyway, Anyhow, Anywhere" as featuring the first recorded use of feedback, though the short burst which opens The Beatles' "I Feel Fine" is generally recognized as the first true instance. Stuck on the front end of the record it makes an interesting intro, but it's used more as ornament than structure. Nonetheless, it does seem to have been a planned part, rather than the "electronic accident" the press reported.

Though the exact chronology is hard to verify at this distance, I asked Mick Green about feedback and also if he remembered The Detours, High Numbers, or Who opening up for Johnny Kidd and The Pirates:

> For *Kidd*? Naaah . . . don't remember them. First I heard was when Terry Goldberg from The Mark Leeman Five took me down to see them play. This was a long time ago, mind. Terry told me I ought to come and see a new band who *he* thought were sensational. Plus, he said, they were all tone deaf and liked The Pirates! So I went

along, Townshend was smashing his guitar around, and his use of feedback—which was something I'd been trying to *avoid*—really knocked me out. Talking to them backstage afterwards, I remember they were all very excited 'cos they were just off to support The Beatles on some package tour. Not long after, I noticed feedback on the front of "I Feel Fine."

The High Numbers *did* support The Beatles, just once, on a national package tour in August '64, way down on the bill below acts like Dusty Springfield, Eden Kane, Lulu, and P. J. Proby. When the show played the Blackpool Opera House, the bill was topped by The Beatles. That was August 16, 1964. "I Feel Fine" was recorded on October 18, 1964. According to the Abbey Road recording sheets, eight instrumental takes were recorded, as Mark Lewisohn notes in his Beatles sessionography: "Right from take one The Beatles had perfected the curious sounding introduction, a Lennon idea of which he was especially proud."

On "Anyway, Anyhow, Anywhere" and "My Generation," Townshend made more *integral* use of feedback than anyone (with the possible exception of Jeff Beck) until Jimi Hendrix's appearance. Hendrix made the most *musical* use of feedback—listen to "Drifting" on *The Cry of Love* album for a sublime, melodic example—whereas Townshend produced some of the most aggressive noises ever made by an electric guitar. Pete recalls:

> And it just led to when, one day, I was banging my guitar around making noises and I banged it on this ceiling in this club and the neck broke off, because Rickenbackers are made out of cardboard. And everybody started to laugh and they went, "Hah, that'll teach you to be flash." So I thought what I was going to do, and I had no other recourse but to make it look like I had meant to do it. So I smashed this guitar and jumped all over the bits and then picked up the 12-string and carried on as though nothing had happened. And the next day the place was packed. It turned into another form of expression for me: it was a gimmick of course. It is a very physical thing to be a stand up guitar player—and the way you feel and the way you move and the way you move your body is a big part of it; the fact that to sometimes pull a string up by the right amount you have to give it some momentum, so that you can't

play sitting down in the way you can play standing up. And so for me all that macho stuff became an expression. I've never had any respect really for the guitar. I've respected guitar players of course and I understand their need for a good instrument but for years and years I didn't care what the guitar was like.

*　　*　　*

Pete says the lyrics of "Anyway, Anyhow, Anywhere" were inspired by the dexterity of Charlie Parker's improvisations, "Yardbird" or plain "Bird" being easily the *freest* improviser in twentieth-century jazz. The speed of his thinking and the flow of his ideas are stunning. Generally, even the most accomplished musicians eventually reach the limits of their imagination or of their technique. Listening to an improvisation, there inevitably comes a point when you hear them bump into—or make circuits to avoid—the perimeter wall of their own abilities. At this point they either take refuge in stock phrases, or start repeating themselves. The smarter player knows to stop before reaching this point; though, sadly, the ability to know when to shut up is one of popular music's more undervalued commodities.

These limits don't seem to apply to Parker. His technical mastery of the saxophone was so thorough, nothing intrudes. He sounds free to play, develop, invert, harmonize, reverse, ignore, parody, or expand the melody in any direction he chooses. As Pete acknowledged in 1980:

> When I was younger I used to listen a hell of a lot to Charlie Parker and Charlie Christian and when you hear him play the way he did and as fast as he did without any flash at all, pure expression of the soul literally flying above everything else, why even bother to attempt to come close? I've never liked flash playing really. I don't mind flash *performers,* I don't mind showmanship, or guitar circus. I used to listen to people like Kenny Burrell and Wes Montgomery. And Chet Atkins—clear thinkers.

His remarks anticipate many of the developments of that decade, in which an entire school of extremely flashy guitarists flourished, players with massive facility but nothing to say. The single-minded pursuit of technique as an end in itself misses the point. Parker's technique is superlative, but it's *transparent,* simply a means to deliver his ideas.

Pete may have started with bebop in mind, but Roger's reading of the song brings it closer to R&B. His delivery shifts the aesthetic to something more concrete; a declaration of personal prowess. Townshend called the result "cocky." Sitting up all night with Pete before the "Anyway, Anyhow, Anywhere" session, Daltrey amended the lyrics to suit what he felt should be his stage persona—though, according to Stamp, it was more a process of Pete feeding lines to Roger for approval. The final version is a perfectly respectable piece of R&B strutting, even if Pete had something more abstract in mind when he conceived the lyrics.

Roger's composing credit on "Anyway, Anyhow, Anywhere" has more to do with band politics and the evolving leadership struggle than any songwriting partnership. Circumstance and personality inevitably brought Daltrey and Townshend into conflict over control and direction of the band. Through the Detours/High Numbers days, Roger had been leader. Choosing which material to cover, handling much of the practical detail, his common sense, enthusiasm, and assertiveness probably kept the band running day to day—although his habit of punching the other musicians can't have been popular. Ambitious, single-minded, and physically the toughest member, he seems to have taken it for granted that hitting people was the simplest method of settling disputes in his band. Once Lambert and Stamp arrived and The Who started to make successful records, the internal dynamics changed. Roger still saw himself as leader, but Kit Lambert recognized Townshend's songwriting as the key to the band's development. Daltrey resented the special attention Lambert gave to Townshend and was ambivalent about Kit's undisguised campness, correctly identifying the Lambert/Townshend axis as a threat to his dominance.

Roger wanted The Who to stay with R&B (the same position Brian Jones held as the emerging Jagger/Richards songwriting partnership increasingly undermined *his* status within The Stones) and obviously found it unbearable when the spotlight shifted toward his junior. Essentially, The Who faced the same problem as The Stones—namely, what to do when an original, non-composing "leader" is eclipsed by younger band members who can write—though their respective responses were very different. In the Stones' camp the machinations over the succession were protracted and far more painful, a pattern of shifting allegiances and relationships with Keith and Anita Pallenberg (jointly and severally) at their center; The Who simply had a good punch-up.

The violence peaked at this critical point where control of the band was slipping away from Roger, in the summer of 1965. "Anyway, Anyhow, Anywhere" charted in June and the crucial incident occurred during a short Scandinavian tour in September. On the 25th the band played a double-header, first doing a typical thirty-minute spot on a package show at the Folkets Hus in Elsinore, then driving the short distance back to Copenhagen to play the KB Hallen, where they were supported by a Swedish group called The Namelosers. Going onstage for the second time that day at around 9 P.M., they played their usual set to a crowd of about six hundred. After The Who's performance, Tommy Hansson, lead singer in the Namelosers, was in the dressing room when Roger Daltrey burst in, looking furious. Rushing over to where Keith Moon sat cooling off, Daltrey hauled him from the chair, lifted him up by the collar, and head-butted the unfortunate drummer straight across the bridge of his nose. As the blood started to flow, Roger complained that Keith had been "playing the drums too loudly."

Whether it's a separate incident, or the same story told from an different perspective, Richard Barnes describes a similar scene on the same tour, with Moon being beaten unconscious, though Barnes places it *between* the two sets (meaning Moon had to go out and play again, once he came round). Daltrey, exasperated by the other three members' consumption of speed, recalled: "The band was playing fucking terrible. I had a big flare-up with Moon . . . got hold of his box of pills and tipped them down the loo. And that's when he started, like a fool, trying to beat me up."

In response, Daltrey beat Moon so severely that the other three members decided that Daltrey must leave the band, once they'd returned to England and completed their current commitments. The Who split up every other week, but this one seems to have been deadly serious. Quite apart from the degree of violence, there are ethical considerations: one does not interfere with another man's stash—least of all abroad, where replacements may be hard to obtain. As Townshend said, "He was thrown out really for interfering with our lifestyles. Keith, John and I really liked drugs and he didn't."

For a month or two, there was talk of various recombinations and replacement singers, with the story reaching MM, whose November 20 edition bore the headline "The Who Split Mystery." Lambert and Stamp considered whether The Who might function as a three-piece with Townshend singing lead. Pete's high, rather vulnerable vocals are often more poignant than Daltrey's—listen to "A Legal Matter," or the demo versions of "So Sad About Us" and "Happy Jack"[3]— but his voice wasn't especially robust, and he'd have had a job sustaining an entire set night after night. Stamp comments: "We really fancied Pete's voice . . . he didn't have a strong voice but it was an interesting voice. Eventually Kit and I talked the other three into taking Roger back—which is ironic as things worked out later."

With the other three members resolutely opposed, Daltrey was reinstated, subject to an ultimatum to stop the violence or leave the band. From that point on he became, in his own words, "peaceful Perce." Townshend, on the whole sparing in his praise of Daltrey, called it an "amazing transformation," one which "took a lot of guts." Certainly Townshend could afford to be generous, because from this point he emerged as undisputed leader, spokesman, and writer of the group's material. The balance of power between Townshend and Daltrey remained in roughly this form for the remainder of the decade.

This sense of barely contained violence that surrounded The Who's early live performances made them very exciting to see. It wasn't just a stage act, but a primary expression of the relationships within the group. If the violence was at times ritual (though in my experience, I was too engrossed in the instant to analyze distinctions between ritual and reality), there was no mistaking the physical undercurrent that propelled each performance; its potential crackled in the air like static. Musically and visually, their attack was so immediate, and it came at you on such a broad front. As a schoolboy at the time, I was reminded of that mixture of apprehension and anticipation immediately before a playground fight. NME's Roy Carr described a friend of his being physically sick during a 1966 performance on Morecambe Pier, and Al Kooper writes of "his heart beating three times its normal speed." Irish Jack noted, "you had to take a step back." There's nothing fanciful about any of these descriptions; nobody's dealing in metaphor. In the early days, before the smash-up ending came to be expected, the stuff was uncut. Fuelled by hard drinking and a steady diet of speed, exacerbated by the regular and often awkward travel that touring in those days involved, an atmosphere built up which Pete described as "'orrible."

Speaking years later, Roger Daltrey, trying to identify what lies at the center of The Who's charm, said, "we've never ever captured it properly on record, and the stage always accommodated it." This is not really surprising. All great ensemble performances draw their strength from the interaction between the players, and the most natural performers will automatically commit themselves in front of an audience, take risks, and go for broke. The studio simply doesn't inspire that type of performance.

"Anyway, Anyhow, Anywhere" was a brave attempt to crossbreed a plain pop song with The Who's live act, though for all the talk of "achieving the onstage sound," it is in fact a *pure* studio record, dependent on piano and the overdubbed second guitar to hang together. Played live it seems to have proved unpredictable (as some numbers do), the transitions between sections sometimes sounding awkward and exposed, without the additional instrumentation. The *RSG* performance captured on "The Kids Are Alright" is magnificent, while a take for BBC radio, recorded three days later, is pretty good considering the depredations of nervous BBC engineers—"mind my dials!"—and the gang of old ladies who habitually knitted in the front row of the Playhouse Theatre.

Nonetheless, the song's hybrid nature and patchy structure is probably the reason it disappeared so rapidly and so completely from the band's live set. While the other singles (bar "I Can See for Miles") stayed in the set for decades, "Anyway, Anyhow, Anywhere" lasted only a few months. Released in May '65, we know it was performed at the 5th National Blues and Jazz Festival at Richmond in August, and on the Danish tour in September, but was probably dropped thereafter. Certainly from 1966 on, it was hardly if ever played again. I can find no occasion where The Who played it, though Pete performed it once in 1993, during his *Psychoderelict* solo tour.

Today, "Anyway, Anyhow, Anywhere" seems the most distant of Who singles; possibly the least remembered, and certainly the least fully realized of the singles up to "Miles." Though it has considerable clout in its own right, it's really a stepping-stone, marking the first appearance of ideas that will reappear both better proportioned and more fully integrated into the next single, "My Generation."

MY GENERATION

"THE WHO ARE THE MOST EXCITING THING AROUND."

—**Paul McCartney, 1965**

"THE ONLY YOUNG GROUP DOING SOMETHING NEW BOTH MUSICALLY AND VISUALLY."

—**Brian Jones, 1965**

If "I Can't Explain" and "AAA" created Who fans among one section of the record-buying public, "My Generation," the band's third single of 1965 and the final record of their chart apprenticeship, brought them to the attention of a wider audience, exactly as was intended. This was something of a coup for Lambert, Stamp, and Townshend, a nicely calculated piece of media tickling. It's a great record but an even greater publicity stunt. Suddenly The Who went from being one, albeit the most promising, of a mass of beat groups to spokesmen, stuttering on behalf of an entire generation.

Youth was once again becoming news. At a time when the "generation gap" had recently been rediscovered, Townshend's best-known couplet, "Things they do look awful cold/Hope I die before I get old," proved irresistible, not only to pop writers and social commentators but to every journalist, documentary maker, and writer in need of an easy hook on which to hang a story. Demonstrating once more that the most resonant lyrics often emerge spontaneously, Pete later said:

I wrote the lines of "My Generation" without thinking, hurrying them—scribbling on a piece of paper in the back of a car. For years I've had to live by them, waiting for the day when someone says, "I thought you said you hoped you'd die when you got old. Well, now you are old. What now?" Of course, most people are too polite to say that sort of thing to a dying pop star. I say it often to myself.

Over the years Townshend has adopted various attitudes toward this, the best-known of his songs. Frequently asked how it feels to have done your best work at twenty, his ambivalence is understandable. Though by his own admission the song was an intentional attempt to write

Op Art/Pop Art. Publicity shot, late 1965.
Courtesy Michael Ochs Archives/Venice, CA

a topical anthem exploiting current affairs, its subject matter was much in the minds of young people at the time.

There *was* a gulf between generations, much wider in 1965 than those born subsequently might imagine (the shift in social attitudes between 1945 and 1965 far outstrips the changes between 1965 and 1995). The twenty years that followed the Second World War saw almost every corner of English life dominated by the generation who had won it. While their self-confidence is understandable (and there must have been a considerable number who were happy simply to be left alive), by 1965 the sense of stasis, safety, and smugness had grown unbearable. Now, as the children of the war reached the age of majority, the automatic supremacy of the previous generation was challenged for the first time, an event that some sections of society found exceedingly traumatic. The young people of 1965 were more mobile, better paid, had fewer inhibitions, and thanks to the pill (first licensed for use in the USA in May 1960, and one year later in Britain) enjoyed a freer sexuality than any comparable generation in history. Once their potential spending power was identified by industry, the contest was all but over.

A combination of economic and social factors—among them, minimal unemployment and easy credit—made it a good time for the bright and the self-confident. Young entrepreneurs could launch a venture, no matter how ludicrous, with little feeling of serious risk. At worst, if the whole thing went belly-up, one lost a few quid and had to start again. If things got *really* desperate, then one could always get a job, for a while. This was exactly how Lambert and Stamp operated. First they formed a limited company which they named New Action. Stamp dashed off periodically to earn wages, working as an assistant director on film sets, and as things settled (as much as they ever would in an organization involving Lambert), Kit kept things afloat with multiple bank loans, scammed on the back of a "good" Belgravia address. Even so, a stream of court orders and visiting bailiffs seem to have been consistent features of the company's early years.

Early in 1965, Lambert moved New Action's office to Eaton Place in Belgravia, a prosperous part of Southwest London lying between Harrods and the gardens of Buckingham Palace. Once a rather grand residential area, now home to various embassies and consulates, it carried an air of solid respectability. A good address, said Kit, improved their credit rating—and credit was a vital line to an outfit whose outgoings so greatly exceeded their earnings. The combination of Kit's unmistakably officer-class diction and headed writing paper was enough to extract impressive looking checkbooks from several collecting banks, who would have been more likely to bolt their doors if they'd known their funds' true destination. The entire enterprise was extremely shaky. Daltrey later estimated that after one year, the debt stood at £60,000. Whatever the true figure (and Kit had been brushing up the boys' interview technique; the Lambert Doctrine exhorted "always talk up the numbers and, if in doubt, change the subject"), there's no doubt that the organization was profoundly in debt. While Lambert and Stamp concentrated on promoting The Who's name and image, they had constantly to juggle a spiralling debt incurred by the Townshend/Moon equipment-wrecking habit. Yet where a more pedantic management might have attempted to curb the destruction, they encouraged it, recognizing, either by instinct, reason, or from simply having no choice, that The Who's only way out of debt lay in more rather than less chaos.

Even as he pondered this paradox, Lambert was teaching his boys to order *premier cru* vintages. Having identified Townshend's writing as the key asset, Kit began preparing him (and Keith Moon) for stardom. Pete said:

> He was an old-fashioned manager, giving me advice, taking me out to dinner and generally filling in any cultural gaps in my education. . . . Kit's grooming started with etiquette . . . up to the end of his life, Keith was still ordering the vintage of Dom Perignon that Kit had said was the best . . . but with me it was more a sense of pushing me forward.

Inevitably one notices that Lambert settled on the two most sortable members of the band. As the two men grew closer, Pete moved into Kit's flat for several months while Chris Stamp was off on one of his jaunts, either promoting the band or working on a film set. The ambience—rent boys at breakfast, introduced as hard-luck cases who'd happened to need putting up for the night—can't have been entirely to Pete's taste, but whatever the nuances of the relationship, it clearly marks the point at which Pete changes from being one of the boys to the central figure in the band.

*　*　*

Since art school, Pete had been messing around with tape recorders, initially bouncing tracks between two mono machines. Richard Barnes remembers him improvising a metronome from a piece of card attached to a record turntable (presumably this only offered three tempos—33, 45, and 78 rpms—though a lugubrious funeral march option may have been available at 16 rpm). By the time he came to demo "My Generation," Pete was operating on more orthodox equipment; a pair of Vortexion tape recorders which Kit had brought for him. (Later, in a gesture that won Townshend's heart, he replaced them with a pair of Revox's—high-quality Swiss machines.) The progress, locations, and components of his various home set-ups are detailed in the liner notes that accompany the collected demos on *Scoop* and *Another Scoop* (although for some reason "My Generation" is not among the songs included, a version was "released" on a flexi-disc, with the original edition of the *Maximum R&B* book).

Townshend has written that, despite the early success, he felt very lonely at this time, the only things in his life being Who gigs and his tape machines. When a flat just around the corner from Kit's became available, Pete moved his tape recorders, and the relationship settled down into the form it would take for the duration. Kit regularly stopped by, listening to tapes and offering suggestions. Pete had set up "two big Marshall loudspeakers . . . relics from the stage, and two Vortexion tape recorders. I used to record right through the night, playing back . . . fantastically loudly, but getting away with it because . . . none of the other flats in the block had been let."

Kit told Pete he should write an anthem, a statement, something with a broad sweep—and though he didn't see any special merit in the early takes of "My Generation," his opinion changed as successive demos brought the song more clearly into focus. Like many spontaneous-sounding pieces of music, "My Generation" was laboriously assembled through a number of intermediate stages. It began as a basic, mid-tempo blues vamp, which Pete considered "light weight." Chris Stamp (who was the first to spot the song's potential) told him to make it "beefier." In his notes to *Decade of The Who*, Pete writes:

> Version one . . . rather like a Jimmy Reed talking blues. Version two . . . added backing vocals, handclaps, a spoof bass guitar solo (later improved upon by John) and a stuttering vocal to the original guitar and voice. The third demo [introduced] upward key changes after every verse. Kit loved this, and on the last version there were four key changes!

Once convinced, Lambert exuded enthusiasm—invaluable assistance to a songwriter who isn't yet certain if a work is any good. Kit didn't take rock particularly seriously as a musical form, and the basic sensibility which informed many of his suggestions was "camp." Seizing on "My Generation"'s most distinctive features, he told Pete to exaggerate them: *more* upward key changes, *more* stuttering vocals, *more* of everything. By the final demo, which runs 3'25" the parts are in place and the arrangement is recognizably that of the single. Pete's home studio now contained a Grampian spring reverb unit, which he employs lavishly on the demo. The spoof bass solo, for instance, is so deep in reverb it sounds like a reggae dub plate; and though the stutter on Pete's vocal is not especially pronounced, the echo picks it up and triples it.

Kit's conversion and subsequent reaction marked the start of a new stage in the writing process, in which he became closely involved in developing Pete's songs. Lennon had McCartney, Richards had Jagger—and without Lambert it's probable that we would have never had Townshend as the songwriter we know today. Kit's role as mentor, foil and critic was formally acknowledged when he was credited as producer on "I'm a Boy." This arrangement lasted for the rest of the decade, right through *Tommy*, and didn't end until the recording of "The Seeker" in 1970. Pete observed, "Kit . . . had something, a language. . . . He had a great grasp of musical terms and was able to make a critique. He used to throw in a lot of ideas and make suggestions that seemed completely inappropriate, but whenever I tried them they used to work."

As Kit helped Pete to shape his material, Stamp was busy appeasing Roger Daltrey. Throughout the summer of 1965 a battle was fought, ostensibly over the type of material that should be included on the first LP, though the real issue was control of the band. Roger, who still felt that the leadership, and the whole direction of the group, were up for grabs, wanted to record the James Brown–style R&B material the band played live, rather than what he called "Pete's pop songs" and was implacably opposed to "My Generation" as the next single.

Shel Talmy was on his way out, though the break wasn't made until the first album, *My Generation,* was completed in October and November. Talmy was not a hands-on producer—an engineer friend of mine, who spent his first years in the business working as a tape operator for him, tells me he never once saw Talmy touch the desk—but he *did* like to direct a session. Talmy was puzzled why there never seemed anything much for him to do on Who sessions; the reason, in Pete's words, was because "we never gave him the chance." Determined to keep their own sound and unwilling to accept interference, the band went to town on the pre-production. When a single was due to be recorded, they spent days in rehearsal rooms. With Lambert analyzing and offering suggestions, they refined hooks, pinned down the parts, and worked up a finished arrangement. By the time they went in to record with Talmy, the session was a formality. Glyn Johns placed the mics and set levels, the tape was rolled, and in "one or two" takes the track was in the can.

Another song built around a two-bar guitar phrase of ineffable simplicity—or in Pete's description, "ying-gang ying-gang ying-gang ying-gang"—"My Generation"'s construction needs little explanation. Like all the best pop music its appeal is immediate; either it moves you or it doesn't. A series of simple upward key changes keep the song moving (the riff is so basic that even with the momentum worked up by the band, it could easily have palled over 3 minutes).

Entwistle's bass solo is superb, deft, and understated, so much part of the song that its excellence is often overlooked. By the second Townshend demo, the idea of a solo section comprising four, two-bar stops for the bass to fill is part of the composition. This was a stock Townshend device, first appearing on his "Call Me Lightning" demo circa 1964, where the breaks are filled by guitar. (The Who's recording of "Lightning" wasn't released until 1968, but the song is actually one of

Townshend's earliest compositions.) On the "My Generation" demo, the solo is clearly intended to be carried by the bass guitar, though Pete contents himself with sketching in an approximation on the detuned bass strings of a regular guitar (*smothered* in reverb to cover the fudges!).

Once Entwistle got his fingers on the phrase, he turned in the sort of performance that catches the attention of even the most unmusical listener. Pretty soon, he started showing up in music press readers polls among the ten best bass players. The break is a nicely judged mixture of taste and flash, rhythmic subtlety and blindingly fast runs using all four fingers of the right hand. Not a problem for Entwistle. He often improved on it live, staring into the crowd with an expression that read "so what?"— a demeanor enjoyed by highly competent musicians (of a certain cast of mind) all over the world. Typically, it consists of playing some impossibly difficult lick while half-stifling a yawn and glancing down at your wrist-watch.

To tighten the studio bass sound, engineer Glyn Johns mounted the bass amp on a heavyweight paving slab, though much of the *twanginess* of the recorded tone came from the eccentrically shaped Danelectro bass guitar, with its "lipstick tube" pickups and fast action. By now, everyone must know the official yarn—the broken strings, the unavailability of replacements, the purchase of a new bass in order to finish the session—like a good fishing story, the number of breakages and replacement basses grows with the telling, the most I've heard being four. As far as I can determine the real total was three Danelectro's, at which point Entwistle said "sod this" and bought a Fender Jazz bass. The Fender did the job, but John says it "slowed him down." Lambert subsequently scrapped the "Danelectro" session and re-recorded the song, so the version we know is a totally different take. There are four strings on a bass, and John's problem was that only two of them would produce the tone he wanted. One outcome was that he started working with string manufacturers, experimenting with cores and windings, in order to perfect a set of strings which would all resonate correctly. The successful product was memorably advertised on *The Who Sell Out* album ("Hold your group together with Rotosound Strings").

Harmonically the two previous singles stay at home—that is, they start and finish in the same key—whereas "My Generation" contains an unprecedented three key-changes (four keys equals three *changes)*. The idea of a single, upward key change is a well-known and eminently respectable arranging device, of long standing and good pedigree. Well placed, it can convey a range of sensations in broadly the same emotional area: excitement, uplift, a changing of gear. Usually introduced toward the end of a song, typically where a circular riff or refrain is repeated, a semitone raise is inserted to prevent the audience from actually dying of boredom. Conventionally, such a key change moves upward by either a half step, or a whole step as in "My Girl" or for that matter, "So Sad About Us." The Who influenced almost every young band who saw them play, so once they'd employed the device so generously, others quickly copied it.

The prize for the most literal implementation must go to fellow Track artists John's Children (featuring Marc Bolan on lead guitar and second vocal). Their song "Desdemona" with its sensitive, haunting refrain, "Lift up your skirt and fly," consists of a simple 24-bar combined verse/chorus, followed by an upward key change after *every* chorus. If they ever got cooking when playing live, they could easily have gone round the clock, arriving back at the key from which they started. Along with its atonal guitar noises and feedback, "My Generation" is obviously the presence behind "Desdemona." More mainstream, the constant upward movement of Tommy Roe's "Dizzy" uses the idea to similar effect.

Writing about the structure in the illustrated chord book *My Generation—A History in Music and Photographs*, Pete says, "On the stage we play [it] in the key of A. The record however was made in G, changing up to A, through B and ending in D. I had made the original demos in a variety of keys but the song tends to sound best in A, with the guitar tuned normally."[1]

So the song moves up a fourth from its starting point—hard luck on the singer! By the time the final key is reached, the vocal is high, even starting from the lower key of G. Most vocalists choose, if they make any alteration, to pitch a song down from the recorded version, to give themselves a little more headroom. Daltrey handles the range very well. Considering his original opposition to recording the song at all, he makes a truly excellent job of getting into character as the stuttering, incoherent, speed-addled Mod with an attitude problem. Scribbling hurriedly in the back of a car, Townshend may not have had time to tailor the lyrics carefully, but so well does Roger wear them you could be forgiven for thinking that they'd been made to measure for him.

You can judge The Who's competence as a live band by comparing the studio version of "My Generation" recorded in October with the BBC session recorded on November 22, 1965.[2] Hosted by Brian Mathew, the Light Programme's leading pop show *Saturday Club* aired weekly from 1958 until 1969. Live sessions were recorded during the week and were then included in the show. In the days before the BBC/Musicians Union "needle-time" agreement was ruled to be "restraint of trade," BBC radio was limited to playing only ninety hours of records per week—across all of its channels—which meant that the station's *own* recordings were an essential source of program material. These recordings took two forms: live broadcasts before audiences at BBC theaters, and sessions recorded in BBC studios. Both were likely to be rebroadcast several times, often in two or three different shows. If considered sufficiently interesting, transcription disks might be sent out to India, Africa, and the Far East, for use on the World Service.

In addition to these mainstream performances, there were also lower profile single or "network" sessions—another way of working around the needle-time restriction—where a version of a current hit record would be re-recorded in one quick session. The BBC could then broadcast it in place of the actual record without incurring PPL (Phonographic Performance Limited) charges, or using up precious needle-time. This was an odd, typically English approach to bureaucracy, in which the record companies connived at breaching their own regulations. Regardless of the reasons, the result is a library of live performances unmatched anywhere in the world.[3]

The BBC version of "My Generation"—a live recording without overdubs—confirms beyond all doubt what those who saw the band's '65 and '66 shows already knew: the "My Generation" *single* was no studio construction, but a true representation of the sound these four musicians produced onstage, night after night. A natural finale, the song quickly found its way to the closing spot where it became the cue for the wrecking to commence.

Straining to make his voice heard above the thunder of the band left Roger little room for vocal nuances, though where he could hear himself, he contributed some fine performances, often improving on the single. On the 1967 Smothers Brother's clip of "My Generation," where he's the only one who's actually working live, he sings as well as he's ever sung. His voice, always tending toward harshness, is perfect here, its tone approaching that of the soul singers he so admired. He exaggerates the stutter without overdoing it, and that in turn is picked up by the particular type of echo that's applied to his voice, creating little rhythmic eddies against the beat. (It's impossible to tell whether he's using this effect, or whether it's simply a good piece of engineering, possibly added after the performance. . . . Either way, it's tremendous.) Keith substitutes stick-clicks for the handclaps which fill the stop-time vocal passages on the record, and Entwistle improves his bass solo, playing on some instrument whose brand name he felt constrained to cover up with electrician's tape. In fact, the whole Smothers Brothers appearance is wonderful, an opinion probably shared by the band members themselves, since the clip is placed at the front of *The Kids Are Alright* film.

Shot at the NBC-TV center in Burbank late in '67, the band look great and sound pretty good, despite being impeded by Vox equipment. It was a constant complaint throughout '67, that while their Track labelmate Jimi Hendrix was allowed to bring his Marshall amps over from England, The Who were always stuck with inferior, locally rented gear, in order to save air-freight costs. The contrast is clearly documented in *Monterey Pop,* Pennebaker's film of The Monterey Festival. You only have to compare the richness of Hendrix's tone to the brittle, toppy sound that Townshend is saddled with to understand the complaint. The Vox amps wouldn't feed back with any conviction, and when Pete goes for an atonal passage they squeak like frightened rabbits instead of squealing like stuck pigs. Essentially, they *just weren't loud enough.*

Monterey was won by main force, as became a major international festival, but *The Smothers Brothers Comedy Hour* was basically just another mimed television date. Keith had bribed the stagehands to put a massive amount of explosives under his drum kit. What follows is worth running frame by frame if you have the video. After a couple of regular explosions, Townshend starts twirling his guitar and catching it. Turning from center-stage back toward his amp, he's just about to bash the instrument down on top of the Vox when the Big Bang occurs. In slow-motion the entire screen solarises for a second and Entwistle, who's already started walking away, turns and looks back. He's not, however, turned into a pillar of salt, though Townshend might easily have been vaporized. Catching the worst of it, from no more than two or three feet away, his hair is singed and chunks are left standing upright. If any single occasion contributed to Pete's hearing loss, this was probably it. Contrary to Dave Marsh's account, Keith isn't blown off the drum riser. He'd already kicked away most of the kit and is standing with one foot up on the remaining bass drum when the explosion hits. His exit off the back of the riser looks more like the timed retreat of someone escaping blame. When the smoke clears, Moon's lying in *front* of the riser, dead to all intents—till he rises, bravely clutching his shrapnel wound and putting on his most innocent "whatever happened?" expression. And this all occurred on network television.

*　*　*

As a group grows in stature, a change can be seen in the style of their record reviews. Initial reviews compare the new group to existing bands. Then, as a group becomes established, they stop being compared with others, while new groups are compared to them. The process took about twelve months and three singles in The Who's case. For the "Blind Date" review, *Melody Maker* gave "My Generation" to a mainstream, old-school disk jockey, Pete Murray. Run in the October 30th edition, Murray's response says more about The Who's position in the rapidly changing London pop scene of 1965 than about the record: "The Who, isn't it? This is a group I really shouldn't like but do. This has a wild beat. I think it might offend a few people though. But The Who are a very, very good group."

"My Generation" became easily The Who's most successful record thus far, reaching number 2 and staying on the chart for a total of ten weeks, figures that they would never beat, although they were equaled the following year by "I'm a Boy." "My Generation" became the Who song known to people who knew no other, and, as such, inevitably became something of an albatross around the band's collective neck. The single, and the album of the same name, were the last recordings made with Talmy at the controls, and the last time they'd ever enter the studio with anyone but a producer of their own choice. Townshend himself would take the controls for the next single, "Substitute."

SUBSTITUTE

"YOU HAVE TO RESIGN YOURSELF
TO THE FACT THAT A LARGE PART OF THE AUDIENCE IS SORT OF
THICK AND . . . UH . . . DON'T APPRECIATE QUALITY, HOWEVER
MUCH YOU TRY TO PUT IT OVER. THE FACT IS THAT OUR GROUP
HASN'T GOT ANY QUALITY. IT'S JUST MUSICAL SENSATIONALISM."

—Pete, age 20

The remainder of the audience—that small part who weren't "thick"—might have noticed a considerable improvement in The Who's standing as 1966 began. Twelve months previously they'd been a good live band, but essentially a local one. Now they'd had three solid hits, broad media exposure, and praise from the highest quarters—and, of course, they hated each other. Nineteen sixty-six looked like their year. A deal struck with Robert Stigwood's Reaction label in the U.K. (for the States, Chris Stamp did a one-off deal placing "Substitute" with the Atlantic Records subsidiary Atco) freed them from Talmy's influence in the studio, although the true cost of this freedom was not yet apparent. "My Generation" had put them on the national stage, and Pete wasn't short of songs with which to consolidate their success.

Survival in the pop world of 1966 resembled nothing so much as a game of snakes and ladders. Hit singles were the sole currency, and only a handful of artists were sufficiently well placed to survive more than two

"Substitute" U.S. trade advertisement, 1966

England's hottest new group
THE WHO
now on ATCO!
"SUBSTITUTE"

ATCO #6409
By arrangement with Polydor Records of Great Britain.

...already a smash in Britain*

* 13, Disc, March 19   * 15, New Musical Express, March 19   * 18, Record Mirror, March 19   * 20, Melody Maker, March 19

or three flops. Without hits the most powerful live band in the country would be back playing their local ballroom circuit within nine months. Nobody was looking at pop as a "career"; even The Beatles famously estimated their band's life expectancy as no more than 3 years. To stand any chance of rising above the scrimmage of beat groups, all playing broadly similar material, it was essential to have good songs and gain national publicity, the more the better. Publicists regularly had desperate, no-chance bands climbing Nelson's Column, boxing with kangaroos, or insulting cabinet ministers—any stunt stupid enough to gain a couple of lines in the national press. This was one problem The Who never had to worry about. With a couple of inspired idea men like Lambert and Stamp, and a self-propelled, one-man publicity machine in the form of Keith Moon, the band soon began attracting serious interest from the various media. The BBC show *A Whole Scene Going* gave Pete his first extended television interview. The Italian director Michelangelo Antonioni wanted them in his new film, and while Keith's antics endeared him to the music press, Stamp was busy cultivating an upmarket Sunday paper, *The Observer*.

Any song that followed "My Generation" was going to have to be strong. For the all-important first post-Talmy single, Pete set out to make as commercial a sound as possible. Given the degree of attention "My Generation" had already attracted, a weak follow-up would have been crucified by the press. From a selection of Townshend's home demos, Kit expressed an interest in a song called "Substitute" that Pete had recorded at his latest home studio in Old Church Street, Chelsea. Over the years Pete has cited various songs as influences on "Substitute," at one moment naming an obscure English beat-boom single by Robb Storme, heard during a *Melody Maker* "Blind Date" record review session, at another describing The Who as "a substitute Rolling Stones." In the liner notes to *Another Scoop* he says:

> I made this demo after hearing a rough mix of "19th Nervous Breakdown" by The Stones. The lyric . . . was thrown together very quickly. Smokey Robinson sang the word "substitute" so perfectly in "Tracks of My Tears"—my favourite song of the time— that I decided to celebrate the word with a song all its own.

Plenty to choose from there, though the clearest cop I hear is a Motown bass line, not from a Miracles record but from The Four Tops. "Substitute" follows Pete's demo faithfully. All the components are present on the demo, including the looping bass guitar riff that drives the verse. Thus we know it's an integral part of the composition, not something worked up in the studio as an embellishment. This riff, which dominates the verses, is *very* closely related to The Four Top's "I Can't Help Myself." Take Jamie Jamerson's bass line, iron out the syncopation, and you have the bass line of "Substitute." Pete writes, "Interesting that in eulogising two of my most important influences (and ripping off a few ideas) I should end up with one of the most succinct songs of my career."

"Ripping off" is a matter of context. Everyone steals; it's not what you nick but the way that you nick it. As a rule, *interesting people steal more interestingly,* because they can't help putting something of themselves into what they steal. Exact copies lead nowhere, and are a bore anyway. Nothing develops. Flawed copies have far greater appeal. Someone sets out to copy an idea but can't quite get it right. In the process, the original idea mutates into something new and unexpected.

Listening to "Substitute" when it came out, one never thought "Oh, Motown!," but traces of its influence are all over the record—the tambourine, pushed right upfront in the mix and the bass line in the verse. Considering that Tamla was a Mod staple (and enormously commercial) it's hardly surprising that in going all out for a "blatant" hit single, Pete should use parts of their formula. "Substitute" was also Pete Townshend's first credited attempt at production, and for such an ardent home-taper the opportunity to control the session from the desk—unhindered—must have been a joy. It was Townshend's opinion that Talmy was "too passive" in the studio, and that engineer Glyn Johns had done all the work (though one hardly imagines a more active Talmy would've met with much favor, either). With Talmy out of the picture, the Who abandoned IBC in favour of Olympic Studios, not yet at its famous Barnes location, where Hendrix, Traffic, Jimmy Miller, and The Stones would record, but off Baker Street in central London.

"Substitute" is a very different sounding record from the three singles that precede it, more controlled, more calculated. Where the first three are passionate and in many ways quite earnest, "Substitute" is cooler and more knowing. Townshend no longer employs every weapon in the band's live armory as he had on "Anyway, Anyhow, Anywhere" and "My Generation," but selects only the instrumentation needed to carry the song. Based around a 12-string acoustic guitar which plays the main figure, plus a tambourine and that circling bass riff, "Substitute" demonstrates that Pete's confidence as a writer had grown to the point where he could successfully take a step back from his own work and construct a custom-built commercial song.

The first three singles are all in their various ways quite heated in expression, but "Substitute" represents a cold, more focused anger. The fury, which had previously been taken out on the equipment, is this time channeled into the lyric and directed primarily against the writer himself. "Substitute" is a song about artifice, about the second rate being passed off as the real thing, and is also a confession of personal inadequacy. It can be argued that Pete was a sense of disillusion waiting to happen. In a notably sullen *Melody Maker* article printed a couple of months before his 21st birthday, he's already saying

Keith Moon used to be a lot of fun but he's turning into a little old man. He used to be young and unaffected by pop music but now he's obsessed with money. I still like him . . . he's the only drummer in England I really want to play with.

The turning inward of anger and the self-disgust expressed in "Substitute" seem to have several strands. Pete was maturing as a songwriter. Where most writers welcome the perspective and distancing that come with mastering a craft, Pete seems to have regarded them with a degree of suspicion, as though they might represent a betrayal of spontaneity on his part. Then, his description of The Who as "substitute Stones" is a rather depressed way of saying that he likes The Stones— and a very partial perspective on The Who. To understand the atmosphere, consider just how much speed was being consumed. The upside is obvious—and much talked about when people describe The Who's performances—but everyone seems to forget that the come-down is as much part of the experience as the rush. Gobbling pure, pharmaceutical amphetamine by the handful, month after month, the come-downs would have been ferocious.

The relationship between The Stones and The Who is fairly convoluted. As The Detours, The Who first played on the same bill as The Stones at St. Mary's Hall Putney, on December 22, 1963. Introduced to them by Glyn Johns, Pete seems to have been awestruck and amazed at their charismatic scruffiness. Jagger and Brian Jones were communicative, and Jones praised the band, which Pete likened to "God touching me." Keith Richards was "sardonic and unapproachable" (no change there for a while) but provided the inspiration for the famous Townshend windmill: "he just swung his arm up . . . before the curtain opened . . . brushed the curtain away . . . and went into 'Come On.'" Twelve days later they supported The Stones again, this time at The Glenlyn Ballroom in Forest Hill, a South London venue on agent Bob Druce's circuit, and a regular Detours/High Numbers gig. At this venue, a girl accused Pete of copying Keith's gesture, though Richards himself couldn't have cared less. The move may have started as a tribute, but it soon developed into something unique.

For the rest of the decade, The Who often crossed paths with The Stones, even covering two of their songs, "The Last Time"/"Under My Thumb" when Mick and Keith were briefly imprisoned, but not until the early '70s does Pete seem to have felt free of their shadow. In 1966, The Stones' domination of London was total, but to young Who fans outside the capital, the relative status of the two bands hardly mattered. The Who's core audience was predominately male and younger than that of The Stones, who were in any case going through their teenybop phase. Still very much Brian Jones's group, The Stones were almost impossible to see playing live. They only came through town on the occasional package tour, which meant buying a ticket months in advance, in order to watch a twenty-minute appearance at the top of the bill, rendered inaudible by screaming girls. To the typical teenage male Who fan, this was a very poor substitute for The Who in all their glory. Until The Stones reinvented themselves in '68 with "Jumpin' Jack Flash" and *Beggar's Banquet*, there was a period where, like The Beatles, they looked to be part of an older, slightly out-of-date sector of the pop world.

"Substitute" soon became a garage band standard, mainly on account of its dramatic opening chord sequence, which is irresistible to guitarists. It seems exceedingly simple, though as Pete notes in *The*

Decade of The Who, trying to get it right has "caused many people much worry." He's absolutely right. If you'd ventured behind the bicycle sheds of any English school during the spring and summer terms of 1966, you'd have found small groups of boys with guitars, and intense disagreements raging. Though Pete says "it's very simple," it's also very simple to get wrong. The confusion lies in the way the chords are voiced. They're the most elementary chords, but they're played in a specific position, over a ground bass or pedal note (the name comes from the bass pedals on an organ, and refers to a chord sequence with a single sustained note running beneath it). Normally, as chords change, the bass note changes with them: an A chord has A in the bass, B has B, etc.; but a pedal note stays put, which alters the sound entirely. The "Substitute" chords—D A G D— all have that single note D held at the bottom, which is what gives the intro its special sound.

The practice of opening a track with Pete's solo guitar was now becoming a custom (three of the first four singles), though on "Substitute" the electric guitar is exchanged for a 12-string acoustic. Nothing better illustrates the true source of the band's power, which lay not just in the unprecedented banks of Fender, Vox, Marshall, or Hiwatt amps, but in tight ensemble playing, crisp rhythmic lines, and, above all, the *drive* of the three instrumentalists. Much of Townshend's guitar tone came from laying into the strings with real force. To get enough attack on the "Substitute" intro it was necessary to silence the unwanted fifth and sixth strings by palm-mutin them at the bridge. If only that information had been available behind the bicycle sheds . . .

When the instrumental break starts, it's the bass guitar that takes the solo, adopting the role of lead instrument (a commonplace of mid-'70s reggae arrangements, but highly unusual in 1966), while Townshend builds an atmosphere in the background with indistinct, sustained, organ-like tones. In the days before multitracking allowed every element of a song to be recorded on a separate track, it was up to the musicians to keep a balance between instruments. If a player altered his level in mid-take, there was little anyone could do. As the solo approached, John Entwistle decided it was time to step forward: "Sod this! I'm gonna make it into another bass solo like 'My Generation' so I turned up the volume. When they eventually started mixing it they couldn't reduce the bass."

Entwistle was well represented, but Keith Moon was absent from the record—or so he believed. When he heard "Substitute," it came as a considerable shock to him. Who was drumming? Evidently, he reasoned, he'd been thrown out, replaced by some new drummer who was playing on the record. Bearing in mind the band's own descriptions of themselves at this period—"absolute bastards," "complete cunts," "selfish sods," etc.—nothing was more likely. Moon had been the last to join, and he'd never formally been told he *was* a member. Geographically he was something of an outsider, too, coming from the wilds of Wembley into a group of Ealing and Acton boys. Confronting the band, Moon demanded to know what they meant by recording without him. Apparently it took much reassurance and many plays of the record before he accepted that he *was* playing on it—extraordinary when you listen closely and hear the yell emitted during the drum fill that follows the false finish (audible at 2'38"). How many other drummers howled like that in mid-take?

Moon often felt insecure about his place in the band, which is absurd considering his complete originality. Though other drummers are rumored to have played on later Who recordings (c.f. "The Seeker"), his sound, his attack, and above all, his improbable ideas—the way he *heard* the beat—make him central to all great Who records. When Keith was off, it never quite *happened*. He must already have given his brain a terrible hammering to experience memory loss on that scale at the age of nineteen; but then he gave *everything* a pretty good hammering, not least the drums. Keith's playing relied on energy more than technique. In retrospect, it should've been evident that such an intensely physical style of drumming was not going to be sustainable for very long, even if he'd trained like an athlete, and sure enough, by his mid-twenties Keith's playing was slowing down. On "Substitute" though (as on "I'm a Boy" and "Happy Jack"), you hear the teenage Moon at the peak of his inventiveness—even if he didn't remember the session! The drumming throughout is utterly unlike anyone else's playing, doubling up beats on the bass drum, playing fills straight through vocal lines, and maintaining a constant swirl of white noise from two or three crash cymbals.

The American release of "Substitute" (Atco 45 6409) is a shortened version of the English single—the second verse is cut, so the solo comes in straight after the first chorus—and has a different vocal. A second vocal had to be recorded when the line "I look all white but my dad was black"

was deemed too controversial for American sensibilities, though Townshend clearly didn't waste too many hours perfecting the replacement ("I tried going forward but my feet walk back"). *Meaty, Beaty, Big & Bouncy* uses the full English version (you can always tell which version you have by checking the lyrics). Atlantic reissued the track (Atco 45 6509) in August '67.

Presumably, even on the 4-track machines of the day, Daltrey *could* just have dropped in the replacement lines, though there are a number of possible problems: the new vocal sound may not have matched the old one, or punching-in may have meant the tambourine and backing vocal would have had to be redone as well. For any number of reasons, it was probably simpler just to record a whole new vocal from top to tail. Roger Daltrey's confidence was waxing audibly as studio sessions became more familiar. You can almost hear him learning his trade. The studio is always unnerving at first, and singers are especially vulnerable because any nervousness tenses the muscles and constricts the throat. Roger's performance on the U.S. version of "Substitute" is as assured as anything he'd yet recorded. Though he sings very much the same part, with the same inflections, there is a difference in vocal quality. The English take is sung squarely on the beat; the American version is more relaxed, with Daltrey phrasing slightly behind the beat, creating space and leaving himself more room for expression and nuance in the lyric. Fractionally slowing down the phrasing, he manages to squeeze considerable *contempt* into the take, using the flat diction and exaggerated clarity with which one might address the outstandingly stupid. It's a great vocal. Whatever problems Daltrey had accepting the loss of leadership, Townshend's new material would be the making of him as a vocalist.

Antonioni was filming *Blow-Up,* his Swinging London tale of murder, voyeurism, and fashion around the capital that summer and, wanting to include the hippest new act in town, approached The Who to appear in a sequence set in an Oxford Street club. Perhaps if the lead had gone as originally planned to Terence Stamp, The Who might have appeared, but as it was they were unable or unwilling to oblige. The relative lameness of the footage which was eventually shot illustrates—by default—the force of The Who's visual presence. Denied his first choice, Antonioni had to find a replacement, and eventually employed The Yardbirds to impersonate The Who. One understands exactly the process that led to this choice.

Jovial Keith Moon, New York, March 1967.
Photo © Don Paulsen

The Yardbirds were a happening band, with a strong, word-of-mouth underground following, and legitimate, post-Stones Crawdaddy Club cachet. But their reputation rested entirely on the *musical* prowess of their star guitarists. Visually, they had the impact of five live sheep.

Briefly, the hero David Hemmings wanders into a club where a group is playing. A lead guitarist—played by Jeff Beck—is driven mad by a series of highly improbable buzzes and squawks emanating from a malfunctioning amp. Such is his rage, so uncontrollable his fury, that he smashes a semi-acoustic Hofner guitar (a brand noted for its propensity to fall apart unassisted) worth several pounds. Beck is a marvelously quirky guitar player but he has never sought a career in acting. Looking as though he'd be far happier tinkering round underneath a car, he breaks the Hofner and throws the remains to the crowd. Hemmings wins the scramble to grab the broken neck (many might have scrambled to *avoid* it), bears his trophy out of the club and, in an incisive comment on consumer culture and the disposable society, throws it away. The Yardbirds made some highly original singles, but in *Blow-Up* they look utterly unreal—more like the sort of group you'd see in a film.

The Who began 1966 with an appearance on the first edition of *A Whole Scene Going,* a new BBC pop and fashion series that debuted on January 5. Introduced by Wendy Varnals and Barry Fantoni, the show promised to tell us what youth should be wearing, dancing, and listening to in 1966. After the opening titles—incongruous footage of a heavily side-burned, Bluesbreakers-period Eric Clapton strumming a Les Paul to the sound of some notably guitarless Hammond Organ vamping—we get straight down to business, as guests Lulu, Spike Milligan, and Frankie McGowan (sister of *Ready, Steady, Go!* presenter Cathy McGowan) discuss spots, clothes, and boy trouble. To the tune of Keith Moon's favorite song, The Beach Boys' "Don't Worry Baby," we cut to footage from California about the coming craze: skateboards. Next an odd assortment of pundits attempt to predict "The Sound of '66." From Liverpool, Alun Williams, who'd managed (and lost) The Beatles, foresees a Trad Jazz revival, while a Mancunian club owner, seated in front of a piano-accordion trio, correctly anticipates a heavily promoted classical music boom—some twenty-five years too early. The most timely judgment comes from George Melly, then music critic at *The Observer*:

Nineteen sixty-six it's very hard to say. . . . The Liverpool sound's right out of the ring. If I had to put my money on anything, on any group in particular I'd put it on The Who, because what they do is to exaggerate and caricature everything that's gone before, and this seems to work with the kids at the moment.

Then we get down to business. Barry Fantoni announces that

each week we intend to look closely at a group through the eyes of its leader. We let him explain himself to us on film, then we put him on the hot-seat and ask him what *we* want to know. So who better to start with then, than Pete Townshend of The Who.

This was Pete's first major television interview. After some live footage of The Who playing "Heatwave" at The Witch Doctor Club in Hastings (filmed the previous August), Pete shows us around his flat. In the corner, a pair of four-by-twelve Marshall speaker cabinets meant for the stage are serving as a domestic hi-fi; on top of one, a black and white television is showing Test Match cricket. The principal decoration is Pop Art posters stuck on the walls. Pete discusses The Who's audience:

When for a brief period I stopped smashing guitars on the stage, cos it *was* costing a lot of money, kids started shoutin' out "smash your guitar Pete!" and getting quite annoyed cos I wasn't, cos to a large percentage of boys, not girls . . . geezers that had come to see the group . . . they paid their money to see me hit my amplifier with the guitar and p'raps see a guitar break.

He goes on to talk about the girls in the audience coming to see them because of the clothes they wear, but as he lists the items—the Union Jacket, Keith's target T-shirts, John's medals—he sounds less than wholly convinced. Quite right, too. At the shows I saw that year, the crowds were about 80 percent male, and the girls who were there looked as though they'd come reluctantly, dragged along by boyfriends. I have a clear memory of The Who playing a provincial ballroom show in January '67, by which time they'd started to get a slightly more balanced audience (the same venue in July '66 had only been three-quarters full; the January

'67 show was a complete sell-out with crowds turned away). Right at the front, up against the crash barriers, was a row of girls. Daltrey kept stretching an arm out toward them until eventually he was pulled off-balance and had to be righted by the crew and a bouncer, but it was still only a *single* row, where they would have been stacked twelve-deep for Dave Dee, Dozy, Beaky, Mick, and Tich. "My Generation" signalled the end of the show (rather like an alternate National Anthem), and as the smoke cleared and the DJ played something they liked, girls started appearing from the darkened corners of the room. Slowly the dance floor filled with piles of handbags, around which little knots of girls danced in simple formations, relief evident on almost every face now that the dreadful, incomprehensible noise had stopped.

Pete's most memorable line from the *A Whole Scene Going* interview is his famous quip about speed. Asked if the band's taste for pills means that they are "blocked up when they're onstage" he replies, "No, it means we're blocked up all the time." A friendship developed between Pete and Barry Fantoni, who recalled, "After we met on *A Whole Scene Going* we instantly liked each other. We looked alike too, both rather beaky, gangly looking men." Fantoni was himself an interesting '60s figure. Another art school boy (though ten years older than Townshend), a multi-instrumentalist, painter, novelist, and sportsman, he was the sole working-class outsider to penetrate the public school inner circle at the satirical magazine *Private Eye*. Employed in 1967 to teach Pop Art at Croydon Art School, two of his earliest pupils were Malcolm McLaren and the Sex Pistols' graphics man, Jamie Reid, the latter a good footballer who played in a team with Fantoni and Ray Davies. Looking back thirty years to the broadcast, Fantoni remarked of Townshend:

> He's young [20], but in a sense very mature. It's his first public interview on television and his candor is very charming. It was what people wanted actually. . . . They'd had all the jokes from The Beatles: Jagger's interviews were just ridiculous; and Pete was that much closer to an audience of twenty-year-olds—which was who the program was aimed at.

Soon a mutual admiration society was flourishing in the music press. Reviewing "A Legal Matter" for the March 19 *Melody Maker*, Fantoni calls

The Who "the best of their kind," while the following week, *MM* ran something called a "Pop Think-In," in which Townshend opined on Vietnam, James Brown, vandalism, and the general election. Speaking of Pop Art, he said, "My favourite artists are Barry Fantoni and Peter Blake. What I like most of all is English. . . . Foreign Pop art I hate" (so much for Lichtenstein and Oldenburg). A "Pop Think-In" was not the sort of forum in which anyone was likely to do himself much justice, and Fantoni (who knew his way around contemporary art) sensed that Townshend's interests were broader than many of his more famous peers:

> Pete was interested in music and painting much more than most of the other people in the pop world. Paul McCartney *affected* an interest in these things, but I don't think they were very close to his heart. Lennon was so unsympathetic as a person . . . he was just very distant . . . I don't really know *what* he thought. . . . anyway, I got on well with Paul and therefore not with John—it seemed you couldn't be friends with both. Jagger had nothing much to offer anybody at all. From the very, very early days—perhaps because he'd been at the London School of Economics—he was just interested in money. Middle-class Englishman who could see there was a lot of money to be made out of Pop and went ahead and did it. All of that, including Jagger, was *incredibly* dull. Mainly interested in all the things that pop singers are always supposed to be interested in—except that Jagger led a double life, in that he wasn't *really* interested in that either—what interested him was Power and Money and the spotlight.

Few people today would be surprised by the opinion that Jagger's financial instinct was stronger than his aesthetic sense; but Fantoni also considered Townshend's and Ray Davies's songs far more original than those of The Stones or The Beatles:

> They were all very good friends. I spent many evenings in the same apartment—Marianne Faithfull's apartment in fact—with Mick and Paul listening to the same Ray Davies record and working out what they could copy off it. Of all the British songwriters he is in my view, the truly genuine article. They bought "See My Friends" and

Jagger and Paul were both sitting there spellbound by this sort of Indian sounding thing—and the simplicity of it.

Fantoni is interesting, too, on the differences between Townshend and Davies:

Pete's compositions were very wordy, but the structure of the songs were incredibly simple. From watching him compose, from being there with him, there wasn't actually much attempt to produce hooks—say, an instantly engaging catch-phrase or melody line—he seemed to have ideas about wanting keep things very simple. Ray Davies had exactly the same attitude about composition, but he was incapable of *not* producing hooks.

The hacks at *Melody Maker* were a cheerful bunch, suspicious of anything, "arty," but a soft touch for anyone prepared to down a few pints with them and talk soccer. By now, as far as MM was concerned, The Who were on the team. As well as the clinical interest in various manifestations of "mania," it was editorial policy to promote healthy, mutual antagonism between artists perceived as being at all similar, thus typical headlines read: "now it's Stones v. Kinks!"; "Dylan v. Donovan—it's war!"; "Dusty v. Marianne!"; etc. This rule was immutable except when the demanding disciplines of pop journalism ruled it expedient that two acts should be *paired*. Mod provided an easy yoke to link The Small Faces and The Who (both London bands with members who knew about beer and soccer) so the Old Pals Act was invoked—not once, but twice.

The March 5, 1966, "Blind Date" was handed to Stevie Marriott (and five months later, Small Faces bassist Plonk Lane had a Blind Date with "I'm a Boy"). Back in March, though, imagine Marriott's astonishment when out of the bag popped "Substitute"! My word, it's Pete and the boys!

Oh great. It's just too much. They sound like Billy Fury (falls on floor laughing). I think they'll get a number 1 with this. That'll please Pete—and Keith's mum. I can honestly say it's not as good as "My Generation" but it's definitely a number 1. Pete's writing more and more commercial stuff—this actually conjures up a visual picture of them.

If January's appearance on *A Whole Scene Going* gave the band, and especially Pete, their first prolonged national exposure, they still only reached a limited audience. The show was aimed solely at the youth market—and a market split with *Ready, Steady, Go!* at that. On the Sunday following "Substitute"'s entry onto the charts, The Who were introduced to a different public when Britain's oldest Sunday newspaper, *The Observer* (established in 1791), gave them the cover story in their March 20, 1966, Colour Supplement, with a seven-page spread inside [see pages 157–166]. Stamp understood the prestige that would result from positioning the band in the quality press, and spent months setting up the story. The magazine went to town on the feature, deciding that the band stood a pretty good chance of being the next big thing:

> For two months John Heilpern followed round The Who and their managers, watching, questioning and cross-questioning the machinery, intrigues, finances and gimmicks, from London to the north to New York. He pieces together how a group is made and promoted—first in the clubs, then on TV, then on records and finally in quest of the real prize—America.

The article featured some of the best pictures yet taken of the band, including Colin Jones's lovely study of Townshend hunched on his bed, before the carcasses of five eviscerated Rickenbackers, and the now-famous cover shot with Union Jack backdrop, and Townshend staring straight into the camera, wearing his Union Jacket. The paper's hunch paid off, and the timing was perfect for the band. "Substitute" went straight into the chart as the story went to press.

The record did nothing much in America, despite the band's move to a new label, Atco. In England, however—where the record reached number 5, staying nine weeks on the chart—the move to the Reaction label produced spectacular results. First released on March 4, "Substitute" was eventually released with a total of three different B-sides. "Instant Party" and "Circles" are the same song (Townshend's production, not Talmy's), and "Waltz for a Pig" is an instrumental by the Graham Bond Organization, billed as "The Who Orchestra." It also provoked an injunction from Talmy and, within seven days, a rival Who single on Brunswick: "A Legal Matter" backed with "Instant Party."

A LEGAL MATTER/THE KIDS ARE ALRIGHT

"Kit Lambert is insane."

—Shel Talmy to Alan Betrock

Talmy's response to The Who's breakaway was immediate. He issued an injunction against Polydor (who distributed Reaction), a single on Brunswick, and a press release, which *Melody Maker* used in their March 12, 1966, cover story.

Pete Townshend: "I don't really mind what they do."

"Substitute," released last week, is owned by Polydor. DECCA, the company who previously issued the Who's records, have now released a single by the group called "A Legal Matter Baby."

Pete Townshend says, "I don't mind . . . 'Substitute' is a blatantly commercial number and certainly an easy hit. It's had 2 weeks more sales than 'Legal Matter' so I don't think it'll make much difference."

Shel Talmy says, "I have a valid contract with them. 'Legal Matter' is their current single release as far as we are concerned." At presstime Shel Talmy was reported to be seeking a court injunction to restrain Polydor from issuing 'Instant Party' which is on the b side of 'Substitute.'

Out in the street.
Courtesy Michael Ochs
Archives/Venice, CA

A LEGAL MATTER/THE KIDS ARE ALRIGHT   59

The situation in which different companies simultaneously released their own Who singles grew out of simple managerial inexperience. In the beginning, Lambert and Stamp didn't know very much about how record deals were obtained, let alone how contracts were drafted and percentages allotted. Drawing nothing but rejection letters from the major labels, they were delighted when Kit's assistant, Anya, was able to put them in touch with a freelance producer who'd just had a sizeable hit with The Kinks: Shel Talmy. Signing a production deal directly with Talmy put the band straight into the studio, and removed at a stroke the problem of how to find a record deal. Talmy would take care of it! This probably appeared a wonderful shortcut to everyone in The Who camp for a week or two, until all the implications were properly appreciated. Broadly, the terms of Talmy's standard production deal (by no means atypical of the time) gave him:

Control over the recording and production process.
Ownership of the tapes (thus control over their placement).
A five year term (as producer).

Once a track was cut, he would "use his best endeavors" to sell it to a company (no massive effort being required, since he had a standing arrangement with Decca in the U.S.) and guarantee to pay the band a royalty of, let us suppose, 3 percent. What Lambert and Stamp initially failed to appreciate was that Talmy might be getting a royalty of anywhere between 6 percent and 10 percent from the record company—and was free to pocket the balance.[1]

In large, bureaucratic organizations, keeping your job can depend more on avoiding responsibility for failure than on producing success. A&R people at record companies who don't have much idea of what's going on can hedge their bets by accepting the judgment of a trusted middle-man: a familiar manager or a known producer with a track record. The middle-man (should he feel the need) can justify his disproportionate cut along the lines "without me, this act would be nowhere"—or, as Townshend summarized Talmy's attitude, by making "groups who were nothing, Stars." The company might pay out a slightly higher royalty rate, but the risks are minimized. The whole ethos rests on the idea of "The Man with the Magic Touch": the producer-asalchemist turning base groups into gold records. Implicit is the notion that artists are interchangeable; there are always plenty more good-looking boys working on building sites. In the case of some pop groups, especially those who didn't write songs, there may be something to be said for such an approach, but clearly it wouldn't do for a group as sure of their own direction as The Who.

To this day there are record companies who'll sign almost anything if it comes packaged and presented by a weighty enough figure. The alternative is unthinkable, because it involves actually discovering new talent, then—as if that wasn't bad enough—backing your judgment with large sums of money, in full view of everyone who works in the company! This approach is simply asking for trouble. Alternative A&R strategies include signing nobody or poaching proven, successful acts from smaller independent companies with the use of hefty financial inducements.

Lambert and Stamp's inexperience caused them to agree to too long a term—five years—and too low a percentage—2.5 percent renegotiated after "I Can't Explain" to 3 or 4 percent (depending on Chris Stamp's memory)—but still low. What Talmy appeared to offer was safe passage through unknown waters, with a guaranteed record release. In practice, of course, placing the product with Decca was a formality, but by the time Kit and Chris saw the trap it was too late. Once The Who's records started selling, and the management began to get a clearer idea of the way music-biz finance worked, discontent grew rapidly.

The main points of contention may be summarized thus:

No creative control in the studio (Talmy forcing in session men).
Too small a slice of the profits (approximately two-thirds of the royalty paid by the company was going to the middleman).
The group was stuck with Talmy for five years.
The group was stuck with Decca for the U.S. (a totally unsympathetic label).

Eventually, having exhausted what Stamp called "all the polite things," The Who's lawyer, Ted Oldman, advised them to simply break the contract and sue Talmy. After talking to their new agent, Robert Stigwood, with whom Lambert and Stamp's "New Action" company shared an office, they decided to issue their next single on Stigwood's Reaction label.

With Townshend producing, they recorded "Substitute." Then, in what Stamp called a "political move" they deliberately recorded a version of "Circles" for the B-side (a song which had at one time been considered as the next Decca single) and renamed it "Instant Party." This, reasoned Stamp, would force Talmy to injunct the record and face them in court (though as Dave Marsh points out, if this was the core of their strategy, it was "fairly absurd").

On the March 4, 1966, they released the record on Reaction, then sat back and waited for the writ from Talmy. This duly appeared—along with Talmy's version of "Instant Party" which Decca released on March 11 as the B-side to "A Legal Matter." "Substitute" was climbing the charts, so to prevent its progress being impeded, another of Robert Stigwood's artists, Graham Bond, quickly recorded a track which was named "Waltz for a Pig," and "Substitute" was re-released with this on the B-side on March 15. The track features no members of The Who and is a plain jazz waltz instrumental.

Thereafter, between March and December 1966, each time The Who released a new single on the Reaction label, Decca took a track from the band's first album, *My Generation,* and issued it as a Brunswick single. Thus "Substitute" was shadowed by "A Legal Matter." In August, Decca's "The Kids Are Alright" just beat "I'm a Boy" into the shops (though not the charts); and late in the year, Reaction's *Ready Steady Who!* EP and "Happy Jack" single were dogged by "La-La-La-Lies." In the hothouse singles market of 1966, where trends changed in a matter of months, a less distinctive band than The Who might easily have been damaged by unrepresentative 1965 album tracks promoted as though they were new singles; and if sales had split equally between the two rival releases, it's probable that neither would have charted. Happily, public taste accorded with that of the band, and while the Reaction records were all hits, none of the Decca singles troubled the chart compilers.

The dispute was settled out of court, on terms that suited Talmy far better than they did The Who. Talmy was granted a 5 percent override on all Who records for the next five years, a term that included the best-selling albums *Tommy* and *Who's Next* (thus making a bundle of money from work in which he had no part), while all The Who got was rid of Talmy.

"I WROTE THIS WHEN I WAS SEV-
ENTEEN. NOBODY HAD ASKED ME TO MARRY THEM, BUT IF THEY
HAD, I WAS GOING TO SING THIS."

—**Pete Townshend, Supper Club,**

NYC, May 3, 1996

As a pleasant album track, suddenly plucked from relative obscurity and thrust into the ring to do battle with "Substitute," this song never
stood much of a chance—even with a bit of help. It appears that the
Pirate stations could not only be "influenced" to play a record; if you knew
how to go about it, you could also get them to suppress a competitor.
Thus, as Richard Barnes points out, while Radio Caroline played both singles, Radio London would only play the Decca record, "A Legal Matter."
It made no difference. "A Legal Matter" stalled at number 32 while
"Substitute" reached number 5.

"A Legal Matter" is a brisk, country-flavored two-step, concerning
(possibly autobiographical) problems with girls, in the days before such
matters were solved by *ex gratia* payments from Lambert's slush fund.
The circumstances of its release shouldn't be allowed to obscure the fact
that this is a fine song. Less of an anthem than "Kids," a pleasant—if
lightweight—tune carries some of the crispest, most concise lyrics
Townshend has ever written. Updating Cyril Connolly's dictum—the threat
to the young artist posed by "the pram in the hall"—Townshend celebrates a narrow escape from entrapment by dangerously marriage-hun-
gry women: "Bet you thought you had me nailed/But I freed my head from
your garden rail."

The vocal is taken by Pete and, though his voice is relatively weak,
the result is surprisingly poignant. There's a definitive Who quality somewhere in the contrast between the attempted swagger of the lyric and the
vulnerability of Pete's rather high-pitched vocal that's very affecting. It's a
pretty tune, too. Various commentators have suggested that Pete sang the
number because the subject matter too closely paralleled Daltrey's own
experience at the time. This is possible, although Pete was always keen

to sing. This contrast between subject matter and vocal tone is similarly exploited in Pete's high tenor vocal on the *Sell Out* track "Odorono." In this case the lyric is low farce—a singer fails an audition when her deodorant lets her down—while Pete's vocal is beautiful: sincere, moving, and pitched almost in the range of a boy soprano. By the time of *Sell Out* (late '67), Pete was probably playing with the idea of juxtaposition, but on a track as early as "A Legal Matter" (late '65), it's more likely just the natural sound of his voice.

"A Legal Matter" has a circular structure, starting and ending with the same simple, high guitar riff, and with the same lyric appearing as both first and final verses. Recorded in October '65, the song anticipates some of the attitudes toward women from Jagger's "ruthless" period, e.g., "Stupid Girl," "Mother's Little Helper," and "Under My Thumb." Townshend's lyric is wittier than those of Jagger, more observant and less crushing, though as a singer, Pete can't hope to match either Jagger's sexual confidence or his effortless misogyny. Ultimately, "A Legal Matter" celebrates escape rather than domination.

As on so many tracks from The Who's first album, the late Nicky Hopkins plays piano. Though his part is far more conventional than on a track such as "Anyway, Anyhow, Anywhere," his playing is beautifully judged; he plays rippling little riffs in the right hand, high up in the "Floyd Cramer" register. However, Hopkins's piano is pretty low down in the mix, as if to take away none of the hard edge of the guitar and drums. To a degree unusual for The Who, this track swings. Keith's drumming is restrained enough most of the time—sufficiently conventional in its time-keeping role—that Entwistle is allowed to function as a normal bass player. Check out his walking bass line after the first line of each chorus.

Townshend always depicts himself as having been purely a rhythm guitarist in the early days, playing no lead at all. This is misleading, though not altogether surprising in a milieu where "heavy" overdriven blues playing was considered the only style for a *real* guitarist. In fact, he seems to have been quite a fluent picker in the country and western style, showing clear tone, clean picking, and major-scale tonality in a manner reminiscent of James Burton's style, itself derived from Chet Atkins. On the odd occasions when Pete broke away from rhythm guitar, he played this style fluently (e.g., the solo on "Don't Look Away" from *A Quick One*) long before he mastered the more common '60s blues-rock medium, as did George Harrison, who shared with Townshend a feeling of being overawed by Eric Clapton. "A Legal Matter" features a nicely articulated lick in this country style between verses. The country flavor extends to Pete speaking the final verse in a knee-slapping meter, reminiscent of Woody Guthrie's talkin' blues style.

"LEAD GUITAR SEEMED MORE SURE OF HIMSELF THAN THE REST."

—Head of BBC Light Programme

audition board, passing The Who by four votes to three,

February 12, 1965

Almost from the first listening, "The Kids Are Alright" fascinated me. The more I listened, the more it seemed to be a decidedly ambiguous song. Instantly attractive, the song is a model of one type of straightforward power pop (before that phrase took on less appealing connotations), yet possessing some musical quality at odds with the context and the lyrics. I couldn't place it. As nearly as I could describe it at the age of fourteen, it seemed to share something of the tonality of the hymns we sang each morning in school assembly. I needn't tell you what my aspiring mod friends at school made of my attempts to articulate this theory.

"Kids" was released as the second of the Decca spoilers—Lambert was reportedly "furious" with the company, because he believed he'd extracted an agreement from them to release "La-La-La-Lies" next—but questions of its legitimacy as a single are sidelined by the charm and longevity of the song. With a punchy title, well suited to the band's perceived relationship with their fans, the song has come to assume a central position in Who mythology. Still, the lightweight sense of the lyric never entirely accorded with an undertow I heard in the music. Why? A song which opens, "I don't mind other guys dancing with my girl" makes a fairly clear statement of intent concerning its subject matter; one immediately senses that it's not going to be about rain forests. We know where we stand. This song is about girls and dancing, about kids . . . and their evident alrightness. Whether heartfelt, or bashed out in fifteen minutes (or both), the words are about as close as Townshend comes to the "Youth Club" or "Teen Etiquette" styles of writing—not surprising, since this is a very early Townshend song, dating back to High Numbers days—yet heard as a whole, the record always seemed to connect with something altogether more baroque.

Two quite separate currents flow through "Kids." First, the influence of The Beatles, whose pre–Rubber Soul style of pop writing is clearly the starting point for "Kids." This strain is general rather than specific, though the second half of the verse—" but I know sometimes I/ must get out in the light"—has a hint of "All My Loving." The debt is nicely acknowledged in the guitar chords of the second break (1'57" on *MBBB*),[2] reminiscent of the vocal stacked harmonies in "Twist and Shout," though Moon's playing alone prevents any similarity to the Beatles' overall sound. The second component is a diversity of influences which collectively we'll label Constant Lambert, since Kit Lambert had been hard at work on Pete's musical tastes:

> He played me a lot of music that his father had unearthed. I listened to people like Purcell, Corelli, William Walton [Kit's godfather] . . . and lots of Baroque stuff. Kit would buy me the records and I would listen to them, and they were harmonically very influencing on the way I wrote. I think the first manifestation of it was on the song "The Kids Are Alright" where I actually started to use baroque chords, suspended chords. It did a lot to create that churchy feel and had a lot to do with the way I play.

The "churchy" feel is clearly heard in the chorus of "Kids," where the chords roll away after the word "alright," and throughout the verses, where Pete is playing suspended chords, letting a note from one chord hang over into the next, weaving a countermelody around what is otherwise the simplest of chord sequences. With no rhythm guitar cluttering things up, the bass and drums carry the song, and the chord voicings have space to create the maximum effect. Partly due to this, and partly because of the way the vocal harmonies are arranged, an apparently bright, up-tempo number carries a considerable air of distance. The harmonies may have been an attempt to evoke Jan and Dean or The Beach Boys, but the result is much more poignant, containing none of the primary colors found in the cheerful, breezy, Californian vocal groups.

All songwriters, composers, and players have key phrases that underpin their work. These aren't the "stock phrases" that the improvising musician develops with experience, but brief, usually very simple, two-

or three-note themes that lie at the core of an individual's musical personality. They have much to do with the way a person hears as with any conscious approach to note selection. When you're familiar with someone's work, you can pick them out as these themes reappear in their various forms.

The song starts with the typical Townshend pyramid opening:

- solo guitar statement
- brief unaccompanied vocal passage
- band entry

Much like, "Anyway, Anyhow, Anywhere," except that the first line—"I don't mind"—is sung as a full choral effect, like a shorter version of the intro to "A Quick One." This intro type appears in its simplest form on "Kids." Instead of the more common fanfare, the guitar plays a single chord—D R O N G G G G—a timeless way of establishing pitch for unaccompanied singers.

Another trademark occurs in the vocal. Listen to Pete's high harmony in the final chorus, on the word "right." Previously he's held a single note, the obvious one, a third above Roger's melody line; now at the close, he extends it up, then down. The suspended chord is transposed to the vocal harmonies. Much like the "ooh-ooh-ooh"s on the front of "I'm a Boy," it's instinctive, charming, and entirely characteristic of the early Who.

*   *   *

In England, the legal dispute caused the "genuine," Who-approved singles to be interspersed by three tactical releases from Decca, though nobody was in much doubt as to which was which since they appeared on different labels. American record buyers would not have found the distinction so easy, since all Who records (with the exception of "Substitute") came out on Decca. In the event, the only tactical single issued in the U.S. was "The Kids Are Alright" / "A Legal Matter," which was released in July '66 and failed to chart. "A Legal Matter" and "Kids" both demonstrate the power of simplicity, but ultimately they're album tracks rather than planned singles. The real successor to "Substitute" is one of the finest pop singles of all time: "I'm a Boy."

I'M A BOY

"I've written eleven songs with 'boy' in the title."

—Pete Townshend

The "I'm a Boy" single is the perfect manifestation of The Who as pop group—punchy, melodic, funny, concise, possessing incredible momentum—one could list its virtues at almost infinite length. It's traditional pop music in the sense that it features an immediately catchy tune, a good hook, and a memorable chorus, but so full of energy and played with such controlled intensity that the record threatens to burst at the seams. Any fool can play with intensity; the skill lies in controlling it: paying it out, reeling it in, knowing when to let it breathe, and when to go for the kill. Such judgment is rare in pop music, and even where it is present in an individual it may be smothered by unfavorable surroundings. Townshend's gift was the ability to compose poignant, melodic pop, and his good fortune was to find a drummer as sympathetic to his style as Moon, *and* a bassist as temperamentally well suited as Entwistle.

The trouble with writing successful singles is that with each hit, the stakes are raised. What's next? How do you follow "My Generation"? "Substitute"? Difficult. The answer—if you're capable—is with something as exquisite as "I'm a Boy." As The Who's run of hits continued, the pressure on Townshend as writer intensified. With one album out and another needed later in the year, The Who's career already seemed more like a series of crises than the smooth rise many other groups seemed to experience. A new wave of blues-based music was rising from the under-

U.S. trade ad for "I'm A Boy", 1966

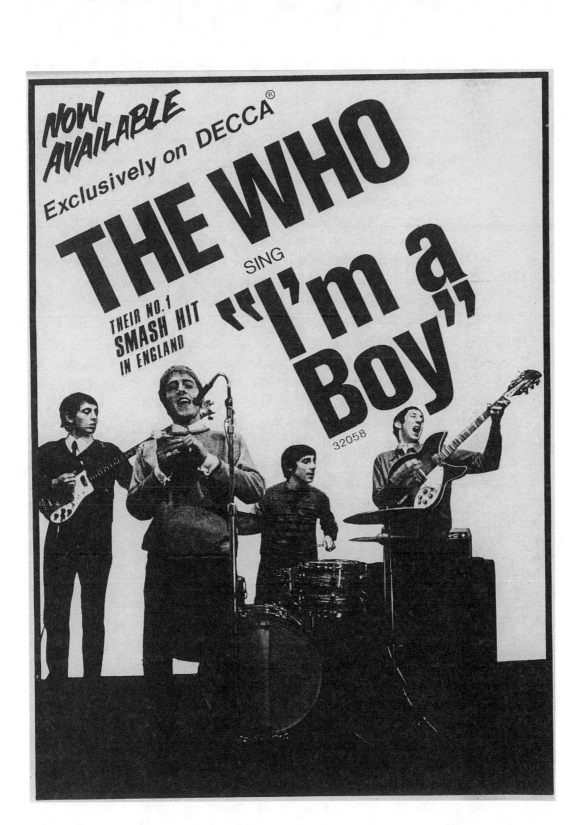

ground, led by groups like Cream, with the emphasis on instrumental prowess and lengthy improvisation, miles away in spirit from the focused, quirky, song-based material that The Who dealt in. If Townshend had run out of songs by this point, The Who could easily have vanished beneath the combined weight of power trios like Cream and the Jimi Hendrix Experience (Hendrix arrived in England fourteen days after "I'm a Boy" charted). Fortunately, Townshend didn't dry up, and "I'm a Boy" reached number 2, spending a total of ten weeks on the charts, exactly matching the success of "My Generation."

Many writers would have been content at this stage to stick with a tested formula, and rework one of the preceding songs into a fairly safe chart bet—but not Townshend. "I'm a Boy" strikes out in several new directions. Musically the song is more complex than its predecessors, with augmented chords and sixths used in the bridge—familiar enough in Beatles songs but new to Who singles, which tended to use the simplest of chords. Lyrically, it marks the point where simple slogans are exchanged for a more personal approach. Above all, it's a wonderful per-formance—or at least, the single is. Unfortunately, *Meaty, Beaty, Big & Bouncy* uses a different version.

Apparently the surviving fragment of a planned opera (there seem remarkably few Townshend songs from this era that aren't) to be called *Quads*, "I'm a Boy" fits a detailed, internally consistent narrative onto a two-and-a-half minute single, the aural equivalent of writing a story on the back of a postcard. Though the words of the four preceding singles are all perfectly convincing, "I'm a Boy" marks a new phase in Pete's writing. "I Can't Explain" is self-explanatory; "Anyway, Anyhow, Anywhere," cowritten with Roger, ends up as a fairly standard piece of pop/R&B machismo; and "My Generation" derives much of its vigor from the simplicity and repetition of its slogans. "Substitute" seems to be the bridge between styles, the point at which the move toward the greater detail and emotional depth of "I'm a Boy" begins. Discussing the mechanics of songwriting in a 1968 *Rolling Stone* interview, Townshend told Jann Wenner:

> Our manager will create artificial pressures to try and get me to operate, but I know they're artificial so they don't work like they used to. "My Generation" was written under pressure [to] . . . make

a statement. It's a very blustering kind of blurting thing. A lot of our early records were. "I Can't Explain" was . . . a bluster, and "Anyway, Anyhow, Anywhere" . . . was just a brag. "Substitute" was a take off on Mick Jagger or something equally banal.

This type of critique is pure Townshend—simultaneously self-deprecatory and defensive, defusing criticism by anticipating it—and marks him out from his peers. You can't imagine, for example, Keith Richards publicly reviewing and reassessing his work in quite the same manner. As brag and bluster go, those early songs don't do so badly either, though one understands what Pete means—and the remark should be taken in its cultural period and context. San Francisco in 1968, spiritual home to *Live Dead*, was not the epicenter of the punchy two-minute pop single form—whatever you make of "Dark Star" as a 45! The earlier songs don't so much express feeling as set up a series of personae for Daltrey to act out the role of Disenchanted Youth. So far as that's what the songs were designed to do, they're pretty successful—not least when you consider that they're the work of a youth aged nineteen or twenty.

In the eighteen months since the release of "I Can't Explain," Pete gains confidence and gradually broadens his range as a songwriter. Encouraged by Kit Lambert, Pete's writing moves from the general to the personal, from the formulaic to the individual, and with "I'm a Boy" we see the first signs of a unique and genuinely unusual creative imagination at work. The song is recognizably Pete, and couldn't have been written by anyone else. Compare its contemporaries in the top 20 and you'll see the subject matter dealt with in "I'm a Boy" is not typical of the average pop song circa 1966. Open to a range of interpretations—and one wouldn't want to limit the fun by defining it too closely—the song is certainly about gender confusion and muted sibling rivalry. It extends "Substitute"'s general concerns about identity into the specific area of sexual identity, a recurrent theme in Townshend's work.

"I'm a Boy"'s protagonist, Bill, is a normal, healthy lad, born the only boy into a family of women—a mother and three sisters. This gender imbalance creates constant problems for Bill, whose life is seriously disrupted by such a surfeit of femininity. All those sisters! Bill would far rather be with the boys. Wishing only to spend his time in healthy, everyday boyish pursuits—fishing, playing cricket, riding bicycles through streams, or messing around with knives and rolling in mud—his attempts are constantly frustrated by a dysfunctional mother. Whether the woman is scatterbrained, malicious, or simply exhausted from bearing and raising four children we don't learn, but it's clear that she cannot be bothered to grasp the vital distinction between the girls Jean-Marie, Felicity, Sally Joy—and poor old Bill. Her delusional state is obviously deeply engrained, capable on occasions of producing physical violence, because Bill's life is made dangerous if he even raises the subject: "I'm a boy, I'm a boy but my ma won't admit it/ I'm a boy, I'm a boy but if I say I am I get it."

The pernicious effects on his day-to-day life are immediately obvious: his cricket is made a nightmare and his cycling ruined. Faced with the appalling prospect of going out to bat in a wig, or having to field in the covers[1] sporting a print frock, it's no wonder Bill feels "lucky if he gets trousers to wear." Even today no self-respecting lad likes to wear *too* much makeup while bicycling—how much worse in the sexual climate of thirty years ago!—and hairpins frankly are a bore when one is trying to drum up a satisfying wrestling match in the mud. They're unsightly, unsporting, and potentially dangerous to one's opponent.

Nor does the coercion stop with the mother's unsuitable ideas about clothing and coiffure. A second front is opened up in the form of the constant threat posed by the three wicked sisters, who, denying Bill's essential identity as an individual, enjoy him as a mannequin on which they practice their cosmetic skills and conduct interesting experiments in hairstyling. Bill's father is never mentioned, which may be significant. Perhaps he's absent, or perhaps simply too weak-willed to take a stand against this monstrous, domineering houseful of women. Either way, his influence is so ineffectual that he's never alluded to. In the face of such an overt, concerted program of feminization, Bill can only shriek over and over to his mother, his sisters, and the world at large: "I'm a Boy—I'm a Boy—I'm a Boy."

It's tempting to speculate what becomes of Bill in adult life, whether he slips effortlessly into a half-life of covert transvestism, or manages to put aside his adolescent problem along with other childish things. Do the scars still show? Does a dark, repressed neurosis drive Bill to a life of furtive assignations and shabby consummations? Does he remain a Head Case? Does he perhaps have himself photographed wearing corsetry, like that worn in Keith Moon's own portfolio of "glamor" shots? We shall never know, although Townshend manages to cram enough narrative detail into three verses to engage our attention and stimulate our curiosity.

Pete's later lyrics sometimes suffer from being over-wordy, but nothing is further from the case here. Like a good novelist, he constructs a detailed portrait with a couple of lightly sketched episodes. Nor, as befits such an ambiguous tale, does he anywhere tell you how the characters themselves feel; he merely provides a few facts, reports some incidents, and allows you, the listener, to fill the gaps. If you love the song as much as I do, you'll be interested by the omitted verse. Present on the demo, it's dropped from both studio versions, probably because its rather awkward scansion makes it hard to sing—though it's also the one occasion on which Townshend allows Bill to speak directly about his private responses:

> They never wanted a boy I know
> But surely one boy's not too many to own?
> Sometimes I feel I could destroy
> Jean-Marie, Felicity and Sally Joy

Everything discussed so far, especially the marvellous, precarious balance between the players, refers to the firstborn "I'm a Boy": the English single (Reaction 591004). In the realm of the Who back catalogue there is frequent potential for confusion, so let's stress that first refers here simply to the order of release and has nothing to do with which version was recorded first. Nobody who remembers hearing the single when it came out could ever be in any doubt that this is the finished masterpiece—we'll refer to it as v.1—or that the alternate version which appears on *Meaty, Beaty, Big & Bouncy* is just a curio—which we'll call v.2.

However many versions of "I'm a Boy" are extant (and it may be dozens once you include issues of stereo/mono/simulated stereo/cleaned-up remasters, etc.), even two different takes are quite bad enough, when the original is perfect. Generally, it's fascinating to hear outtakes and alternate versions, such as the various "Mary-Anne with the Shaky Hands," and Bob Dylan's work provides frequent instances where the best performance isn't the released version, but "I'm a Boy" v.1 is, for me anyway, so fine a performance that alternate versions detract. I formulate no

General Theory here—I just find that when it comes to v.2, I don't wanna to listen to it.

The two versions are completely different takes, as distinct from an edit, or alternate mix. They are different from start to finish. Since the original single failed to chart in the U.S., it's doubtful whether the American listener, buying *Meaty, Beaty, Big & Bouncy* in 1972, would have been unduly disturbed by the switch; and English buyers who already had the single may have welcomed a new version. I still think it's a shame that a lesser version was used, when the single is among the most engaging and enjoyable noises the band ever made.

The Reaction single (v.1) is tougher, more compact, and so well pressed it positively leaps off the vinyl. Perfection. It starts like a greyhound out of the trap and never lets up. *The Meaty, Beaty, Big & Bouncy* version is a good-natured mongrel. When you play the original 7" single, the guitar has the ideal mixture of brittleness and compression, and the drums are so powerful they shake the whole mix. Separation is not an issue. This is the open sound of a *kit* of drums being hit very hard (mostly, all at once), the antithesis of the contained, discrete, modern, processed drum sound. John Entwistle compared it to the sound of biscuit tins; I like it. But then I like biscuits, too . . .

Crucially, the arrangement is trimmed down to exactly the right length, so that the song builds relentlessly to its climax and resolution in 2'28". Listen to the opening; few bands in the world can develop that much power from a standing start. Pete sings the first verse; Roger enters at the second: "My name is Bill and I'm a head case." Their voices match so well you'd hardly notice the transition unless you were listening for it, and when they combine in harmony at the first chorus the blend is definitive Who. Daltrey adds exactly the right degree of petulance to the later verses, and the bass part is so good it needs to be considered separately.

Version 2 is gentler and more than a minute longer, with small differences of lyric and scansion. Townshend describes it as "more relaxed . . . [with] fancy voices added." The fancy vocal harmonies lean more toward Beach Boys territory, which is a pity considering the decidedly English choral quality of the best Who harmonies. In most other cases, the more they try to sound like surfers, the closer they resemble choirboys— a considerable part of the charm. Maybe Pete likes his extended guitar solo on v.2. It rambles around the same harmonic territory as v.1, developing a series of chords, but without that most vital ingredient of all great Who singles: tension. On v.1, the progression is reduced to eight chords, arranged for voices singing "oohs." But if it's guitar you want, the place to look is the Townshend home demo, where the sequence is much more "out," at times rattling around Pete's newly acquired "luxury" Grampian spring reverb (an echo chamber) like a piece of experimental music.

Both versions 1 and 2 feature John Entwistle's French horn, though the phrases are better chosen and better incorporated into the mix on v.1. At about the two-minute mark on v.2, you hear John trying out ideas, some of which work, some of which are passable. They don't sound like lines that a musician of Entwistle's quality would have intended for final release. John's bass parts always reveal someone who's thinking in terms of the whole song, and with "I'm a Boy"'s structure running verse 1/verse 2/chorus, the bass is used to distinguish verses. For the first verse, John plays a staggered, syncopated pattern (not exactly funk, but making plenty of use of rests), then changes for the second ("My name is Bill and . . .") verse, to the simplest possible idea, an "oom-pah" bass line, more often found in Euro-beat MOR and Bavarian Bier-kellers—where it's usually played by brass instruments.

It's clear from Pete's demo, where the 2/4 "oom-pah" beat is used prodigally in verses and chorus, that the feel was part of the original conception. On v.2, John plays the part on bass guitar, doubling it with French horn high in the mix. What's potentially an extremely corny beat is transformed into rock by the momentum of the band. John plays the two bass notes dead straight, on the beat, left-right, left-right; Pete's guitar pushes against them double-time, duh-duh-duh-duh duh-duh-duh-duh; while Moon thrashes around like an octopus with a weakness for crash cymbals.

The two versions demonstrate Moon's intrinsic importance to the sound. An on-form Moon is vital, not just for his own part, but because everything that Townshend plays is rendered doubly dramatic by the interplay. Keith plays much straighter on v.2—if indeed it is Keith—and though some extra tympani flourishes are featured in very broad stereo, and in one verse a little half-time drum figure out of "Ticket to Ride" is rather tentatively introduced, all the ecstatic fills that thunder through v.1 are absent. On that version, Moon is unquestionably the lead instrument. Listen to the four bars between the end of the verse "put this wig on, little boy" and the start of the chorus. Roger sustains the word "boy," while Keith builds a compound phrase—too long to call a "fill"—that owes very little to any formal notion of drumming and everything to his own personality.

In a direct comparison between the two versions, there's no contest. Everything that makes the single so joyful is missing. Version 2, sounds ultimately, like a decent monitor mix of a work in progress or a rehearsal—perhaps given the context, a dress-rehearsal.

*   *   *

Kit Lambert had been playing various classical pieces to the young Pete Townshend, who expressed an interest in Purcell. Certainly a touch of distinctly classical harmony, and of the hymnal, can be heard in the resolution of the suspended chord to the major, a classic Townshend figure. These harmonic ideas first appear in the chorus of "The Kids Are Alright," and again in the final "You Are Forgiven" section of "A Quick One":

> I got very into Baroque music with people like Purcell and I started to be interested in the fact that they used melodic transitions very rarely and there would always be suspensions and tension and it would be another level of tension and it would drop. This was mainly Purcell . . . who I was deeply influenced by. . . . "I'm a Boy" did that as well in the solo.

By and large, when rock musicians start talking about the influence of Classical music, it's kinder to have them shot; in this case though the influence is audible, all through "I'm a Boy" (and many other of Townshend songs). Right from the top it's clear that two separate forces have been harnessed. The rhythmic drive that Entwistle and especially Moon supply is pure rock 'n' roll, simple in conception and beautifully executed—Moon's eccentricities balanced by John's formal approach and irreproachable sense of time; on top, the harmonic element of the guitar and voices come from an older tradition.

The solo section marks the first appearance of an harmonic idea that will reappear often in later Who works. In this case, stacked harmony voices unfold a progression of eight chords over a pedal bass. Gradually, while his bass guitar still pedals an E, Entwistle's French horn joins the stack, playing unison with the chord progression until the last two bars, where he breaks out into a trill heralding the final verse. From here to the end, the song builds all the way with Moon creating a great joyous wash of noise, all his cymbals ringing at once.

As The Who grew more confident of their ability, there was less reliance on aggression and wrecked equipment as means of covering musical limitations, and greater use of vocal harmonies, although none of their attack was lost. While American groups of the period had a hard time matching the onstage power of the best English bands, they outsang them effortlessly when it came to harmony (or part-singing). One listen to a Byrds record tells you a lot about close harmony (though their attempts to play instruments, and the unredeemed squalor of their live performances on their 1965 English tour, are still cackled about today). The Hollies were about the best of the English vocal groups—and they could reproduce their harmonies onstage—but it remained an essentially American form. No matter how hard The Who tried to sound as slick and American as Jan and Dean or The Beach Boys (whom they greatly admired), the result always came out as something essentially English. In time, The Stones would get the hang of country and western harmony, helped along by Gram Parsons, who taught Keith Richards about texture and tone and high country fifths, although Jagger could never entirely resist the urge to lapse into parody.

Compare the West Coast groups, or the doo-wop/barbershop/four- or five-part harmonies that dominated New York vocal stylings, with the early recordings of The Beatles, The Kinks, and The Who, and you'll hear at once that they're worlds apart. Much is written about the art-school influence on English pop, but less about the numbers of rock 'n' rollers who sang as choristers. Both Keith Richards and Stevie Winwood had voices pure enough before they broke to sing in notable choirs. Keith sang in both Chichester and Westminster Cathedrals, while the Birmingham-born Winwood sang in the Three Choirs, an annual West Country Festival held since 1724 in the cathedral cities of Gloucester, Worcester, and Hereford. Just as the Baptist church in America was explicit in shaping soul music through its gospel roots, the choral influence is implicit in the way that English musicians hear harmony.

With the exception of regular church-going families (a small and decreasing minority), and children such as John Entwistle, who learned music at home, most English schoolboys made their first practical acquaintance with music—and thus with notions of harmony and descant—singing hymns at school. Though the bearing of hymns on English rock 'n' roll may not seem immediately apparent, its influence rests just beneath the surface. Most rock musicians (at least those of the 1950s and '60s) had little or no formal musical education, and self-taught musicians learn from listening, grabbing onto whatever music surrounds them as they're growing up.

By contrast, American kids of the '40s and '50s grew up with a wide range of diverse regional and ethnic music available on the radio, especially at night when under good conditions a strong signal might travel 1,000 miles across the heartland of America. In Hibbing, Minnesota, next to the Canadian border, the young Bob Dylan could hear music from Shreveport, Louisiana. According to Dylan,

> Late at night, I used to listen to Muddy Waters, John Lee Hooker, Jimmy Reed and Howlin' Wolf blasting in from Shreveport . . . I used to stay up till two, three o'clock in the morning. Listened to all those songs then tried to figure them out.

Nothing remotely similar existed in 1950s England. Young visionaries could hear *Music While You Work* or *Three-Way Family Favourites* (always an intriguing title!) broadcast on the one official channel, the BBC Light Programme. "Popular" music consisted largely of an archaic mix of Variety, strict tempo (ballroom) performed by regional BBC dance bands, and bad English covers of bad American schmaltz. There were exceptions, of course, but on the whole the listening was not easy. Radio Luxembourg could be heard playing a certain amount of pop in the evenings and occasionally AFN—Armed Forces Network—broadcasting from Germany, might bring a little cultural diversity. Nothing much changed until the advent of the pirate radio stations in Easter 1964, which was fine for those born, like myself, in the 1950s, but too late to have much influence on those born in the '40s.

"I'm a Boy" was The Who's fifth consecutive English hit, and the band was now a major live attraction, playing, on average, fifteen dates per month throughout 1966. Their strongly visual show helped in countries where a language problem existed. In Europe, they were popular in

Germany, and were especially well received in Denmark and Sweden, where they toured in June and again in October. In November they recorded most of the tracks for their second album, *A Quick One* (*Happy Jack* in U.S.), working quickly, because they still managed to play at least ten shows that month, including a six-date German tour. Territories were falling to them everywhere it seemed, except the one market which they most wanted to crack: America.

HAPPY JACK

"Happy Jack" was the single chosen to launch The Who's assault on America. Released in England in December '66, it was held back three months to coincide with the group's first American dates in March '67—or that at least became the official Decca line. In fact, the company hadn't considered the record worth releasing in America. They'd already released five singles without any notable response[1] and had already passed on their option, only exercising it months later, when it was learned that The Who was scheduled to visit America, playing on a high-profile package show with serious promotion. Such were the circumstances surrounding the band's first, unlikely, American hit.

Aside from some film clips shot in England for *Shindig*, The Who had received very little U.S. exposure. The reluctance of American radio to program their singles—even as they charted one after another in England—was evidence either that something was getting lost in the translation and The Who's music was an exclusively European taste, or that somebody was not doing his job. It is possible that Decca failed to promote the records properly or perhaps simply didn't know how to present a group like The Who. Artists whose work is not easily categorized

Fear and Loathing in the Goldhawk Rd. Ralph Steadman's "Happy Jack" advertisment, 1966.

80

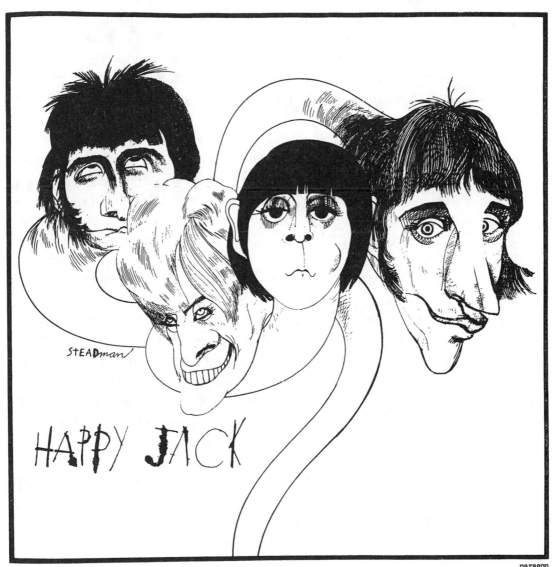

are usually more interesting, though they often pay for their independence in public or professional neglect. "Happy Jack" was eventually released in the U.S. on March 18, 1967, and at last The Who began to pick up some radio play as a run of New York shows got underway.

Murray the K's Fifth Dimension opened on March 25, at the RKO Theater on 58th Street in New York, and ran until April 2. The scene had changed a great deal in the three years since the heyday of Beatlemania, but this annual event, promoted by the "fifth Beatle," would still have attracted considerable attention in the business. Murray the K was an influential DJ, and artists appearing on his bill would have quickly seen their records playlisted on New York radio stations—and beyond, as stations round the country followed his selections. Not that Murray was interested in oddball stuff like The Who or Cream; what he really wanted was Mitch Ryder and The Detroit Wheels. The Who only got on the show as a result of a complicated trade-off between Frank Barsalona of Premier Talent and Murray the K, who was desperate to have Mitch Ryder on the bill at any cost. Neither man had the least interest in The Who (Barsalona had repeatedly rebuffed Stamp's attempts to get The Who signed to Premier), but at last the band's U.S. affairs came—at least temporarily—within the influence of two people who knew how the business worked and had a mutual interest in seeing the record promoted. Murray the K gave "Happy Jack" plenty of airplay, and Barsalona persuaded Decca to hire three independent pluggers, sufficient to give The Who their first U.S. top-40 entry. "Happy Jack" was a medium-sized hit, eventually reaching 24 on the *Billboard* chart, and Decca grudgingly began to treat the band with slightly more respect.

Murray the K's 1967 bash was the last of this particular type of package show—whose roots ran right back to Alan Freed—with the acts playing five or six shows per day. The final roster was an improbable mixture of the new and the old, U.S. and U.K., top-40 mainstream and fledgling underground, including Cream, Smokey Robinson and The Miracles, Wilson Pickett, Al Kooper's band The Blues Project, and others. The Who performed well up to standard, smashing copious amounts of rented equipment—their Marshalls had been left at home to save air-freight bills—and making a point of wrecking Murray the K's gold-plated emcee's microphone. With five or six houses daily, it was important that the gear should not get too smashed, so Pete and his faithful assistant Bobby

Pridden spent the time between sets with gluepot and soldering iron, performing open-heart surgery on guitars.

Pete's favored Rickenbackers had a tendency to disintegrate "like light-bulbs," spoiling the show by breaking too quickly, and usually proving impossible to repair to any playable standard. He discovered that the American-made Fender guitars were far cheaper in the U.S. than at home, and considerably more robust. The two main Fender guitars, the Telecaster and the Stratocaster, whose design hasn't changed since the late '40s and early '50s, are basically amplified planks, good solid lumps of wood with bolted-on necks. Pete discovered they were tough enough—on a stage made of boards—to pull off a new trick. If the guitar was held out at arm's length with its neck pointed up toward the ceiling and speared downward to the stage (like throwing a dart into the ground), it would bounce. On a well-sprung stage, it would bounce right back up, like a yo-yo. The Fender was so robust, it would even stay in tune!

Back in England "Happy Jack" had already reached number 3, spent seven weeks on the chart, and disappeared before the band even set out for New York. Released in early December '66, it was The Who's third hit single of the year, and the sixth successive Townshend composition to enter the English top ten. The band seemed to have settled into an enviable rhythm, steadily issuing successful singles at approximately four-month intervals, over a period of two years. The record also continued an established Who tradition of wasting no time between a single's recording and release. While all but the top groups were expected to cut both sides of a single in one session, the period between recording and release was entirely in the hands of their record company. Groups of lesser importance might find their single held back—or brought forward—to accommodate the schedule of major acts on the same label (or for that matter, to fit in with holiday arrangements in the press room). Whereas the whole process often took The Beatles three months, "Happy Jack" was recorded in one day (November 10, 1966)—half a day according to John Entwistle—and was on sale three weeks later.

The Who's tally of three hits per annum in 1965 and 1966 matched The Rolling Stones and actually exceeded The Beatles, who released only two singles in 1966: "Paperback Writer" and "Eleanor Rigby." The individuality of Pete's work meant that he could now be regarded as one of a handful of writers at the top of the English pop scene, like Lennon and

McCartney, Jagger and Richards, or Ray Davies—a select few whose work is immediately recognizable and unmistakably their own. Pete had found his voice. Along with Dylan, whose influence was universal, each of these writers was a sufficiently strong personality to stamp a song with his own character. All are readily identifiable from a few bars of any of their records.

The growth in self-confidence that was evident in "I'm a Boy" continued with "Happy Jack," an even more singular and quirky composition than its predecessor. Pete's growing maturity as a lyricist enabled him to approach subjects beyond those traditionally considered "suitable" for popular song: girls, lust, cars, requited and unrequited love, and of course, boasting. With less need to bluster and rant, he was able now to speak in his own voice, and a personality starts to emerge, rather than a collection of attitudes. The character behind the song is distinctively Pete, even when the voice on disk is Roger's. This new-found freedom would soon result in singles with lyrics concerning arcade games, masturbation, eyesight, dogs, and buses—but none of the subsequent songs match "Happy Jack" as simple fantasy.

The song concerns a beach-dwelling hermit of indeterminate age who lives on an island in the Irish Sea. Jack is ostracized by "the kids," who sustain a campaign of persistent lies and abuse, culminating in a savage trampling with a furry donkey, although Jack stands accused of nothing much worse than a poor showing during community singing. Rather like Keith Moon—who was currently suffering delusions about his vocal accomplishments—Jack frequently selected "the wrong key." A version of Jan and Dean's "Bucket T," featuring Keith squeaking enthusiastically as lead vocalist, had recently been a runaway hit for The Who in Sweden. Convinced that he should sing—prominently—on all future records, he'd made several attempts on "Happy Jack" before being physically restrained in the studio control room, where he was safely off-mic. Out on the studio floor, John, Pete, and Roger had just finished a vocal overdub when Keith freed himself and popped his head up at the control-room window, eliciting the cry of "I saw yer" from Townshend, which is heard at the end.

The record has a wonderful, fat bass sound. High in the mix (John seems to have liked to be heard), it's the definitive mainstream '60s English pop bass sound: plonky, lightly damped, and played tightly in time

Inspired by a poster of the Monkees, Pete tunes his Stratocaster backstage at the Murray the K show, 1967.
PHOTO © DON PAULSEN

with the bass drum. John didn't always play this style (apart from anything else, Moon's drumming more often than not precluded it), but here John's tone fills the whole track. The bass and drums make such a big sound that they alone carry the arrangement, allowing Townshend to use quite a thin guitar tone without the whole sounding empty. The suitably quirky guitar phrase which opens the song is as singular as the lyric. Similarly structured songs of the period use riffs with clear R&B precedents: "I Feel Fine," "Day Tripper," and "Ticket to Ride" all rework Bobby Parker's "Watch Your Step"; and "Satisfaction" comes from a James Brown horn riff. But if the "Happy Jack" lick has any relatives, they live in unwarranted obscurity.

The song is in 2/4 time—basically a march—with an extra beat thrown in for each line of the verse, which gives the track its lopsided meter. At the end of each line the rhythm has to catch up, with the extra beat falling on the following italicized word:

> Happy Jack was a man but he *wasn't* old
> He lived in the sand at the *Isle of* Man

This sits quite comfortably because the meter of the song follows the phrasing. Unlike some of the "progressive" experiments with compound time, this is not an attempt to squeeze a clever time signature into a piece, but simply reflects the natural length of the line. Many of Lennon's songs, such as "I'm Only Sleeping," "All You Need Is Love," contain bars of odd length and chunks of compound time for the same reason, and the flow of the song is never disturbed.

As you'd expect, Moon's playing is utterly unconventional, and, if the word can be used to describe a drum part, charming. Pete's demo of the song has a strong flamenco influence—complete with mock-Spanish vocal extemporizing—which only really survives on the single in the guitar solo, though something of the style also carries over into the drumming. Moon attacks the piece with a sort of stylized machismo, at times laying out and playing very little, at other times filling every conceivable space. A December 1969 performance at the London Coliseum, included on the *30 Years of Maximum R&B* video, shows this clearly. The video is worth viewing for Keith's performance alone, which is crisp, spot on the beat, tough yet somehow funny. Vintage Moon. During the quiet sections of the verse, he stops playing the top kit altogether and freewheels on his twin bass pedals, using the sticks to mime a mouth singing along with the "la-la-la la" background vocal. When he does come back in, especially for the guitar break, he matches Pete's *rasgueado* strumming, beat for beat—more duet than duel. Sadly, the whole bottom end (Keith's twin bass drums and the bass guitar) is almost inaudible, but Keith's lovely, fluid runs around the tom-toms are well up in the mix, and he's in wonderful form, if anything improving on his part of the single. Once the camera settles on him it can't pull away.

When compared to the best work of his contemporaries, Moon's drum part on "Happy Jack" makes no sense at all: there's no backbeat to hold, it doesn't nail down a groove, it doesn't in any conventional sense mark off the verse/chorus divisions; it's more like an enthusiastic puppy at play, looking for things to join in with, resting for a moment to catch its breath before bounding off in another direction. Keith simply explodes all over the song, his part functioning more as a commentary than a structural role, punctuating the lyric and choreographing Pete's guitar thrusts.

So where did this style come from? Even the most inventive and original innovators generally have clear antecedents. Hendrix certainly broke more ground than any other rock guitarist, but his roots are clear to see. What Parker and Coltrane did on alto and tenor sax was something quite new, but it was clearly a logical step forward from the music they grew up with. Moon seems to arrive from nowhere. His own named influences—Buddy Rich, Gene Krupa, Shelly Manne—give us some clues about flash and visual style, but don't really reveal much else. There were far, far more competent technicians among Keith's contemporaries, but it was Moon who was noticed and singled out for praise by elders like Elvin Jones.

Moon should be regarded as a phenomenon of nature, one of a kind, without whom The Who would never have sounded as they did. Keith's individuality isn't restricted to the parts he plays; the actual sound of his kit is unique, too. Throughout the '60s, his drum sound resembled nobody else's. It's partly to do with hitting the skins hard enough; but others have done that. It's partly to do with the way the drums are recorded; but the same engineers recorded other drummers. It may be partly to do with the metal shells that Keith had made, or the make of drum; though if you know a Premier dealer selling kits that sound like Keith's . . . the world awaits.

It's a rule that only the very best musicians are instantly recognizable from their tone. This has nothing to do with technical ability—among guitarists, for example, you need hear only a second or two to identify Jeff Beck, Jimi Hendrix, Ry Cooder; Pete Townshend, or Keith Richards. It makes no difference whether they're players with great facility like the first three or technically more primitive players, like the latter pair; something in their sound enables the individual personality to come through.

*   *   *

Described by Pete as a "nonsense song," "Happy Jack" is set in a real location rather than in the usual undifferentiated teenage hinterland. The Isle of Man is a small island between England and Ireland, noted for an annual motorcycle race and a mild tax regime. With its sandy beaches, hotels, and holiday camps, it was the location for the Townshend family summer holidays through the 1950s.

Both of Peter's parents were musical. Cliff Townshend was an alto saxophonist, and Pete's mother, Betty, was a featured singer with The Sydney Torch Orchestra. When war broke out, certain occupations seem to have favored a particular service. Writers including Graham Greene, Ian Fleming, and Dennis Wheatley made for the Intelligence Services, while musicians—those who had any choice in the matter—headed for the Royal Air Force, with its stable of bands and more relaxed attitude toward discipline. Certainly a player like Cliff Townshend, who'd already made something of a name for himself in pre-war Dixieland jazz circles, would have chosen the RAF entertainment corps in preference to marching up and down parade grounds, thumping out Sousa marches with The Band of the Royal Welch Fusiliers. The entry of America into the war and the concurrent craze for swing music created a demand for big bands to entertain the huge numbers of servicemen and women stationed on bases everywhere from the north of Scotland to the tip of Cornwall. The RAF bands seem to have been organized in an appropriate hierarchical structure, with the best players graduating to the number one band, and so on. Cliff joined The Squadronaires, led by Ronnie Aldritch, which became one of the best-known bands in the country. Cliff met Betty, also in the entertainment corps, when she deputized one night for an absent vocalist.

After being demobilized, the band decided to retain their name and continue performing out of uniform. Expanding from fifteen to eighteen members, the band began a civilian career which lasted well into the mid-'60s, playing one-nighters through the winter and earning their main livelihood from long summer seasons, which included eighteen-week residencies at a seaside resort. Throughout the 1950s, The Squadronaires returned each summer to Douglas on the Isle of Man, and for that part of the season which coincided with the long holiday from school, Pete and his mother joined Cliff Townshend. Here the young Pete Townshend played in the sand. "Happy Jack" clearly builds on childhood memories, but the holidays also afforded the boy a chance to watch good musicians at close quarters, to fool around with the instruments, and perhaps to absorb something of the particular way in which the various sections of a dance band interact. As Betty Townshend told David Marsh, "Pete was there in front of the stand, watching rehearsals and always trying to sneak in round the back when he should be in bed. Watching the band . . . playing the drums."

War-time swing and '60s rock seem worlds apart, yet the two bands, The Squadronaires and The Who, were working concurrently. Looking through old copies of the *Bristol Evening Post*, a local paper in the west of England, I noticed dates for two forthcoming shows from the year 1966:

Sat 26th February	Winter Gardens, Weston-Super-Mare
	Ronnie Aldritch & The Squadronaires
Wed 11th May	Corn Exchange, Bristol The Who

It was the American practice to feature hit singles on albums, while in England the opposite was true. Decca felt that *A Quick One* was not a suitable album title for America, so they exchanged "Heatwave" for "Happy Jack" and renamed the album after the single, releasing it in May '67. Otherwise the U.K. and U.S. albums were much the same, a mixture of Townshend originals with songs from each member of the band, most notably John Entwistle's "Boris the Spider."

BORIS THE SPIDER

"'Boris the Spider,' both bass and vocals . . . I made the whole thing up on the spot as I went along. I often find my most enduring stuff was written without an instrument, even though it's very difficult writing a song without an instrument."

—John Entwistle

The solitary non-Townshend composition, and the only non-single on *MBBB*, "Boris" is one of two songs John Entwistle wrote for *A Quick One*. (The Who's second album needed two songs from each band member to satisfy the terms of a publishing deal.) Possibly the best-known of Entwistle's songs, its inclusion here is clearly attributable to guilty conscience on Townshend's part. Referring to it in his *Rolling Stone* review, Pete notes that it should have been a single, but band politics and his own insecurities got in the way. There may be a degree of special pleading here—Pete disarming his critics by getting the accusation in first—because the points he makes in the *Rolling Stone* article are every bit as political as the moves they describe. Amusing and original as "Boris" is, it was by no means an automatic choice as a single. At the time of its composition (late 1966), Townshend was turning out work of the highest quality, and "Boris" faced some pretty stiff opposition in the form of songs like "Happy Jack," "Pictures of Lily," and "I Can See for Miles." It might

John Entwistle poses with his custom-made, fur-covered, 8-legged "Boris the Spider" bass, 1967.
Photo © Don Paulsen

90

perhaps have fared better had it been written a few years later, around the time of, say "The Seeker."

Great musicians don't always make the best songwriters; indeed, limited technical knowledge often seems to be the hallmark of the best pop songwriters, while the real virtuoso players are frequently limited composers. John Entwistle—a highly accomplished bass player and easily the most musically literate member of The Who, who'd studied piano and trumpet from childhood—suffered the same difficulties that many competent players find when it comes to writing, namely that their critical faculties are far ahead of their composing abilities. As each idea presents itself, the trained musician tends to think, "No, that's nothing special," while the player of restricted musical knowledge is delighted at having discovered such a satisfactory concept. In the same way, the self-taught, nonreading musician (such as Pete) is often better placed to write songs than the literate musician. The former hears a new sound that suggests a mood and inspires a chain of ideas, the latter just hears a Ninth chord with the Seventh raised. Too often the result for the literate musician is that ideas are dismissed before they're given the chance to grow. As John Entwistle put it, "Knowing which chords I should go to next hindered me when I was writing a song; I couldn't do anything out of the ordinary."

Pete, who had written all the important material up to this point, never considered himself a lead guitarist in the Clapton/Beck/Hendrix sense. Where a solo was called for, as often as not Entwistle or Moon took it, while Pete nailed down the beat on rhythm guitar or—as on "Substitute"—used long sustained notes to build background atmosphere. Comparing the two very different roles of soloist and writer, he told Steve Rosen, "the joy I would get from expressing myself through a solo would never be as great and would never be as fulfilling as the joy I get from expressing myself through a song." Entwistle, who'd always wanted to be a lead instrumentalist (the role of the conventional pop bass guitarist being about as far away as you can get), was ideally suited to a three-piece lineup where the guitarist stuck to playing chords. In addition to the standard role of holding down the bottom end, he could play long, connecting runs, functioning as a front-line instrument (which just happened to be voiced in the bass register).

For some reason, most attempts at combining the two jobs result in hideous overplaying. Lead guitarists who switch to bass are traditionally the worst offenders, though rhythm guitar players often play good bass. Keith Richards played bass on many Stones tracks, and Hendrix (a superb rhythm guitarist who also happened to play lead guitar well) was a fine, subtle bassist (as demonstrated on "All Along the Watchtower"). The reason for Entwistle's success isn't hard to pin down: there's nothing technically difficult about the dual role, but the player does need to have *taste*.

For an idea of how The Who might have sounded with a bassist of no more than average ability, listen to the Stones-Aid single "The Last Time"/"Under My Thumb," recorded and issued in such a hurry that there was no time to wait for the return of the honeymooning John Entwistle. The tracks had to be completed before Keith and Mick's prison sentences were quashed (everyone knew that were never going to be imprisoned for long), so Pete played bass. On both tracks he takes a very conservative line, both musically and rhythmically. Hardly moving off the root-note of each chord, Townshend's bass sticks rigidly to the most basic on-the-beat rhythm, like a motorboat engine. "Under My Thumb" needs a much more syncopated feel at the bottom in order for the rhythm guitar chops to sit properly; those distinctive Richards' chords are up-strokes, and they need the bass to play downbeats and leave gaps in order to create that push–pull feel. Without this looseness in the rhythm section, it's just not sexy. Though Entwistle's contribution over the years was less flamboyant than Moon's, this single makes it very clear how big a part of the band's sound was his.

*   *   *

Of all The Who's non-Townshend material, "Boris the Spider" is unquestionably the popular favorite, regularly requested and performed in their live shows even after thirty years. The Spider has replaced the Ox as Entwistle's talisman. As with the other non-Townshend songs on *A Quick One*, the original impetus behind its creation was financial. Though Lambert and Stamp's promotional flair was inspired, they were utterly inexperienced as negotiators. Presumably, because so much of their management style depended on appearances, they approached deal-making in a similar spirit (whatever happens, always look as though you know what you're doing), and some of their early decisions were pretty rancid, even by the prevailing standards. Their first foray into the contractual jungle netted the fateful deal with Talmy, and their subsequent attempts to renegotiate still left The Who with only a very low percentage of the income from their record sales. Despite selling hundreds of thousands of singles, the money actually reaching the organization wasn't enough even to cover The Who's expenses, which is why live shows continued to remain so important, as the band's one reliable source of immediate income. This period of "profitless prosperity" as Stamp dubbed it, lasted right up until the revenues from *Tommy* finally came through the pipeline, around 1970, and was certainly the defining condition in which The Who spent the 1960s.

For a group who'd been earning a respectable wage from gigs before they ever entered the recording studio, this was a depressing state of affairs. Looking to remedy such an obviously dead-end situation, Lambert and Stamp cast around for other sources of income—the terms of Talmy's settlement effectively ruled out any lucrative recording advance—and the obvious choice was publishing.

Though it's not always realized, publishing royalties are by far the largest single source of income for musicians and singers, provided that they write their own material and don't sign any stupid contracts. As late as 1979, the standard recording contracts offered by several of the major record companies contained clauses automatically assigning all composers' rights to a publisher nominated by the record company, on a 50-50 split between writer and publisher (the nominated publishing company would usually be an arm of the record company). If the artist knew enough and was in a sufficiently strong position to enforce it, the clause could be deleted, but poorly advised or over-enthusiastic young musicians who were just keen to make a record could easily find they'd given away half of their single most important source of income for no reason at all.

Songwriting generates far greater sums than record sales. A group receiving, for example, a 10 percent recording royalty, have to split those ten points between four or five members, *and* pay their manager a percentage, whereas a lone songwriter could be earning an additional 7.5 percent all to himself. In bands where one or two members compose all the material, huge gaps in relative wealth open up between writers and non-writers, a situation that good management has to address, since the issue provokes more band splits than any other single cause. Where songs are worked up communally but only credited to one or two individuals the situation is acute; although this wasn't the case with The Who. In fact, if ever a band existed where this was demonstrably not the case, it was The Who. As the demos clearly show, Pete provided the band with completed arrangements, parts all worked out and little or nothing of the essential structure left to chance in the studio. The songs really are the work of one man.

It is extraordinary then, in a band so clearly dominated by one writer (a band moreover, which had nearly split up in the process of establishing that dominance), that Lambert and Stamp negotiated a publishing deal that called for the whole band to write! Essex Music, one of the major publishing houses, paid each member an advance of £500 to contribute two songs to the next album, *A Quick One*. The money certainly helped keep rivalries under control for a while, and appeased the group's shop-steward (as Lambert dubbed John Entwistle's mum). Roger probably felt less annoyed by Townshend's American cars once he could use his advance to buy a Volvo sports car. Barry Fantoni remembers:

> Pete was driving round in a van, maybe his mother's. I had some American car, cream with red leather seats. One of the ideas that was common to all of us at that time was the notion that American pop culture and that style of life was bigger and better than ours. What we did was a British version of it—which had its own value—but you knew that somehow the Union Jack was never quite gonna be the same as the Stars and Stripes. So a left-hand drive pink Lincoln Continental with whitewall tyres would be what you wanted. Pete rung me up and he said "look there's a place down the road from you in Balham that do second-hand American cars." He'd just got his first big song-writing royalty cheque for "My Generation"—five grand. He turned up at my flat in Clapham and I drove him down the road to this showroom. The guy instantly knew who he was, banked the cheque, and Pete drove this thing home. Now I never saw that car again. I understood that he hit a tree on the way to Brighton—or maybe it broke down on the M1—and just left it! Abandoned it. . . .

Buying cars is easier than writing songs. At least many people find it so. One imagines a certain amount of panic as the studio deadline approached. Two excellent musicians, Entwistle and Moon, and a decent frontman/vocalist in Roger—all good professionals in their own spheres—were now called on to demonstrate mastery of an alien craft. Not only that, but the results had to be produced in an atmosphere as competitive and potentially rancorous as you'd find in the entire country, *and* before a natural songwriter of Townshend's proven ability. Surprisingly it all seems to have gone rather well, with Pete helping them polish the numbers, and without any broken noses. Roger wrote one song and quit while he was ahead; John, having already used up all his ideas on his first number, "Whiskey Man," was stuck when it came time to record a second. When Pete inquired if he had a song ready, John calmly replied "sure" and extemporized a quick melody. Asked what it was about, he added that the lyric concerned spiders.

Once he'd had a chance to flesh it out, "Boris" developed into a far more unusual composition than the competent but routine chord progression of "Whiskey Man." "Boris"'s verse uses a chord sequence that sounds as though it might have started life as Solomon Burke's "Everybody Needs Somebody to Love" before mutating into something altogether more odd. The verse is sung in the normal range, but the chorus drops into the same gravelly bass register that John used for the spoken responses in "Summertime Blues." The chorus is beefed up by the bass guitar, which accompanies the bass voice in unison for the strange, descending six-note melody. The chorus "B-o-ris the Spi-der" is the song's main hook, and must be one of the few choruses in pop or rock built almost entirely on a chromatic scale, (that is, a scale which runs entirely in semitones). It's this tonality—heard in a more usual context on the nursery-rhyme chant of "creepy-crawly"—that gives the song its atmosphere.

What worked as a short-term cash solution could easily have produced a monstrous sounding album, though fortunately it didn't. By the time of the November '66 sessions, the band had a sound that could turn almost any song into a Who number, be it The Everly's "Man with Money," Martha and The Vandellas' "Heatwave," or the non-Townshend originals: Daltrey's "See My Way," Moon's "I Need You," and John's "Whiskey Man" and "Boris the Spider." All sound characteristically Who-like (much more so in fact, than most of the R&B covers which sit uncomfortably alongside Townshend's compositions on the first album), and only the impromptu marching band extravaganza "Cobwebs and Strange" sounds alien. As an instrumental, "Cobwebs" is a lot of fun though it's marred slightly by the music. It makes a worthy companion piece, as "drummer-songs" go, to Ginger Baker's "Pressed Rat and Warthog."

"Boris" marks the emergence of a second songwriter within The Who, not an occasional writer like Daltrey or Moon, but a writer capable of work good enough to keep Townshend on his toes. Once he began writing, Entwistle never looked back, and his songs appear regularly as B-sides to subsequent singles. Some of these, most notably "Heaven and Hell," were strong enough to enter the live set in their own right and not just as novelty pieces such as "Boris."

PICTURES OF LILY

"SOME THINGS LOOK BETTER WITH A FEW DENTS IN THEM."

—Keith Moon

The mid-blue Reaction label with its "equal and opposite" overlapping arrows evokes the year 1966 for British Who fans as powerfully as the *Maximum R&B* poster does 1965, but after three singles and an album for Stigwood's label, The Who's first release of 1967 appeared on a new label: their own Track Records. "Pictures of Lily" (Track 604 002) was the label's second release (the first being Hendrix's "Purple Haze"). Whatever Lambert and Stamp's other failings, with Track they succeeded in setting up a genuine independent label when most other attempts crashed. Comparing their own income from Who singles with that of the record companies, they concluded that they were at the wrong end of the business and set about researching alternatives.

As independents everywhere know, making a record is not too hard. Distributing it, however, is a different matter. In America, the sheer size of the country and diversity of musical forms worked in favor of regional independents catering to specialist markets, but the British market in the mid-'60s was a traditional monopoly controlled by the big four record companies: EMI, Decca, CBS, and Phillips. American independents had their difficulties, but at least there was a choice of distributors and a number of small independent pressing plants where the records could be manufactured. In Britain, the business was sewn up tight. Not only did the big four companies control the distribution networks, they also owned

98

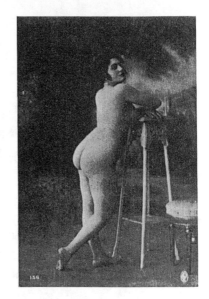

"Pictures
of Lily"
by
The Who

TRACK
RECORD

604
002

Distributed by Polydor

the only available pressing plants, giving them two effective strangleholds. There were any number of ways to freeze out the small operator. Good distribution means getting enough records in the appropriate shops in time to anticipate demand. An independent who somehow managed to get around the distribution problem could still be squeezed at the pressing stage. If a single started to do well, an independent would need more copies pressed, and would need them fast. An initial run of five thousand might easily be followed by an order for twenty-five thousand. On placing the second order, an independent might discover that the plant was mysteriously "overbooked" and couldn't begin work for at least eight weeks—by which time the record would have lost its momentum.

Lambert and Stamp approached Polydor (who already distributed Reaction) to discuss a partnership, but the company was unenthusiastic. Apart from anything else, encouraging mavericks set a bad precedent. The deal would probably never have happened if Lambert hadn't persuaded Chas Chandler to sign the newly arrived Jimi Hendrix to Track, right in the middle of the Polydor negotiations. The felicitous arrival and resultant fast footwork are classic Lambert, from the days when luck was still running his way. The buzz surrounding Hendrix was considerable, but as usual, the companies didn't know quite what to make of him. A deal was struck whereby a first Hendrix single ("Hey Joe") would be issued on Polydor; if it was successful, then Polydor would back Track Records, and subsequent Hendrix recordings would appear on Track. The combined weight of Hendrix and The Who was enough to tip the scales (though the clear inference is that even in England—their strongest territory—with six hits behind them, The Who were regarded as less of an asset than the untried Hendrix). Within a couple of months the label was functioning. Hendrix's "Purple Haze" was released on March 23, 1967, and "Pictures of Lily" was released on April 21st.

"Lily" is the mature sound of the pre-*Tommy* Who. Compare it with any of the three singles from 1965 and what is most striking is the band's poise. For an occasion as significant as the launch of their own label, one might have expected for them to lead with their strongest song, and a completed Townshend demo of "I Can See for Miles" had been around for some time, but their confidence as a unit—management, crew, and band—was very high. Indeed, the first ten months of 1967 are probably the high-water mark of The Who as a singles band. Sure enough, their judgment was correct, and "Lily" received unanimous approval from the English press and public. Only Townshend had reservations. From an English perspective, "Miles" marks the end of The Who as a pop—or power-pop—singles band. This being the case (and "Miles" having already been written), "Lily" was the last single which Townshend sat down to write in the traditional three-minute format. Townshend commented, "When I wrote 'Pictures of Lily' I thought it wouldn't be a hit and although I was getting better at it all the time, I thought I can't write this shit any more. I'd got to come up with something of substance."

The record does a fine job of balancing the requirements of a pop single with the attack of, what was by now, an experienced live band. It's melodic, witty, but at the same time it pushes along with real energy; the band is as comfortable in the studio as they are on the stage. In his own *Rolling Stone* review, Pete Townshend wrote that the track somehow "just *jells* perfectly." It does, and what's more, it does it without any studio manipulation beyond a couple of basic overdubs. If a single microphone had been placed in the middle of the studio floor, the track wouldn't have sounded that much different, save for a little less separation. Anyone who saw the band during 1967 would tell you that "Lily" is perhaps the most faithful representation of their onstage sound.

Townshend dubbed the song "Power Pop—what the Small Faces used to play," and, in a reference to *Pet Sounds*, "the kind of pop The Beach Boys played in the days of 'Fun, Fun, Fun' which I preferred." There's nothing especially innovative about this single, although the elegance of the arrangement and its deft execution make the track seem deceptively simple. The formula is unchanged from, say, "The Kids Are Alright," of two years earlier; it's just a bright, catchy melody played with infectious enthusiasm and ten times the attack of any other group, before or since.

The Entwistle/Moon rhythm section drives the track along with such ebullience, I defy anyone (able) to play along without feeling the urge to start jumping in the air! Throughout The Who's work, the conventional bass and drum roles are reversed, with John acting as timekeeper and Moon racing all over the place in the manner of a front-line lead instrument. Eventually, Moon's time-keeping grew to become a problem for the band—(not until after Keith's death would John be able to play without having to worry about holding down the beat; he speaks of having to "relearn" the bass—but at this stage Moon is still radiating energy. When a rhythm section is able to balance propulsion and control like this, the resulting power is a dream for a guitarist—or any other top-line voice or instrument, for that matter—to play with. The guitarist can play as little or as much as he wishes; he can keep time with the section or sit out, adding only fills and ornamentation. He can play structurally, decoratively, or both. The ability to provide a soloist this degree of freedom only comes from highly competent, intuitive players, usually those who've played together long enough to recognize cues and anticipate each other's moves. You can hear this freedom in Townshend's chording, simultaneously casual and explosive, and in the way he varies his part throughout the song, phrasing one way in one verse, then playing something quite different in the next. There's less of the characteristic ringing sound of his favored Rickenbacker; this time it's a sharper, more stinging tone, probably that of a Strat.

"Lily" is in C major, a new key for Who singles, although Pete's habitual antipathy to the minor keys continues. This time there's an ensemble entry instead of the typical solo guitar fanfare which starts so many songs, and there's also a notable break with tradition in the actual composition of the song. Most of Townshend's songs on *MBBB* sound as though the starting point was the chord sequence. "I Can't Explain," for example, clearly started with the basic four-chord sequence, on top of which the tune evolved. "Lily" is different. It's built not around chords, but around the single notes of a scale, a descending pattern which runs straight down the C major scale. The rhythm guitar, of course, plays chords, but they're an accompaniment to the descending scale. Though Townshend's demo is played on guitar and the bass line is played by detuning the low strings, it's less of an obvious guitar song and more like something that might have been written on a bass or a piano.

There are many deft touches, including John Entwistle's heavily reverbed French horn sounding distant in the mists; but I like the way both verse and chorus modulate at their respective halfway points. The move from C to A minor in the verse is a straightforward use of the relative minor—a musical commonplace—but the modulation from C into a new key, A major, at the same point in the chorus—"Pictures of Lily solved my childhood problems"— is more adventurous. Its effect is to lift the mood of the song. When it returns at the coda—"For me and Lily are together in my dreams"—it establishes a triumphal mood to conclude the song. The key change is present on Townshend's demo, though the coda section is better organized on the single. Otherwise the demo is similar to the single, apart from a few extra bars at the ends of verses, where the build-ups are extended. The resemblance between demo and single is not as precise as on "Substitute" or "Pinball Wizard"—but it's still pretty close.

*   *   *

The English press was rapturous about the record—"The best The Who have ever done" wrote Penny Valentine in *MM*—and there seems to have been general agreement that it marked The Who's coming of age, which is ironic considering Polydor's assessment of the band's market value. A nicely coordinated campaign was put together by Track for their first Who single. Trawling the Portobello Road market stalls, Chris Stamp found half a dozen saucy postcards, risqué in that stylized Victorian/Edwardian manner then fashionable—though hardly pornographic— which were used as an ad for the single in England. Again, this proved too much for American mores, where a cartoon of the four band members was substituted to promote the Decca release. At least one of the pictures was eventually seen in the U.S., as a repeated image on Keith's "Pictures of Lily" drum kit, custom-made for him by Premier, which bore the legend KEITH MOON PATENT BRITISH EXPLODING DRUMMER.

Despite clear references to masturbation, the song wasn't banned by BBC radio and, after rave reviews in all the music papers, reached number 4 on the English chart, staying six weeks. The scandalously poor showing of the song on the American chart seemed initially to indicate lack of taste on a quite prodigious scale; a more likely explanation was the ban imposed on the record by those in charge of radio programming, afraid as ever of offending their sponsors. Pete's comment "it's just a look back to that period in every boy's life when he has pin-ups" failed to pass the record off as an innocuous sequel to "Calendar Girl." In the U.S., limited airplay and minimal exposure prevented the single from reaching any higher than number 51.

Inspired by a postcard of 1920s vaudevillian Lillian Bayliss seen on his girlfriend's wall, the lyric which Pete later described in *Rolling Stone* as "merely a ditty about masturbation and the importance of it to a young

man" is the most direct treatment of the subject to be found in rock music at that time. Precedents don't seem too hard to cite—until one tries! The references in "Lily" are fairly oblique. The subject is addressed with wit and with an absence of smutty innuendo, the most direct lines being "now me and Lily are together in my dreams," which echoes the Felice and Boudleaux Bryant's song from 1958, "All I Have to Do is Dream," or perhaps "Pictures of Lily have solved my childhood problems." It's hard to see why U.S. radio found that offensive, unless perhaps they interpreted in the lines "I got so sick of having sleepless nights, I went and saw my Dad / He said, 'Son now here's some little something'"—as a reference to the abuse of prescription barbiturates. Referring to long nights spent alone with his tape machines, Townshend noted that "Masturbation . . . and making demos is not far off." Let the final thought on lyrics go to a music critic:

> In modern songs it is taken for granted that one is poor, unsuc-
> cessful and either sex-starved or unable to hold the affections of
> such partner as one may have had the luck to pick up. Even when
> the singer says that he has a woman crazy about him he hastens
> to point out that her attitude is clearly eccentric.

Who do you suppose is writing here? Paul Williams in *Crawdaddy* or Chris Charlesworth in *Melody Maker*? John Mendolsohn or Greil Marcus in *Rolling Stone*? Nick Jones? Dave Marsh? Chris Welch? The writer is actually Kit's father, Constant Lambert, in his book *Music Ho!,* written in 1934.

It's a great shame, thematically, that "Lily" wasn't paired with the lovely "Mary-Anne with the Shaky Hand" on the B-side; what a two-hander that would have made!

Keith Moon on drums, with Roger Daltrey, 1967.
PHOTO © DON PAULSEN

I CAN SEE FOR MILES

"THE REASON 'I CAN SEE FOR MILES' CAME OUT GOOD WAS BECAUSE I SAT DOWN AND MADE IT GOOD FROM THE BEGINNING."

—Pete Townshend to Jann Wenner

For three years, Who singles had been entering the English charts with monotonous regularity. "I Can See for Miles" was the eighth consecutive hit, but none had fulfilled Townshend's avowed aim of achieving the number-one spot, nor had any of them made much of a impression on the American chart. Convinced by now, in his own words, that he had the business of writing hits sussed, Pete pulled his best song out of the locker and focused his powers on creating the definitive Who record, one that could surely top both English and American charts.

From its conception, Pete considered "Miles" something special. It was his "ace in the hole," the secret weapon with which he could redeem matters if The Who were ever in deep trouble. His comment that it was written "probably around the same time as 'I'm a Boy'" dates its composition to the first third of 1966, and various qualities common to the demos of both songs bear this out. Richard Barnes suggests that it could've been released before, or instead of, "Happy Jack." Certainly everyone in The Who camp seems to have sensed that the song was something unique, and felt a degree of trepidation about actually recording it. Pete waited for Kit Lambert's confidence as a producer to reach suitable proportions before attempting the song, which in itself is an

The Who at their first performance at the Fillmore East.
PHOTO © DON PAULSEN

106

insight into the complex relationship between the two men. Kit's qualities as a producer, over and above the guidance he gave Townshend at the writing stage, lay neither in musical knowledge nor recording technique, but in the ability to motivate the players, manage their excesses, and create a suitable studio atmosphere, so his own state of mind and level of self-confidence were critical. Pete told Jann Wenner that the demo "was just so exciting and so good that for a long time we didn't dare make a single 'cos it was blackmail. I was more or less blackmailing Kit Lambert into doing better. So we always put it off until Kit was very sure of himself."

Excitement is an unstable and notoriously elusive commodity. Captured one day, it can prove impossible to repeat on another, as musicians and producers everywhere know. Like any work that relies on balancing form with spontaneity, there are times when it just won't happen—and of course, the harder you try, the more elusive it becomes. Trying to recreate the magic of a great demo has defeated many top bands and famous producers; some parts can be reproduced with ease, but the spark that ignites them, the feel that binds them, are entities of an entirely different order—volatile, capricious, and utterly unresponsive to coaxing.

A great recording is more than just the sum of its parts. When the interaction between those parts proves unrepeatable, it's sometimes simpler to abandon the attempt and use the demo, polishing it up as much as possible. When The Jimi Hendrix Experience had finished cutting "Purple Haze," they spent twenty minutes banging down a rough take of a new song, called "The Wind Cries Mary." Try as they may at subsequent sessions, they could never recapture the ease of that spontaneous run-through, so the rough version was released, mistakes and all. There are small timing glitches—the production could not be called glossy—but the atmosphere is relaxed and intimate, and the fluid guitar lines are Hendrix at his most graceful. The record is living proof that nonchalance is damned hard work.

It would seem that "I Can See for Miles" wasn't attempted during the *Quick One* sessions of November '66. When the band re-entered CBS London Studios in the spring of 1967, the time felt right to Kit, and the basic track was laid down. Pete recalls: "One night he just turned around and said to us 'Let's do "I Can See for Miles."' I had the demo there and we put it on and we dug it again ... and he did it. He got it together."

The moment was obviously propitious. The track is rich sounding, skillfully assembled, and stunningly recorded, and it must've been clear from the start that the track was *happening*. Atypical among Who singles, this is very much a studio record, arranged for several guitar parts, and was consequently seldom ever played onstage. Whereas "Anyway, Anyhow, Anywhere" tried to evoke the live performance by throwing in as much as possible, "Miles" took the opposite tack, compressing the band's onstage excitement into the grooves of a single by paring down the cardinal Who qualities to their essences. Despite multiple guitars, there's not a superfluous note in the entire four minutes, just the vital elements precisely positioned to create an atmosphere of refined menace. The result, by miles, is the most ominous sound The Who ever recorded. Pete commented:

> The real production masterpiece in the Who/Lambert coalition was, of course, "I Can See for Miles." The version here [on *MBBB*] is not the mono, which is a pity because the mono makes the stereo sound like The Carpenters.

It does seem a bit of a shame, considering that three of the songs on *MBBB* appear in the original mono. The only apparent way to find the mono version is to buy the original (U.K.) single, or else mono versions of *The Who Sell Out* (1967) or *Direct Hits* (1968) LPs. It is scarcely worth the trouble. The 7" single does sound wonderful, though that has more to do with vinyl than mono—and there's a distinct advantage to owning the stereo mix,[1] discussed later in this chapter.

With the basic track captured at the CBS session, there was little time to develop the song. As usual, lack of funds meant that the band had to get back out on the road. Through the spring they played U.K. and Italian dates before making their long-planned U.S. debut on Murray the K's Easter show. They came straight back to Europe to make a short German tour—in Dusseldorf, a show with fellow Track artists John's Children turned into a pitched battle and full-scale riot—then traveled on to Helsinki, and a week in Scandinavia. "Pictures of Lily" was released (prospering as always in the U.K., but, once again, failing in the U.S.), then in June the band made a second trip to the States, playing shows in Ann Arbor and San Francisco, before their vital appearance at The

Monterey Pop Festival on June 18. The band returned for a brief spell back in London, during which they recorded "Under My Thumb"/"The Last Time," following the Stones' Redlands bust, before a third, and far longer, U.S. tour from July 14 to September 16, supporting Herman's Hermits. Finally, during a break in this tour, time was found to resume work on "I Can See for Miles," at Gold Star studios in Los Angeles.

The best American studios of the mid-'60s had equipment far outstripping their English counterparts and engineers with greater experience recording rock music. The Stones had been taking advantage of U.S. tours since '64 to record with engineers like Ron Malo at Chess and Dave Hassinger at RCA Studios in Hollywood; the results, including "It's All Over Now," "The Last Time," and "Satisfaction," speak for themselves. In the U.S., The Who discovered a new depth and clarity of sound. Gold Star was the studio in which Phil Spector had produced his "little symphonies for the kids," and was known to possess an enchanted echo chamber. Pete describes his enthusiasm for the studio:

> We cut the tracks in London at CBS studios and brought the tapes to Gold Star studios in Hollywood to mix and master them. Gold Star have the nicest sounding echo in the world. And there is just a little of that on the mono. Plus, a touch of home-made compression in Gold Star's cutting-room. I swoon when I hear the sound.

Even the best recorded tape can still go wrong in the mastering or pressing, which are the final stages of record production. Many a well-recorded tape has gone down with all hands.[2] "Miles," however, was safely delivered onto vinyl in time for an October release.

Inevitably, the most beautifully arranged and recorded single in The Who canon—the certain hit held back for an emergency—failed to sell anything like the quantities expected. Townshend was infuriated, then despairing. Like Spector, after his Gold Star masterwork "River Deep, Mountain High" failed to crack the U.S. charts, Pete withdrew from the singles arena, expressing disgust with the stupidity of the record buying public. He told Ray Tolliday: "To me this was the ultimate Who record and yet it didn't sell. The day I saw it was about to go down . . . I spat on the British record buyer."

The relative failure of "Miles" signaled the end of The Who's days as a pop group. Eight singles, spanning March '65 through November '67, starting with their debut "I Can't Explain" and ending with "I Can See for Miles" had each entered the top-10. The unbroken run stopped there. On the English chart, "Miles" only reached number 10. It wasn't that the record was a miss, just that expectations for it had been so high. The Who had never had a number 1 and Townshend, justifiably confident in his own writing ability, had clearly set out to score one with this single. Unbelievably, a record which managed to create a perfect balance between the excitement of hard rock and the catchiness of a mainstream pop single, the distillation of everything The Who had set out to do on 45, achieved the lowest chart showing thus far—equaling "Anyway, Anyhow, Anywhere," though even that record stayed six weeks on the chart while "Miles" only lasted for four, the shortest duration of any of the singles.

Yet in America "Miles" was the first Who single to do any serious business, and the first to enter the top-10. It reached number 9 and stayed five weeks on the *Billboard* chart. However, even this long-awaited U.S. breakthrough failed to alter Townshend's perception of the record as a flop, though it permanently altered everything else. The Who's priorities changed. The sustained American touring in the summer had certainly prepared the way for "Miles" to enter the top-10, and from this point (October '67) they turned their full attention to the pursuit of success in America.

*   *   *

In 1966 The Who were probably the loudest thing that anyone outside of artillery circles had ever heard. But anyone can play loudly. What distinguished them from the myriad thumpers who followed them was their intelligent use of dynamics. As a unit they recognized that effective live performance is all about expansion and contraction, tension and release; that triple *fortissimo* is more effective when it follows a passage of quiet; that contrast is more powerful than relentless sledgehammering; and they possessed the musicality and ensemble understanding to deploy that insight. From early in their career they used light and shade to greater effect than any of their rivals. Their live trademark—the ominously steady passage that suddenly erupted into overpowering crescendo—is brought to perfection on "I Can See for Miles." Abrupt rushes of guitar jump out from simple pedal bass parts, the drums sound more like a bombing raid than an exercise in timekeeping, and Daltrey's vocal strikes the exact tone of cold superiority implicit in Townshend's lyric. Gone are the sprawling, lashing, tongue-tied Who, stuttering in frustration at the inability to articulate their rage, replaced by an altogether cooler, more focused proposition, in which detachment, clarity of vision, and a nicely controlled violence converge with such precision that the actual threat never needs to be expressed.

The spareness of the arrangement allows the listener to hear how good the individual instruments and voices sound. The instrumental sound is so clear, the quality of the arrangement is revealed. The overall effect is lean and concise. The bass pumps away unchanged on a single note, creating a flat plain on which the action occurs. For most of the song, Entwistle's eight-to-the-bar pedalled E underpins the changes, even where the sequence moves through four or five different chords. One of Pete's guitars doubles this part. The atmosphere is tense but unhurried. It builds in its own time. After Townshend's opening chord, nearly two bars pass before anything else happens. Then, at the seventh beat, Moon comes in with an introductory drum fill and proceedings begin. The slow buildup throughout the track is beautifully managed, with new elements introduced as the song progresses. Unlike, for example, "Pictures of Lily," which is basically a live performance with fixed instrumentation, "Miles" obeys Keith Richards's precept that a hit single should feature "something new every ten seconds." The stereo mix gives much better separation, presenting a clearer picture of the disposition of Pete's three guitars—two electrics and an acoustic. The two main guitars, panned hard left and right in the stereo image, conduct a dialogue, alternate lines, and suspend mildly dissonant chords, while the acoustic adds an almost subliminal presence.

Perhaps my favorite guitar moment in the song comes at the final chorus. The nagging unison bend on E that runs through the penultimate chorus suddenly leaps up an octave (at 3'51") and plays to the fade. It's simple and effective. (A unison bend is played by holding a note on one string, while bending an adjacent string upward, until both strings are at the same pitch. As the near-unison slips in and out of phase, the result is a sharp, stinging tone.)

Townshend was never technically dazzling in the Hendrix/Beck mould— "when I should of been practicing I was writing songs, and when I was writing songs I should've been practicing"—but more than any other guitarist of his era he learned to make a virtue of his limitations. Simple devices such as the octave leap described above are placed to great effect within the context of the songs. Frustration at his relative inability also produced the power chord, which forces maximum expression from the simplest of components. Before 1968, Townshend rarely attempted lead breaks, preferring to let other instruments take the solos, such as the bass on "My Generation" and "Substitute," the horn on "Pictures of Lily," and harmony vocals on "I'm a Boy." Or, if he did play, he used noise and effects as on "Anyway, Anyhow, Anywhere" or a chord solo as on "Happy Jack." For "Miles," he came up with a device perfectly suited to the uncompromising mood of the song: a one-note solo. A single mid-range E is hammered out at the tempo of a pneumatic drill, then finished up with a quick one-handed trill. Once heard, it's so obviously right, you know that nothing else would do.

Every instrument has keys that suit it and keys that don't. "I Can See for Miles" is in the key of E, a classic guitar key that allows use of the lowest note the instrument can produce in normal tuning. It gives a song a "grounded" feeling. Interestingly then, the demo was recorded in F sharp. Given the verse progression and the layout of the guitar neck, this makes sense, though once the low pedal bass is introduced, E makes better sense. Possibly too, the key was shifted to accommodate Roger's range. A potential problem is worked around in third verse, where the song has changed key to A. The stop-time section, beginning with "Here's a poke at you," which worked fine in the first two verses with Roger going up, is now too high, so he drops down to deliver it.

Most songwriters, even the very best, have three or four basic songs—templates, if you will—to which they return; not from laziness, nor as any conscious reworking, but because these are the core forms on which their musical sensibilities rest. Townshend has his "home" keys— first position Ds and As, useful for their chiming tone, distinctive character, and the ease with which open strings can be left ringing through the changes—as well as his favored arranging devices, but the songs themselves are amazingly diverse. One of the most impressive things about the first run of singles, which ends here with "Miles," is the consistent variety of the material. The similarity of "All Day and All of the Night" to "You Really Got Me," of "I Can't Help Myself " to "It's the Same Old Song" finds no echo in Townshend's writing. Amazingly, given this much diversity, not one of the songs is in a minor key—-perhaps the simplest, most obvious variation Townshend could have employed to create a new atmosphere. To generalize, minor keys convey a sense of sadness, or distance. Yet even setting out to write a song as intentionally downcast as "Melancholia" (an out-take from the *Who Sell Out* album), Townshend uses a major key.

There isn't one song in a minor key on *MBBB*; as far as I know, Townshend has never indicated why this might be, though his guitar style offers a clue. The basic chord has a bottom, a middle, and a top—the 1st, 3rd, and 5th notes of the scale, respectively—and like a sandwich, the note in the middle (the 3rd) gives the chord its flavor. It also determines whether the chord is major or minor. Instinctively it would seem— "I didn't start to actually understand the fundamentals of music until I started playing the piano and I didn't start playing until I was 22"—the young Pete Townshend settled on a way of voicing guitar chords so that they used only the 1st and the 5th. Omitting the 3rd gives a starker, tougher sound than the standard chord by removing the melodic, sweetening element. It's other effect is to preclude minor chords: no 3rd, no minor. This construction crops up all through Townshend's work. Instead of playing, for instance, a standard G triad (1st, 3rd, 5th—G, B, D) he stacks up 1sts and 5ths so the chord consists solely of the notes G, D, G, D, G.

> It's only two notes—G and D. Even though I know it's only got two notes in it, I can *hear* another note in there. It doesn't sound like two notes. The distortion throws in other notes.

A good place to hear it uncluttered is the lone D chord (or D with no 3rd, to be pedantic) which opens "The Kids Are Alright." Pete comments:

> If you're playing what are two-note chords in octaves it leaves you freer melodically and it takes you back to more ancient music principles. It's almost like using a chord as a drone.

Drones are found in early music, in plainsong, and in ethnic music all over the world, from Scotland to China. The bagpipes are a perfect example.

The most common drone uses two notes, the 1st and 5th measures of the scale. Twentieth-century popular songwriting, by contrast, is built around the entirely different notion of chord progressions. Drones became slightly more common in popular usage after John Coltrane grew interested in Indian music around 1960 (and, as a result, directly influenced, among others, The Byrds and The Doors) and overwhelmingly more common after 1966, when people heard the Beatles use of the sitar on "Norwegian Wood" and on *Revolver*. Townshend's adaptation, however, sounds entirely instinctive, rather than copied from any of the obvious sources; the sort of quirk that self-taught musicians often develop, as much by accident as design.

*　*　*

In a way it's fitting that the record that ended The Who's first era should come at a time when the supremacy of the 7" single was passing to the 12" LP. Before long, the whole nature of the music business would change as the companies realized that albums were more lucrative than singles. In England, the record stands too as a fitting epitaph to pirate radio, which was put off the air in mid-August 1967. No band had been better served by, or identified more with, pirate radio than The Who.

At the start of 1964, radio in Britain was still subject to the same tight government controls that existed before the Second World War, with a single centralized body, the BBC, transmitting programs to the whole country. As a relatively small territory in broadcasting terms, Britain never had local radio stations, and FM was unknown. The national service broke down into three branches. The Home Service broadcast news and current affairs, while the Third Programme broadcast classical music and cultural items. The Light Programme delivered Variety and a tiny quantity of pop: three hours per week comprising a two-hour slot on Saturday mornings, *Saturday Club*, and *Pick of the Pops*, a rundown of the top-20 on Sunday afternoons. (The names tell you everything you need to know about how hip these shows were.) With the exception of Radio Luxembourg, whose English-language pop-music programs, broadcast from the European mainland, could be heard fading in and out after dark, that was it.

During the 1950s, The Musicians' Union had negotiated a complicated deal with the BBC known as the "needle-time" agreement.

Intended to protect the livelihoods of M.U. members (principally dance-band musicians), it was a relic of the days when the top-20 was calculated by the sales not of records, but of sheet music, and made no sense at all in the new, disposable world of pop. When the BBC's monopoly was finally overturned, the attack came from a totally unexpected quarter. On Easter Saturday—March 28, 1964—*Radio Caroline* went on the air. Broadcasting from a ship anchored three-and-a-half miles off Frinton on the Essex coast—outside of British territorial waters—the new station could broadcast non-stop pop to London and the whole of Southeast England, beyond the jurisdiction of English law and the crippling "needle-time" agreement.

There had been a dozen non-English speaking shipboard stations, broadcasting mostly to Scandinavia and northern Europe since the late '50s, but by this time most of them were off the air. According to author Christopher Booker, the idea of English pirate radio came from a London music publisher named Alan Crawford, who started researching the idea in 1960 but rather rashly talked about his plan to a young Irish entrepreneur named Ronan O'Rahilly, the manager of the Scene Club. This was the same club into which Pete Meaden had booked the High Numbers. It was a dive notorious even by Soho standards—"you felt like it was gonna be raided any minute" according to Townshend. O'Rahilly acted quickly, found backers, and got his station Radio Caroline on the air first. Raising funds from some surprisingly Establishment figures, O'Rahilly rented a former passenger ferry, the *Frederica*, and moved it from Holland to Greenore in southern Ireland where, outside of English jurisdiction, he had it fitted out with a rudimentary studio and transmitter. It was then moved to the Essex coast, and pirate radio began.

In May a second pirate, Radio Atlanta, began transmitting from a converted coaster, the *Mi Amigo*. Moored close to Caroline, this ship had a 50,000-watt transmitter and broadcast on the same frequency, during the hours that Caroline was off the air. As more and more stations popped up around the Essex coast—some on ships; some, like Screaming Lord Sutch's "Radio Sutch" transmitting from ghostly looking abandoned wartime towers at the wonderfully named Shivering Sands—in July '64 the two most powerful, Caroline and Atlanta, merged. Renamed Caroline North and Caroline South, the combined stations were soon claiming a listenership in excess of eight million. Whatever the true figure, the 1964 sales of U.K. singles were almost 20 percent above figures for 1963. A single that might have been heard on the BBC once—in a good week—could now often be heard five times a day. It's no exaggeration to say that pirate radio was the medium most responsible for the mid-'60s boom in English pop.

Just before Christmas 1964, the last and probably the most influential ship arrived, broadcasting as Radio London. Approximately half a million pounds were spent fitting out a thousand-ton, former U.S. minesweeper, the *MV Galaxy*, with a 212-foot mast and a 50,000-watt transmitter, making the station audible over most of England. With its fast-paced programming, professional sounding DJs, and slick U.S. jingles and station IDs, it was unlike anything ever heard before in England.

The *Who Sell Out* album, which features "I Can See for Miles," was conceived as a tribute to pirate radio, and especially to Radio London, with the tracks (on the first side at least) being linked by imitation commercials and "Big L" jingles. In a precursor to the whole 1990s sampling squabble, The Who were later sued by the company who had originally created and supplied the jingles to Radio London. Nik Cohn approved the album's "obvious reaction against the fashionable psychedelic solemnity," but complained that the concept was only half-completed, something which he identified as a traditional Who failing. Though "I Can See for Miles" was a U.S. hit, the album only reached number 48, and got no further than number 13 in England. Its U.S. release in December '67 marked the end of the era of the Who as Britain's classic singles band.

Though the changes would take several years to work through, here was the moment when the paradoxical, embattled, melodic, quirky, constantly gigging English 'pop group' changed course, eventually becoming a multinational, mid-Atlantic, stadium-filling success story on the grand scale. Much was gained, but a good deal was lost too—and they would never again make singles as powerful as "I Can See for Miles."

MAGIC BUS

"WHAT IS THERE TO SAY? THE ONE
MAN BAND VERSION, A VOODOO-DUB-FREAK-OUT OF A NOTHING
SONG THAT WAS DESTINED TO BECOME THE MOST REQUESTED LIVE
SONG . . . ALONG WITH 'BORIS THE SPIDER.' DAFT PUNTERS."

—Pete Townshend, *Scoop* liner notes

There seem to be two schools of thought about "Magic Bus." On the one hand, thousands of concert-going Who fans around the world view it as quintessential "rock-out" material; the opposing view is best expressed by John Entwistle, who regards six or seven minutes stuck on a single note playing the Bo Diddley beat as Purgatory. "Magic Bus" was considered another of Townshend's "special" demos, essentially just a groove set up by simple percussive sounds treated with repeat echo. As the echoes multiply, rhythms and counter-rhythms pile up; a polyrhythmic playground for the acoustic guitar to bounce off, and a gift of a rhythm track for any decent guitarist. Inevitably, much of the effect is lost when it is shunted across to a regular drum kit and claves.

Nonetheless, the finished single is one that many people would include among their all-time favorites. The critic Paul Williams, who has a decent ear and impeccable credentials, includes it in his 100 Best Singles book, along with "I Can't Explain" and "I Can See for Miles." (Where these songs appear in the one hundred is irrelevant because the choices are arranged chronologically, not in order of merit; in the words

"Magic Bus" trade advertisement, 1968.

118

THE WHO

Magic Bus c/w
Dr. Jekyll & Mr. Hyde

of Williams himself, "number 78 is as good as number 1.") On this basis, the "Bus" ends up parked (as did the Who at Monterey) between Otis and Jimi. Paul includes it as "one of a handful of records . . . that's genuinely pushed me over the top," calling it "cathartic, overpowering, unforgettable" while at the same time acknowledging the near impossibility of defining the irregular process by which a piece of music can affect us so powerfully at one time in life, and then fail to do so on demand on another occasion.

The song became a live favorite, taking on a life of its own, equal some would say to "My Generation," which it sometimes replaced as the closing number of the live set. Others, Townshend included, might simply say that coupling a beat as simple and repetitive as a Bo Diddley rhythm with an easily memorized two-word slogan is the surest way of appealing to the lowest-common-denominator stadium crowd, the "daft punters." Ultimately there's nothing to be gained from trying to resolve such fundamental differences in taste. *De gustibus non est disputandem.*

For "Magic Bus," Townshend repeated the trick that Jagger and Richards had used for "Not Fade Away," returning to his R&B roots and borrowing the Bo Diddley beat from the 1950s. In his art school days, Pete had inherited a considerable rhythm and blues record collection when his student mate from Alabama, Tom Wright, was deported back to the States. So much of The Who story consists of luck stretched almost to breaking point, with people and things turning up at the right moment. It was exceptional good fortune for a young songwriter to suddenly find himself with the complete recorded works of Chuck Berry, Jimmy Reed, Bo Diddley, John Lee Hooker, James Brown, Slim Harpo, and Jimmy Smith, as well as albums by Howlin' Wolf, Big Bill Broonzy, Ray Charles, Bobby Bland, The Isleys, The Shirelles, The Miracles; jazz from Charles Mingus, John Coltrane, Charlie Parker, Miles Davis and Wes Montgomery, plus comedy albums by Lord Buckley—and the full list is far longer.

"Magic Bus" is one occasion where Townshend's demo and The Who single really do differ. The band recording cleans up the demo considerably. Pete's acoustic guitar is far tidier and works up an impressive momentum. The record features what is a memorable piece of rhythm guitar by any standards; simple in conception, precise in execution, and monumental in effect—but it is different from the demo. The single is driven by the guitar, while the demo is propelled by the percussion, with the guitar sitting out for whole verses at a time.

Pete and Roger do a good job of sorting out coherent vocal parts from what, on the demo, is at times just a rant—recalling a cross between those Bo Diddley dialogues like "Say Man" and something out of *The Goon Show.*[1] Lyrically, there's not much to say—although the couplet "Thank you driver for getting me here/you'll be an inspector have no fear"—will ring a bell with public transport officials everywhere. The work carried out is thoroughly professional but, unlike "Miles" which improves on its demo, the spacey feel of Pete's original is never quite nailed down; the voodoo doesn't happen. As Townshend suggests, it *is* a fairly slight composition, and whatever energy it builds is mainly due to the wonderful, hypnotic quality of the Bo Diddley beat.[2]

*   *   *

After three good years, The Who's fortunes slumped in 1968. The year started on a bad note, when a short Australian tour with The Small Faces ran into a hostile press and accusations of hooliganism. The flight from England to Australia remains a long haul, but in those days it was a wretched journey. Stumbling off the plane, tired, irritable, undoubtedly the worse for wear and probably the worse for drink, the band were greeted by a press corps eager to know their views on—of all things—the devaluation of the pound. Townshend took the only reasonable course of action and whacked the reporter, which set the tone for the rest of the tour.

Then everything went quiet. To the English audience it seemed as though every feature that had distinguished The Who since late 1964—the constant strings of gigs and regular hit singles—abruptly ceased. The band that sometimes played towns four or five times a year suddenly disappeared from the English stage. Through 1968 they were busy trying to break America. February, March, and April were spent there, notionally promoting the "Call Me Lightning" single (March '68)—though they never seem to have played it—and *The Who Sell Out* LP (December '67), though the only tracks they ever played from it were "Relax" and occasionally "Tattoo."[3]

The months of June, July, and August '68 were also spent touring the States, mainly to generate cash. Pete needed time to organize songs for the new, extended work he had in mind. As they crisscrossed America in their customized bus, still attempting to crack the major market, they were performing what was essentially their 1966 English stage act. Despite regional breakouts, success on a national scale continued to elude them, and the two singles "Lightning" and "Magic Bus" only reached 40 and 25 respectively on the *Billboard* chart, despite heavy touring. In September, Decca capped this with the bogus *Magic Bus— The Who on Tour* album—excellent timing for a tour that finished on August 22!

Dividing their energies in this manner was something of a risk. America had shown real interest only in one single, "Miles," while at home, the combination of eccentric singles like "Dogs" and a prolonged absence from the stage threatened the ground they had gained. Trying to reconcile two fundamentally different markets, they were in danger of losing in both. When they did play, their concert price in England had dropped, and they were accepting some odd gigs. At this distance in time, it's easy to forget how swiftly fashions moved in the singles-based pop world. In Bristol on January 8, 1968, I saw them play a half-full ice rink, crammed onto a stage no larger than that of the average bar venue, such as CBGB's. The rink was in the same building as the considerably larger Locarno Ballroom, where just twelve months earlier a magnificent, sell-out show on January 26, 1967, had left so many enraged fans locked outside, that they'd assiduously smashed everything in the car park—including Daltrey's sports car. In due course, parking lot battles with the police became a standard feature of U.S. stadium shows, but were a sensation in mid-'60s English life.

"Call Me Lightning," released in the States in March '68, was not initially considered for release in the U.K., being "too dated for the U.K. market" according to Richard Barnes. It did, however, appear in June as the B-side to "Dogs"—though neither "Dogs"/"Call Me Lightning" nor "Magic Bus" entered the English top-20. Roger Daltrey, practical as ever, hated this "strange, in-joke phase"; Townshend was working away at the material which would become *Tommy* but to the public at home it looked as though the group were running out of steam.

As the nucleus of *Tommy* began to take shape in Pete's imagination, his belief in the single as the definitive expression of Pop seems to have wavered. He wrote, "I felt that if I had to say everything on a record in three minutes maximum, then I wasn't ever really going to say very much." The fact that he chose to follow his masterwork "I Can See for Miles" with a song that was at least four years old clearly indicated something was amiss. "Call Me Lightning" was one of Pete's earliest songs, written in the days when he still lived with his parents, and demoed in the first of his home studios on the top floor of their house in Ealing. In his liner notes to *Another Scoop,* Pete describes the song as "a clear example of how difficult it was for me to reconcile what I took to be Roger's need for macho, chauvinist lyrics, and Keith Moon's appetite for surf music and fantasy sports car love affairs." "Magic Bus" was old news too, having been written and demoed in early 1966, approximately two and half years earlier. If Pete really did hold "Magic Bus" in such low esteem, might he deliberately have chosen a "dumb" proven crowd-pleaser as a single in the hope of scoring a hit? Certainly it was an old song, released during a lean period chartwise—but it is more likely that Townshend's attention was on his new material.

The Who's comparative obscurity in the U.S. assisted them in one respect: American audiences had no difficulty accepting them as part of the new underground movement, which was closely associated with FM radio and albums, rather than the world of top-40 AM pop and singles. In England, The Who were caught between two camps. With their long tenure in the top-10 and song-based repertoire, they didn't fit into the new crop of psychedelic and blues-rock bands, but neither had they ever been a straight ahead pop group—they were too aggressive and far too ugly, and had too many ideas. Nor had they established anything like the unassailable positions The Stones and The Beatles occupied, above the fray. By mid-1968, their position in the English marketplace was looking increasingly isolated.

The first new market the record companies targeted was the underground. Then came the backlash. Much of the traditional, singles-buying market felt deeply alienated from what it identified as the drug culture, and it didn't take the companies long to start marketing a second, post-Beatles wave of easily digestible, lightweight pop, aimed at an increasingly youthful market. In addition to a new generation of teenage girls wanting their own pop stars, a group of disaffected working-class youth had formed a new subculture, Skinheads. Their tastes included Soul, Ska, and Bluebeat, soccer and violence, and their enemies were queers, immigrants from the Indian subcontinent, and the type of middle-class and hippie crowd who now formed a growing proportion of the audience of bands like The Who.

The irony, of course, is that the skinheads came from precisely the same suburban working-class backgrounds as the Mods. One of their earliest public appearances en masse was at the Rolling Stones free concert in Hyde Park in July 1969. The stage was located next to the lake, known as the Serpentine, and the ground before it formed a gently sloped natural amphitheater. It was a long, hot day, and by the time The Stones came on everyone was tired. Almost abandoned when Brian Jones drowned, the show was hastily remounted as a "tribute" to Brian. As Jagger began drawling out the elegaic passages from "Adonais" (which Marianne Faithfull had selected for him), it became clear that sections of the crowd were growing restive. "Peace peace 'e is not Dead . . . 'e duff not. . . . ARE YOU GONNA BE QUIET OR NOT?" I looked over to my right and there was an extraordinary spectacle. A flying wedge of shaven-headed youths were chanting rhythmically—football terrace style—chucking cans, and forcing their way toward the stage. This was unprecedented behavior at free festivals of the time.

While the singles chart filled up with bubblegum records and "manufactured" groups, a clutch of bands every bit as contrived were aimed at the more lucrative album charts. Sharper operators recognized that the self-regarding underground was every bit as susceptible to manipulation as the teenybop market; they had only to alter the imagery to appeal to a different sensibility. Stress "musicianship" and "authenticity," season lightly with the "Wisdom of the Mystic East," bung in a generous helping of Hobbits—some bits of tat acquired from the estate of bankrupt Occultists never hurt—and you were in business. Correctly calculating that a mass audience would prefer heavy rock with most of the subtlety removed, the second wave of "heavy" groups sold records, filled stadiums, and made money on a scale never dreamed of by their immediate forerunners—but there was still no place for The Who among these bands—yet.

The Who had returned from their U.S. tour of '67 with a pretty low opinion of American bands, especially the much-publicized San Francisco acid bands. The only group of whom they all spoke well was

Moby Grape (both sides of the Moby Grape single "Hey Grandma"/"Omaha" became staples in the sets of every second division rock 'n' roll band in England between '67 and '70). Most of the San Francisco bands grew out of the folk or folk-rock scene and had little grounding in practical R&B or in performing live with powerful amplified instruments. Tripped out crowds full of top-quality Oswley acid were never going to provide the sort of critical appreciation that sharpens a band's performance—and many of the musicians were as spaced out as their audience. The ethos (or at least the public face) of the San Francisco acid-rock scene was to eliminate the gap between the stage and the crowd, creating a unified communal experience, a gestalt in which "artificial" notions of stardom could be dispensed with. Songs were largely dispensed with too, or treated as staging posts from which interminable improvised rambles could set out, then meet up again every hour or so before wandering off on new tangents. In some ways a brave attempt, but I guess you had to be there; by and large the music didn't travel well.

The passage of Cream through San Francisco seems to have been a momentous and influential event on the west coast. The Fillmore audience was packed with members of the Grateful Dead, Jefferson Airplane, The Quicksilver Messenger Service, Country Joe and The Fish, and others, and the power, volume, and extemporized skills of the (Fresh) Cream impressed everybody. Speaking in 1981, Jerry Garcia told me of the effect of these shows, which he described as "a revelation. Something completely new. We didn't know music could be presented that forcefully." As things turned out, I was sitting in a car with Jack Bruce, not long after, so I repeated Garcia's remark. The effect was dramatic. Jack screwed up his face, and made one of those distinctly Scottish sounds in the back of his throat, "Aaaaaach." He remembered those same 1967 shows as "terrible. Horrendous—everything wrong." A similar example of the Anglo/American impasse is quoted in Robert Greenfield's book *Stones Touring Party*. Nicky Hopkins—the pianist on the 1965 *My Generation* album—who'd moved to Mill Valley and joined The Quicksilver Messenger Service, spoke of the effect on a musician of the wonderful San Francisco atmosphere, the warm nights, the sense of community, of receiving praise and rapturous applause from halls full of people you knew and liked, and of the shows themselves:

I remember . . . people coming backstage at Winterland to tell us how great we all were, and everybody in the band being so wiped out, they were a semitone off—either way—-through the whole set. It was so awful. . . . God, it made me want to puke.

1968 proved a strange, transitional, and divisive year for rock in general, with wretched second-rate bands prospering, while major acts allowed themselves to become distracted. The Beatles were squabbling, Dylan was changing horses, and The Stones were at their lowest ebb, with much of their vitality draining away through the rapidly fading Brian Jones. Lacking the confidence to sack Jones outright (a favorite with the band's female fans, and still regarded as the group's leader in mainland Europe), they were unable to tour with him, but unwilling to tour without him.

The year closed with the filming in December of an intended television spectacular, *The Rolling Stones Rock 'n' Roll Circus*, featuring The Who (and many others) as the Stones' guests. In a scene where a great deal of subtle, and not-so-subtle, jockeying for position was the norm, The Stones hadn't maintained their position at the top of the London society pyramid by sweetness of nature. They were still undisputed rulers of the scene—but they hadn't played live since April '67. In the recording studio, Keith Richards could cover for Brian by overdubbing extra parts, but onstage it was hopeless; so much of The Stones drive came from the interplay between the two guitars. The *Circus* footage shows a ghostly Brian, hanging on to an inaudible guitar, but the show is stolen by the special guests, The Who. They had played well over fifty major shows in 1968, and at most of them had performed the number they chose for the *Rock 'n' Roll Circus*: their mini-opera, *A Quick One*. They played it superbly, but this was its final appearance; mini-opera was about to give way to full-length opera.

Pete Townsend fingerpicking at the Fillmore, 1967.
Photo © Don Paulsen

PINBALL WIZARD

"I ONCE GOT A GREAT LETTER FROM KEITH RICHARDS AFTER HE HAD READ AN INTERVIEW OF MINE. IT JUST SAID, 'DEAR PETE, SHUT UP!'"

—Pete Townshend

Townshend felt himself "written out," at least as far as the three-minute single was concerned, and hankered after something more "substantial." Various ideas and themes were floated about—an album's worth of singles that would tell a story in "cameos"; Sufi parables; elaborate stage shows which would replace the smash-up ending—but inevitably, given Pete and Kit's predilections, talk soon drifted toward opera. By August '68, Pete was outlining the plot of a new work called *Deaf, Dumb and Blind Boy* to Jann Wenner. Lambert talked the project through with Pete, helping him make sense of the vagaries and trying to avoid the obvious pitfalls that afflicted so many concept albums of the period.

Pete's friend Nik Cohn, a writer/journalist and pop theorist ("he had pop off by heart, he thought in it instinctively—no sermonizing, no crap." said Pete) was appalled by the opera idea, fearing pomp and pretentiousness. Loving everything that was primitive and most exciting about '50s rock 'n' roll and loathing the intellectual baggage which attached itself after 1967, Cohn saw The Who as natural successors to Eddie Cochran. This accorded exactly with one facet of Townshend's character, but there were many others, and some of them dreamed in expansive and grandiose terms of a rock music unfettered, which could shape the world. It was that sort of time. Inevitably, these facets clashed, and when they thought out loud in interviews, as they were sometimes prone to do, attempting to give intellectual expression to everything that was least intellectual and most instinctive about rock, they came out with a fair amount of blather—the sort of thing that occasioned Keith Richards' letter.

As the nebulous collection of songs and ideas that formed *Tommy* began to take shape, was encouraged, and as far as possible clarified by Kit Lambert's script, Pete's attention was fully engaged with the material that would become his opera. The final months of 1968 and the early months of '69 were taken up recording *Tommy* tracks at IBC in London—only an eight-track studio, but all they could afford—and even these sessions were interrupted each Friday as the band broke off to go out and perform in order to pay for the studio time. The studio facilities were clearly very limited, as were funds, and the budget wouldn't run to session players for string and horn parts. For a band as respected as The Who, engaged on a make-or-break magnum opus, this was, once again, a dispiriting state of affairs. In a concession to Cohn—who shared Townshend's pinball obsession and also wrote influential reviews in *The Observer* and *The New York Times*—Pete wrote "Pinball Wizard," which "committed me to turning *Tommy*'s rather mystical plot into a farce." It also gave The Who something they'd been missing of late: a hit.

When "Pinball Wizard" entered the English charts, it ended the longest drought thus far in the band's history: they'd gone nearly a year-and-a-half without a hit. "I Can See for Miles" left the U.K. charts late in 1967 and "Pinball Wizard" made its entry in April 1969. It reached number 4 and stayed a total of eight weeks. Just as The Stones had bounced back from their *Satanic Majesties* doldrums with "Jumpin' Jack Flash," so The Who returned to form with "Pinball Wizard," having spent the whole of 1968 in the wilderness.

It's never easy to convey the effect a piece of music has when it's new. What causes one generation to riot often sounds fairly tame to the next. With all the advantages of hindsight and familiarity, it may seem preposterous to suggest that The Who or The Stones seemed washed up by '68, though at the time it seemed perfectly plausible (ironically, it was The Beatles who seemed best placed for longevity), but eighteen months is a very long time in pop. Both The Stones and The Who were ill-suited to psychedelia. The Stone's last strong work—"Let's Spend the Night Together" and the *Between the Buttons* LP—had come out in January 1967, and right up until the release of "Jumpin' Jack Flash" in May '68, there was nothing but the lightweight "We Love You" single and the December release (already too late) of their *Satanic Majesties'* midsummer '67 psychedelic noodlings. Much of "Jumpin' Jack Flash"'s impact came from the clarity with which The Stones reidentified what they did best, and the accuracy with which they hit it. "Pinball Wizard" (one of Townshend's favorite singles) had a similar effect and, with The Who's 1968 output as far off-center as The Stones' in 1967, the sense of a triumphant return was equally strong. After what seemed like a lengthy absence, it was a reinvigorated Who that burst back onto the English scene in 1969.

The Who's problems were not the same as The Stones.' No band member was (yet) disintegrating before the others' eyes, and a high-profile jail sentence was not an option. Try as he may, Pete could not get busted. An enthusiastic advocate of the underground scene, he identified strongly with the pro-dope lobby, and since the "blocked up" remark on Barry Fantoni's *A Whole Scene Going* show, he'd made all sorts of indiscreet comments in interviews, but as Jagger, Richards, Jones, and Clapton were chased around Chelsea by Detective Sergeant Robin Constable, Pete couldn't get arrested. His reaction to The Stones (albeit short) jailing, and his feeling that Jagger and Richards had been made scapegoats for the habits of an entire sector of their generation, resulted in the Who covers of "The Last Time"/"Under My Thumb."

Pete was certainly shrewd enough to recognise the PR potential of minor martyrdom. The Stones' bust at Keith's country house, Redlands, and the subsequent trial at Lewes, generated acres of national coverage ranging in tone from the salacious to the morally improving. 1967, in fact, was the High Summer of a particularly English attitude toward drugs, best illustrated by the full-page ad which appeared in *The Times*, advocating the legalization of cannabis, above the signatures of a surprising range of people, including many of the Great and the Good. By the time "Pinball Wizard" came out in '69, Pete's attitude toward drugs had changed. He was now a Meher Baba devotee, permanently put off powerful hallucinogens by an horrific STP experience, which occurred while he was returning from the Monterey Pop festival and the Fillmore West shows that followed it.

For a number of reasons, being stuck in an airplane on a long transatlantic flight would appear very high on most people's list of "Locations in Which Not to Have a Bad Trip." You can't seek solace in movement; "walking it off" is not an option. You're unlikely to be flying with a group of people sympathetic to the loud, eccentric, or energetic expression of the extremes of the psychedelic experience. And while most people are superficially relaxed about air travel, there is a high background level of ambient terror, a latent atmosphere which the unfortunate tripper might well have the misfortune to tap into. Stuck inside a pressurized metal tube at thirty thousand feet with nowhere to hide is a recipe for the full horrors. A bad acid experience would have been unpleasant enough, but STP was a relatively new strain of psychotropic drug, similar in effect to LSD though more intense and—critically—far longer lasting.

With LSD, the peak (the most anxious period, as the rushes commence) lasts between thirty minutes and an hour. Once these rapids have been navigated, it's a fairly gentle five- or six-hour drift downstream. From the terms in which Pete describes his experience, it's obvious he was no stranger to LSD, but equally obvious that he'd no real appreciation of the differences between LSD and STP. Whether this was a result of improper briefing (San Francisco in the "dosing" years was probably not the best place to get an accurate account of the substance you were being given) or acid bravado on Townshend's part ("I can take it!") is unclear. Pete recalled:

> It was bloody terrible. I had to leave my body . . . the hump was about four to five hours . . . I said "Fuck this, I can't stand anymore" . . . and I was free of the trip . . . floating in mid-air looking at myself in a chair.

Although he doesn't seem to have spent the flight tearing up and down the aisles, screaming "I got The Fear," it's little wonder that Townshend overhauled his attitude toward powerful psychedelics. Some tracks on *The Who Sell Out* (November '67) make perfunctory nods in the direction of acid rock, but stop well short of full-blown psychedelia. Though it was never much of a serious threat, any danger that The Who might have drifted irretrievably into pyschedelia was effectively dead by the time Townshend made his way off of that aircraft in June 1967.

*   *   *

Townshend's method of arriving in the studio with a completed work for the band to reproduce was unique among English pop groups. Plenty of musician/writers demoed their songs, then used the studio or rehearsal room to develop the arrangement with their musicians, but Pete's position was closer to that of a Classical composer delivering a written score—except that the music wasn't notated on manuscript paper but recorded on tape. In almost every case, the band was presented with a finished arrangement that they followed faithfully, retaining the structure, following key changes, and altering details only where superior technical ability dictated (e.g., John's upgrading of the "My Generation" bass solo).

Most writers preferred variations on the organic model. Dylan and The Stones, for instance, generally arrived at the studio with an outlined arrangement, then allowed the song to evolve as the musicians ran through it. The Stones often waited six or eight hours while Keith chipped away at a riff until it assumed a shape he was happy with. Dylan preferred to assemble players and attack the song immediately—often without telling the musicians the chords. If they hadn't picked it up within two or three takes, he moved onto something else. The results of this approach are audible all over Dylan's work in occasional fluffed notes. Most often the bass player gets caught out (bassists are most vulnerable; guitarists and keyboard players can bluff or hedge their bets, but the bass must commit himself once or twice in every bar), but the take is used because the feel is right.

"Pinball Wizard" meets three of the traditional criteria for a Who single: it's in a major key, it features a solo guitar intro, and it is based harmonically on a sequence of chords unfolding over a pedal note, played in this case on a sweet-sounding Gibson acoustic guitar, a J-200. Pete told Steve Rosen:

> The beginning of "Pinball Wizard," on the demo, that chord sequence runs for about 15 minutes. It's just an exploration of how many chords I could make with a running B: the B was in every chord. It went through about 30 or 40 chords very slowly and then into the song.

For the single, the sequence is trimmed down to nine chords, as on the *Another Scoop* demo. There may well be earlier versions, because this is definitely a late demo, and virtually indistinguishable from the single. Though there are no bass or drum parts, and no Roger Daltrey, the overall feel is so similar (and the quality so high, compared with earlier demos) it's easy to forget you're listening to a home recording. Track might just as well have issued this demo!

Even drastically shortened, this is still by far the longest of Townshend's guitar intros, and as pastoral an opening as you'll find on a Who single. The intro is in two sections. First comes the progression of nine chords descending in steps; relaxed but with a definite sense of leading somewhere, driven by that insistent pedal note:

> I became very interested in the drone. I listened to a bit of Indian music and that influenced me, and country music has a drone going through it as well. They call it pedal bass, but of course on guitar and banjo work it's not a bass but a running note that runs through all the chords.

What makes any such sequence of chords interesting is the relation between each chord and its successor. Anyone can string a series of random chords over a pedal bass and call it counterpoint, but it won't actually do anything. Pete had been working away with his Mickey Baker chord book investigating the jazzy, more exotic, or "difficult" chords for a while and knew his way around suspensions and "broken" chords. On the "Pinball Wizard" intro, most of the eight changes are accomplished with the smallest possible movement, so that any chord may have three notes in common and only one note different from its predecessor. It's the closeness of the voicings which makes the progression flow.

The second, more flamboyant part of the intro is the flamenco section, with Pete strumming furiously from the suspended chord to the plain major, and the acoustic guitar close-mic'd to maximize the percussive sound of plectrum on strings. Not until thirty-two seconds into the track does the first verse begin, and then it's sung with only guitar and bass accompaniment; the drums don't enter until the end of the verse, with the first refrain of "sure plays a mean pinball." When the electric guitar re-enters with the main riff straight after that punchline, the "crunch" tone is delicious, and it's balanced on the opposite side of the stereo image by the stringy, percussive scrub of the acoustic guitar. The twin parts are perfectly weighted; two different aspects of Townshend's guitar style run in parallel. In mono, or heard on AM radio, the two merge into one impeccable guitar sound.

Townshend was now an accomplished songwriter and record-maker, able to incorporate key changes seamlessly into his work. "Pinball Wizard" moves quite naturally back and forth between the two keys of B and D. The bridges ("How do you think he does it?") are in D, but the main body of the song, verses and chorus, always come back to B. The Who always liked to use strong dynamics—sudden shifts between loud and soft—to create light and shade, and (at 2'14") the full band drops out, leaving the solo acoustic guitar, which reprises the flamenco intro. Effectively, the song begins again, but in a new key: D. Thus the structure is circular. The new key is much higher, so for the final verse, Daltrey is pushed to the very top of his vocal range. (To hear the bottom end of his range, listen to "The Good's Gone" from the group's first album, *My Generation.*)

If you've ever noticed how many good things are tucked away on fadeouts, you may have noticed this one. If not, check it out. Playing the main riff for the last time (it too is in the new key of D), Townshend alters the final chord to a B flat, a deliberate change in an unexpected direction. It's also a comfortable chord-shape from which to play this brief, off-beat, picky, melodic passage—a classic example of one of the best, and often overlooked, facets of his guitar playing.

*   *   *

"Pinball Wizard" is the last great Who single of the '60s. A part of *Tommy* yet a viable single in its own right (its release preceded the album by two months), it marked the end of an era. *Tommy* was undoubtedly the making of The Who; but at what cost? What are we to make of the fears that Nik Cohn voiced about The Who's new direction? If we accept Cohn's notion of The Who as the re-embodiment of all that was most exciting about '50s rock, then the cost was ruinous. If we reject it, then *Tommy* was their crowning achievement, a triumph that led, moreover, to further major works like *Quadrophenia.*

Cohn's critique was formed against a highly stylized backdrop, which dealt in a mythological view of rock, and of Americana in general, a quintessentially 1950s British view of America as an impossibly distant land of tail fins and Little Richard. It makes wonderful reading (wonderful Pop Art, too) and it's a true reflection of a widely shared dream, but it was a dream that could never survive the reality of America, which was what The Who as a business had to do. Though Cohn's terms of reference are often fanciful, there was nothing wrong with his critical faculties, and one

Roger Daltrey in full regalia at Woodstock, 1969.
PHOTO: THE DON PAULSEN COLLECTION

THE WHO

must remember, too, that at the time, his was a minority voice. Most commentators hailed *Tommy* as a groundbreaking masterpiece.

What's my view? I think The Who did what they had to do. Indeed, it's hard to see what else they could have done. But my sympathies are with Cohn. If you were fortunate enough to see The Who play live during their first three or four years, in local ballrooms or at The Marquee, you saw a live rock 'n' roll benchmark established, which as far as I'm concerned, nobody—including the later Who themselves—has ever exceeded. One is immediately open to criticism of élitism, of being backward-looking, of lending support and succor to a phoney golden age, of nostalgia for lost youth—but who cares? If you were there, you know how good they were.

THE SEEKER

"I SUPPOSE I LIKE THIS LEAST OF ALL THE STUFF."

—Pete Townshend

Released in the spring of 1970, "The Seeker" is the final single on *Meaty, Beaty, Big & Bouncy* and stands apart from the rest of the songs for a number of reasons, both musical and chronological. All the other songs come from the era before *Tommy*, and all save "Pinball Wizard" and "Magic Bus" are from the years 1965–67. "The Seeker," which was the first record to be released after the runaway success of the double-album opera, is the sole *Meaty, Beaty, Big & Bouncy* track recorded in the '70s. A non–Kit Lambert production, it's also the only example on this album of a straight, riff-based composition.

The success of *Tommy* altered The Who forever. The scale and duration of the public acclaim that followed, especially in America, moved them from influential cult status to the very top of the rock world. As Townshend told the *NME*:

> I'd spent 2 years writing the thing but it was still more an image idea than a musical idea. And it was the whole thing of it being taken up in the States as a musical masterpiece that threw us. From selling 1500 copies of *Who's Next*, right, we were suddenly selling 20 million copies, or whatever it was, of *Tommy*. It was ridiculous from the sublime. It had repercussions.

The band toured *Tommy* relentlessly in Europe and America, where they played everywhere from massive football stadiums to the Metropolitan Opera House in New York, in the process inventing stadium rock and defining the major rock tour as it's understood today. By the time they finished, John Entwistle was so sick of *Tommy* he never wanted to play it again. The band's accountants declared them millionaires—it may have even been true, though there are many ways to calculate individual wealth. Certainly Townshend, with his individual publishing money, must have experienced a huge change in his personal circumstances, opening another rift between himself and the band. After this time, hardly an interview went by without the subject being alluded to in some way or other (check the footage from *The Russell Harty Show* included in *The Kids Are Alright* video).

For the first time since "I'm a Boy" was recorded in August 1966, the band went into the studio without Lambert as producer, and though he's still credited on the 45, he played no part in the arranging or recording of "The Seeker." Kit's attention, always mercurial, started to wander as the financial success of *Tommy* moved The Who from their long-held position as brilliant outsiders toward a more stable, conventional form of success. A dazzling talker and a master of brinkmanship, Kit was sustained by his belief in The Who as a unique talent, and his temperament had been ideally suited to juggling the band's dubious finances through the 1960s. When the major American breakthrough finally happened—the "ultimate prize" spoken of in *The Observer* piece—the game changed forever. Mainstream success, long overdue, brought an entirely novel condition to the Who camp—a degree of security. Kit undoubtedly enjoyed the money as much as the others—"Baron" Lambert was now the owner of a Venetian Palazzo—but he missed the improvisation and the scams, and had little patience or aptitude for the mundane day-to-day business of running a successful enterprise.

Lambert's management philosophy rejoiced in a mixture of nerve and outrageous front; the discovery that with a combination of momentum, money, and panache you could get away with almost anything. When confronted with some apparently insuperable difficulty, Kit would reply, "It's nothing. Once you've rearranged the entire seating of Lancing College Chapel to sit next to the boy you fancy, anything is possible." Kit found chaos very funny and loved telling disaster stories, which grew with every telling. It's quite true that success is nowhere near as funny as truly horrendous screw-ups, but The Who were now operating at the top level of the business, and the climate had changed since the pop days of '66. By the early 1970s, the increasingly self-conscious rock business offered unprecedented rewards to those prepared to take themselves sufficiently seriously. As fewer situations required his brand of inspired recklessness, Lambert started to find himself out of sympathy with the times, as well as out of sympathy with factions within the band, who felt that his system of accounting left something to be desired.

Kit's grand conceit—and perhaps his last great fling—was to take rock 'n' roll into European concert halls as prestigious as those in which his father had worked. Aware of potential animosity from the guardians of high culture, as well as the complex logistics of crossing four European borders with a major touring party and trucks full of equipment, he employed a young Cambridge graduate, Peter Rudge, to manage a short tour in January 1970. Rudge, who went on to organize U.S. tours for The Stones, had already been working with fellow Track artist Arthur Brown. Between January 18 and 30, The Who played the Champs Elysées Theatre in Paris, the Royal Theatre in Copenhagen, and opera houses in Cologne, Hamburg, and Berlin, finishing up at the Concertgebouw in Amsterdam.

"The Seeker" is a different type of song from anything else on *Meaty, Beaty, Big & Bouncy*. Though many tracks on *Tommy* are riff-based, none of the previous Who singles had any use for fundamentalist riffing—that monotonous sledgehammering which would characterize the bastard form heavy metal. Where riffs had once been an element of composition, in metal they became the totality. The methodology is simple. First, steal your riff: take the sort of line that Hubert Sumlin might have played on a Howlin' Wolf record and extract all the nuance and sprightliness. Loop it, and repeat ad nauseam. There's your guitar part. In case any of your listeners are unable to take the point from a single instrument, have the bass guitar play the riff in unison. Perhaps the singer can join in, too? Why waste time with a melody! In no time you can reduce a three-dimensional form based on interplay, into a dumb, brutal, one-dimensional thud. Which isn't such a bad idea as an effect—as one shading among many—but is not an encouraging basis for an entire school of rock music. Because the form simultaneously dispenses with such tiresome concepts as harmony and counter-melody, it proved irresistible to third-rate songwriters everywhere, and consequently is featured very little in Pete Townshend's best work—or that of songwriters like Ray Davies or Bob Dylan—though "The Seeker," with its running bass line in the verse, comes very close.

Unlike successful Who singles, "The Seeker" never adds up to more than the sum of its parts. Where Pete's guitar is alone on the intro, its tone is distinctive, but as soon as the band enters, its character is absorbed into the track. Roger does his usual professional job, but the track never really goes anywhere. The key is Moon's lack of effervescence. Playing with the sort of restraint normally only seen when he was singing "Barbara Ann," there are so few distinctive fills it might as well be a session drummer playing—and a Who track without Moon in top form is unlikely to really take off. If we assume that it *is* Keith playing, there's a possible explanation for his low spirits. Recorded on January 19, 1970, the session came just fifteen days after Keith had the car accident which resulted in the death of his chauffeur, Neil Boland.

Moon was great friends with the well-known satirical rock group The Bonzo Dog Band. You might find him visiting Bier-Kellers in full SS uniform with Vivian Stanshall, or, as a friend of mine discovered him one Christmas, riding up and down in the elevator at Hanley's toyshop dressed as a lift attendant. At a Bonzo's gig I saw, Keith played drums for most of the set, allowing Legs Larry Smith to vacate the kit and fool around upstage. So when Moon was invited to open a disco in Hertfordshire, he took along Larry Smith and their respective wives, plus his roadie Neil. On arrival, Keith's Rolls Royce became surrounded by a threatening mob of skinheads. Boland got out of the car to deal with the oafs. Precisely what happened next is lost in a fog of conflicting testimony, expensive lawyers, and an understandable wish to protect the principal, Moon, from a potential charge of manslaughter.

The skinheads pushed Boland to the ground, and Keith may have panicked. Sliding over to the driver's seat, he put the car into gear and moved off. Boland's skull was crushed beneath the front wheels, and he died before reaching the hospital. The coroner returned a verdict of accidental death, and Keith admitted having taken drink. When the wheels of the formal legal process start to grind, they can crush the participant almost as effectively as a Rolls. Keith, who's widely remembered as being a good guy—"a lovely man" in Anita Pallenberg's words—was devastated. An essentially private tragedy was compounded by a double load of pressure and guilt; not an ideal state of mind in which to enter the studio for an important recording. Years later, the incident still tormented Moon. In her book, *I'm With the Band,* Miss Pamela of the GTOs describes nights with Moon where self-loathing broke through the conventional mix of interesting sex, brandy, and pills:

> Sometime during the night . . . he broke down and started to cry, calling himself a "murdering fuck" . . . he'd gobble reds [Seconal] and Quaaludes to escape himself and still wake up every couple of hours in terror. He would screech and sit bolt upright, switch on the light gasping for breath, and try to calm his wildly racing heart.

*   *   *

"The Seeker" was the first single in nearly a year, since "Pinball Wizard" was released in February '69. Townshend has described both himself and Lambert as being close to nervous breakdowns after the hard touring of *Tommy,* so it's not easy to discern his intentions. If he still believed in the primacy of the single as a medium, this was clearly a crucial recording, symbolically and commercially. It was the start of a new decade, and would be The Who's first single as accepted stars in America—a box-office attraction to equal The Rolling Stones. We can never really know whether Townshend, at the time, regarded the record as a winner or as a mere potboiler.

Perhaps the problem lies not entirely with the song, but with this particular recording of it. A different—though contemporaneous—version, recorded very quickly for BBC radio on April 30, 1970, is far more sprightly. Keith sounds like his usual self, and the instruments are assigned differently. The main guitar part (as on Pete's demo) is given to an acoustic—so much better suited to those flamenco flourishes—which Pete attacks with the fastest over-strumming I've ever heard him produce. Pete described this technique in a conversation with Steve Rosen:

> My acoustic style is very, very Spanish influenced and what I tried to do was to develop a way I could play very, very fast flourishes and still keep hold of the pick. I developed a technique—and this is only analysing backwards because I didn't consciously do this—using a heavy pick. . . . I would float it in mid-air and not actually

hold it. It floats between my fingers, and I somehow managed not to drop it, so it is very, very loose and you can get a lot of odododododododododododo.

The whole track lifts off cleanly in under fifteen seconds, and approaches vintage Who. The guitar break contains a mixture of ingredients, one moment Chuck Berry, the next veering off onto the banjo-based tangent, a Townshend trademark every bit as distinctive as the windmill and the power chord. The ensemble performance is so much stronger that the memory of the single is temporarily expunged.

There can be no doubting the lyric's passion or sincerity—not that either have much to do with quality—but one feels that if, for instance, "Substitute" is anything to go by, Pete does his best work when moved as much by cynicism as by conviction. He says himself that "the best lyrics were always the ones you scribbled out in two minutes." Pete frequently uses his personal uncertainties as subject matter, but in this case he does so in a very literal form. Taking his own search for "meaning" as a metaphor for an entire generation's experience, he catalogues the "Lights That Have Failed": Dylan, The Beatles, even poor old Tim Leary. Leary might have been happy to discuss philosophy, but the others seem a little implausible. Did Pete really ask Bobby Dylan? Nothing would've seen him out the front door quicker . . .

On its release, the critics were not favorably disposed. Nik Cohn noticed "another 'Call Me Lightning' or 'Magic Bus' except it's not as good," and the paying public showed considerable restraint. The song spent one week in the English chart and reached number 19. In America it did less well.

There's a case to be made for ending *Meaty, Beaty, Big & Bouncy* at "Pinball Wizard"—the last of the '60s singles, and a storming record—rather than the slightly downbeat note of "The Seeker," though since both LP and CD are sequenced without regard to chronology (or any other discernible criteria) the album doesn't actually close with "The Seeker" but with the long, alternate version of "I'm a Boy."

Old-fashioned, automatic record players had a stabiliser arm holding the discs in place on the spindle. By lifting it, you could make the machine play a record over and over again. These days though, all you need is a CD player with a Loop button. Hit it.

AFTERWARDS

The period covered by *Meaty, Beaty, Big & Bouncy* ends in early 1970 with "The Seeker," but to all intents it's a classic '60s album—and by and large a mid-'60s album, because so much of its material comes from the years 1965 to '67. It can legitimately claim to be the definitive Who artifact because every important single is here. Not that The Who simply ceased to release singles in 1970—far from it. As their subsequent career shows, Townshend evidently still felt that he should release singles, even if he no longer regarded "the single" with the same passionate belief that fired his early career. Eventually he abandoned the single as a form and went back to his demos. As the '70s wore on, Who singles would either be album tracks or repackagings of earlier material. In both musical and chart terms, these singles were a mixed bunch.

Some, like "Let's See Action" (1971—never a U.S. single) and "Relay" (1972) were minor U.K. chart hits (16 and 21, respectively); some like "Join Together" (number 9 in 1972) were more successful, but none attained that effortless, poised, blend of pop and power that distinguished the '60s singles. Whether you class these songs as true singles or album tracks is a matter of interpretation. Kit Lambert was no longer in the producer's chair and all three songs were unused material from the aborted *Lifehouse* project—-an attempted mystical/multimedia fusion of which Nik Cohn wrote, "Not even Townshend's managers have any clear idea of what he's up to. For that matter, neither has Townshend—his plot has been changing day to day, according to his mood."

"Won't Get Fooled Again" (1971) is a mighty recording, but the single (nos. 9 and 15 respectively on the U.K. and U.S. charts) is an edited-

OBSERVER

Tony McGrath

WHO'S STILL WHO

Pete, Keith, John and
Roger never
broke their promise

ALSO:
JULIANE TELLS 'HOW I SURVIVE THE JUNGLE'

down version of the eight-and-a-half minute *Who's Next* track—not a pur-pose-built, catchy three-minute single in the great tradition with which this book deals. For that matter, *Who's Next* itself is a watered-down ver-sion of what might have been the *Lifehouse* double album, had Townshend not over-reached himself and lost the thread. The first non-Lambert produced LP, *Who's Next* is the album that was salvaged from the wreckage. Treated to a "conventional" (albeit highly competent) Glyn Johns production, it's probably the band's most accessible album, and the only Who release ever to make number 1 in the U.K., though dis-senting voices view it as the beginning of a formulaic Who. Townshend himself called it the band's "first ordinary album."

The 1971 release of *Meaty, Beaty, Big & Bouncy*, just months after the success of *Who's Next*, made excellent commercial sense. The con-sumers who sent *Who's Next* to number 4 on the U.S. album chart were clearly not the same handful of isolated fanatics who'd helped "I Can't Explain" reach 93 on the Hot 100, back in 1965. As far as many in the mainstream U.S. audience were concerned, The Who might well have been one of the wave of new, heavy groups, a late '60s outfit who'd come to prominence with their marvelous rock opera *Tommy*—contemporaries perhaps of Led Zeppelin. The existence of an entire body of previous work was unknown to them, as was the extent of The Who's influence on the entire new breed of heavy rock groups, like Zeppelin.

By its nature, stadium rock demanded a visual language that could be read by ticket-holders sitting a quarter of a mile from the stage. The leaps into the air and grand windmills that Townshend had developed in small clubs translated effortlessly to the grand arena, as did Daltrey's swirling fringes and mic-swinging lasso routines, and Keith's massive drum kits. The vast American stadiums not only required a new type of act, they needed an entire rethinking of the logistical and financial bases—a new form of touring. The days when half-a-dozen acts could pile onto a single tour bus, share back-line equipment, and use whatever PA system they found at the venue were gone. The potential profits from sixty-date U.S. arena tours were vast—but so were the headaches. It was a Track employee, Peter Rudge, working as U.S. tour manager for The Who, who developed many of the methods that became standard proce-dures for large American tours.

Exactly five years later, the Who restage their 1966 *Observer* cover. March 1972.
© *THE OBSERVER* COUR-TESY OF THE BRITISH LIBRARY

A curious side-effect of the band's lopsided development was the formation of The Who's personal mythology, which began to flourish round about the time of *Meaty, Beaty, Big & Bouncy*. Myths and legends evolve around many bands—press agents are employed to see to it—but no group carried its own portable sense of history quite like The Who. It's probably inevitable that a band who opened shop with such a concentrated burst but whose recognition was so belated should become embroiled in their own legend. It traveled everywhere with them, fueled by on-the-road antics, nurtured by Lambert's charm in a tight corner, and expressed as pietas for the Goldhawk Road (as in *Quadrophenia*). Moon's legendary excesses had a charm, quite absent from the coarse thuggery and gross lechery of Zeppelin, while The Stones were more concerned with *preventing* their mythology getting in the way of lucrative American work visas.

THE WHO

Townshend made regular public pronouncements on how he felt about The Who—at one stage issuing what amounted to monthly bulletins—while he struggled sincerely with the problem of how to avoid becoming a mere oldies act performing much-loved material from the '60s. I doubt if anybody tried harder to reconcile the transient nature of classic pop with the long-term demands of keeping a successful show on the road—but the task was Sisyphean. As an individual, Townshend certainly suffered on its account, making several attempts to escape: into musicals, into prose (*Horse's Neck*), into publishing (first Eel Pie Publishing, and later an editorship at Faber & Faber).

As Barry Fantoni remarked:

> There's an energy about him, but there's a part of it which was constantly unresolved. . . . He was hugely loyal, and generous to the people who were his friends, but the genre he put himself into—and I feel this with Ray [Davies] too—is not substantial enough for an intelligent man, for a lifetime.

Once Moon died, the legend became set in stone. Though the band played on, the book was closed, and the myth became increasingly oppressive. At the summer 1980 dates I played in California, opening up for The Who, its presence backstage was so tangible, I'm surprised it didn't have its own dressing room.

Before *Meaty, Beaty, Big and Bouncy* there'd been two attempted Who collections, American Decca's *Magic Bus—The Who on Tour* (1968)—a lamentable album by any criteria—and Track Records' U.K. *Direct Hits*, released later the same year. Suffice it to say that while they may interest collectors, they are of no use at all to the general listener seeking a decent singles retrospective.

Since 1971, there have been many more collections of Who singles, yet for a number of reasons, *Meaty, Beaty, Big and Bouncy* remains the best bet. Including world-wide releases, the total number of compilations runs into double figures, many being badly mastered and poorly selected, one Spanish collection even featuring a sleeve picture of the Dutch band Golden Earring in place of The Who! As Chris Charlesworth mentions in his *Complete Guide*, by 1993 the U.K. buyer had no less than six different "hits" albums to choose among.

The Story of The Who is a 1976 English-only release on Polydor, which mixes the "classic" singles with album tracks from *Tommy* and *Who's Next*, but omits the all important first three (Talmy) singles—though an edited *Live at Leeds* version of "My Generation" is included.

Hooligans (1981) concentrates mainly on singles from the '70s (there are only three of the '60s "classics" included on this two-LP set), and is an MCA U.S.-only release—as is *Who's Greatest Hits* (1984) on CD, which is similarly patchy. Polydor's U.K.-only CD, *The Singles* (1984), contains roughly the same mixture as its U.S. predecessor. Though the balance of '60s/'70s material is more evenly weighted, it's still incomplete, lacking vital Talmy tracks.

In 1985, U.K. rights to The Who catalogue were briefly leased to CBS, who released *The Who Collection* on their Impression label. Along with plenty of '70s material, this double CD does contain all the classic singles—the first CD even sequences the songs in the correct order for a while before losing interest.

A single CD, *Who's Better Who's Best* (1988), was released on both sides of the Atlantic (MCA and Polydor) and contained a booklet written by Richard Barnes. The songs are all there, although their order makes no sense unless you consider the possible sequencing used on the vinyl release; a double LP with four sides each needing a punchy opener. The drawback is the quality of the mastering.

Five years passed before *The 30 Years of Maximum R&B* boxed set (1994), which contains four CDs, a booklet with essays by publicist Keith Altham and writer Dave Marsh, and an introduction by Pete Townshend himself. The most common complaint leveled against this collection is that the U.K. single version of "Substitute" is absent, replaced instead by a 1970 version from the *Live at Leeds* album. Though the quality of sound is much improved, as you'd expect from modern studio equipment, many of the tracks have not only been remastered, but remixed, inevitably altering the overall sound of songs that were, in some cases, made to be played on portable phonographs.

This raises the entire mono/stereo issue. In the days when the *Meaty, Beaty, Big and Bouncy* singles (and the concurrent LPs) were recorded, plenty of time would be set aside for the mono mixing, as befits an operation that determines the entire sound of the finished product. But the stereo mix was typically carried out in a single afternoon, often without the band even being present. The process was regarded as a relatively trivial technical detail, warranting about as much of the musicians' attention as running off safety copies or labeling the tape boxes.

Master tapes of the Talmy-produced tracks (the first album and the first three singles) were unavailable for use on the boxed set, because Talmy is still hanging onto them (presumably pending some financial settlement satisfactory to him), but these tracks also have been "tidied up" by Jon Astley and Andy Macpherson. How far a producer goes in altering the original sound is a question of taste and individual judgment, while the degree to which the alterations are noticeable depends upon the individual listener. Some people may notice no difference. I can only say, truthfully and without exaggeration, that my jaw dropped in disbelief when I heard "Happy Jack." If you can afford it, the boxed set is a luxury well worth having—but it's not the definitive singles collection.

At the time of writing the latest collection is *My Generation—The Very Best of The Who* (1996), a single CD featuring only the singles, as they appear on the boxed set. It contains all the right songs, and it's correctly sequenced, but the same criticism applies concerning remixed material sounding different from the original singles.

In the best of all possible worlds you could just pop out and buy the original vinyl singles, but till the dawn of such a day, my advice—especially if you're looking to replace 45s you once owned, or remember clearly from the radio—is to get hold of *Meaty, Beaty, Big and Bouncy*.

THE REVIEWS

MEATY, BEATY, BIG & BOUNCY

by Pete Townshend
ORIGINALLY PUBLISHED IN *ROLLING STONE* MAGAZINE (NO. 97, DEC. 9, 1971)

On listening to this album, it's very easy to imagine that the whole Who world has been made up of singles. Where Tommy and his lengthy and finally expatriated self come in, it's hard to say. Probably nearer the time of the second album, *A Quick One* or *Happy Jack* as it was called in the States. Before we even approached the idea of making an album that was an expression of our own feelings, or in the case of *Happy Jack*, an album expression of our own insanity, we believed only in singles, in the Top Ten records, and pirate radio. We, I repeat, believed only in singles.

In England albums were what you got for Christmas, singles were what you bought for prestige. It was the whole re-creation of the local dance hall cum discotheque in your own sweet front room. You had to have the regulation tin speaker record player, tin, not twin, housed artistically in a vinyl-covered box under a lid with a two-watt amplifier worthy only of use as a baby alarm, and a record deck on which the current Top 20 singles could be stacked 12 or 15 high for continuous dancing of the latest dance—which differed only from last week's in the tiniest possible hip-waggling details. A long sentence, but a single sentence. One sentence and you have the truth about singles. We made them tinny to sound tinny. If you made them hi-fi to sound tinny you were wasting your time, after all.

Shel Talmy, who produced our first three singles, was a great believer in "making groups who were nothing, stars." He was also a great believer in pretending the group didn't exist when they were in a recording studio. Despite the fact that I go on to say that our first few records are among our best, they were the least fun to make. We only found out recording was fun when we made *Happy Jack* and the ensuing album with our latter-day producer Kit Lambert. However, dear Shel got us our first single hits. So he was as close to being God for a week as any other unworthy soul has been. Of course it was a short week; I quickly realized that it was really the brilliant untapped writing talent of our lead guitarist, needless to say myself, that held the key to our success. Talmy and all following claimers to Who history are imposters.

As you can see, I feel pretty good about my own contributions to this the greatest of Who albums. John Entwistle's contribution should have been a single too, that's why it's here. Without a hint of guilt I shout aloud that singles just could be what life is all about. What Rock is all about. What the Spiritual Path is all about! Ask Kit Lambert about shortening a song two hours long with 24 verses, six choruses and 12 overdubbed guitar solos down to two minutes fifty or preferably shorter. Ask him how he did it without offending the composer. *Deceit! Lies! Cheating!* That's what Rock is all about.

It really is the most incredible thing that after two years of brainwashing himself into being a producer of singles for Top Ten radio play, Kit Lambert actually turned his brain inside out and came up with Rock Opera. Enigmatic paradox. But good thinking for a group who stopped getting hits. Listen to "Magic Bus" and "I Can See For Miles" and tell me why these cuts weren't hits. Tell me why *Tommy* was. Kit Lambert knows some of the answers, and perhaps because this album covers not only a huge chunk of our English success record-wise, but also our evolving relationship with Kit as our producer, it is, in my opinion (doubly prejudiced, and tainted by possible unearned royalties helping to pay for the tactical nuclear missile I am saving for) the best collection of singles by The Who there is.

It's *all* our singles, and it includes all our earliest stuff, excluding "I'm The Face" which might be released soon on the Stones label; "I'm The Face" was our very very first record on an English label called Phillips. It was "written" by our then manager Pete Meaden, fashioner of our mod image. He pinched the tune of "Got Love If You Want It" by Slim Harpo and changed the words to fit the groovy group. That is another, even earlier, story which, if it was ever told, would banish Who mystique forever.

"I Can't Explain," more than any other track here, turns me on. We still play this on stage; at the moment, we open with it. It can't be beat for straightforward Kink copying. There is little to say about how I wrote this. It came out of the top of my head when I was 18 and a half. It seems to be about the frustrations of a young person who is so incoherent and uneducated that he can't state his case to the bourgeois intellectual blah blah blah. Or, of course, it might be about drugs.

"Anyway, Anyhow, Anywhere," our second record, was written mainly by myself, but those were political days in late '64. Or was it '65? Roger helped a lot with the final arrangement and got half the credit. Something he does today for nothing, bless him. I was lying on my mattress on the floor listening to a Charlie Parker record when I thought up the title. (It's usually title first with me.) I just felt the guy was so free when he was playing. He was a soul without a body, riding, flying, on music. Listening to the compulsory Dizzy Gillespie solo after one by Bird was always a come-down, however clever Gillespie was. No one could follow Bird. Hendrix must have been his reincarnation, especially for guitar players. The freedom suggested by the title came restricted by the aggression of our tightly-defined image when I came to write the words. In fact, Roger was *really* a hard nut then, and he changes quite a few words himself to toughen the song up to suit his temperament. It is the most excitingly pigheaded of our songs. It's blatant, proud and—dare I say it—*sassy*.

Musically it was a step forward. On "Can't Explain" we had been fully manipulated in the studio, the like of which hasn't been seen since (aside from my dastardly treatment of Thunderclap Newman). Jimmy Page played rhythm on the A side and lead on the B, "Bald-Headed Woman." He nearly played lead on the A, but it was so simple even I could play it. The Beverly Sisters were brought in to sing backing voices and Keith has done poor imitations on stage ever since. "Can't explaaaain," he screams, hurling drumsticks at the sound man who turns the mike off because he thinks it's feeding back.

"Anyway" was the first time we encountered the piano playing of Nicky Hopkins, who is a total genius, and likes The Who. He likes John Lennon, too, and a lot of other people who give him work. A lot of bands breathed a sigh of relief when he and his missus showed their weary cheery faces in England again this summer. We did, and so on. He's still working.

Kit Lambert described "Anyway, Anyhow, Anywhere" to reporters as, "A pop-art record, containing pop-art music. The sounds of war and chaos and frustration expressed musically without the use of sound effects." A bored and then cynical Nik Cohn, Christ he was even more cynical than me, said calmly, "That's impressionism, not pop art." I repeated what Kit had briefed me to say, mumbling something about Peter Blake and Lichtenstein and went red. Completely out of order while your record is screaming in the background: "I can go anyway, way I choose, I can live anyhow, win or lose, I can go anywhere, for something new. Anyway, anyhow, anywhere."

Then we released "My Generation." The hymn. The patriotic song they sing at Who football matches. I could say a lot about this. I suppose I should say what hasn't been said, but a lot of what has been said is so hilarious. I wrote it as a throwaway naturally. It was a talking blues thing of the "Talking New York" ilk. This one had come from a crop of songs which I was, by then, writing using a tape recorder. Kit Lambert had brought me two good quality tape decks and suggested I do this; it appealed to me as I had always attempted it using lesser machines and been encouraged by results. But when you sit down and think what to play, it's a little hard. The whole point is that blues patterns, the ones groups use to jam with one another, are somehow the only thing forthcoming when you are gazing at a dial and thinking mainly of how good it's going to be to play this to Beryl and proudly say, "I played *all* the instruments on this myself." *All* the instruments being guitar, guitar, bass guitar and maracas.

Anyway, enconsed in my Belgravia two-room tape recorder and hi-fi showroom, I proceeded to enjoy myself writing ditties with which I could later amuse myself overdubbing, multitracking and adding extra parts. It was the way I practiced. I learned to play with myself. Masturbation comes to mind and as a concept, making demos is not far off. "Generation" was then praised by Chris Stamp, our "other" manager, who was worshipped only as a source of money from his ever-active roles as assistant director in various film epics. He was convinced it could be the biggest Who record yet. Bearing in mind the state of the demo, it shows an astuteness beyond the call. It sounded like (I still of course have it) Jimmy Reed at ten years old suffering from nervous indigestion.

Kit made suggestion after suggestion to improve the song. He later said that it was because he was unsure of it. I went on to make two more demos in my den of magnetic iniquity. The first introduced the stutter; the second, several key changes pinched, again, from The Kinks. From then on we knew we had it. I even caught a real stutter which I only lost recently.

Over the period of rewriting I realized that spontaneous words that come out of the top of your head are always the best. I had written the lines of "My Generation" without thinking, hurrying them, scribbling on a piece of paper in the back of a car. For years, I've had to live by them, waiting for the day someone says, "I thought you hoped you'd die before you got old. Well, you are old. What now?" Of course most people are too polite to say that sort of thing to a dying pop star. I say it often to myself. The hypocrisy of accusing hypocrites of being hypocritical is highly hypocritical. See the new Lennon album. See "My Generation."

It's understandable to me, perhaps not to you, that I can only think of inconsequentially detrimental things to say about the emergence of lyrics from my various bodily orifices. "Substitute," for example, was written as a spoof of "Nineteenth Nervous Breakdown." On the demo I sang with an affected Jagger-like accent which Kit obviously liked, as he suggested the song as a follow-up to "Generation." The lyric has come to be the most quoted Who lyric ever, it somehow goes to show that the "trust the art, not the artist" tag that people put on Dylan's silence about his work could be a good idea. To me, "Mighty Quinn" is about the five Perfect Masters of the age, the best of all being Meher Baba of course. To Dylan it's probably about gardening, or the joys of placing dog shit in the garbage to foul up Alan J. Weberman. "Substitute" makes me recall writing a song to fit a clever and rhythmic sounding title. A play on words. Again it could mean a lot more to me now than it did when I wrote it. If I told you what it meant to me now, you'd think I take myself too seriously.

The stock, down-beat riff used in the verses I pinched from a record played to me in "Blind Date," a feature in *Melody Maker*. It was by a group who later wrote to thank me for saying nice things about their record in the feature. The article is set up so that pop stars hear other people's records without knowing who they are by. They say terrible things about their best mates' latest and it all makes the pop scene even snottier and more competitive. Great. The record I said nice things about wasn't a hit, despite an electrifying riff. I pinched it, we did it, you bought it.

"The Kids Are Alright" wasn't a single in England; it was in the States. Funnily enough, this broke really well in Detroit, an area where both Decca Records and the local community were a little more hip to The Who than they were elsewhere. Detroit, or at least Ann Arbor, was the first place in the States we played after New York.

There are a few cuts on this album that are good because they are as simple as nursery rhymes. "Legal Matter," for example, is about a guy on the run from a chick about to pin him down for breach of promise.

What this song was screaming from behind lines like, "It's a legal matter baby, marrying's no fun, it's a legal matter baby, you got me on the run," was "I'm lonely, I'm hungry, and the bed needs making." I wanted a maid I suppose. It's terrible feeling like an eligible bachelor but with no women seeming to agree with you. "Pinball Wizard" is, quite simply, quite pimply, from *Tommy*. It's my favorite song on the album and was actually written as a ploy to get Nik Cohn, who is an avid pinball player to be a little more receptive to my plans for a Rock Opera. Nik writes on and off for the *New York Times*. I know which side my Aronowitz is buttered, mate!

From the superb production of "Pinball" it is hard to imagine that anything produced by Kit Lambert with The Who *before* "Pinball" could stand up. There are two songs that do. "Pictures Of Lily" just *jells* perfectly somehow. Merely a ditty about masturbation and the importance of it to a young man. I was really diggin at my folks who, when catching me at it, would talk in loud voices in the corridor outside my room. "Why can't he go with girls like *other* boys?" The real production masterpiece in the Who/Lambert coalition was, of course, "I Can See For Miles." The version here is not the mono, which is a pity because the mono makes the stereo sound like The Carpenters. We cut the track in London at CBS Studios and brought the tapes to Gold Star studios in Hollywood to mix and master them. Gold Star has the nicest sounding echo in the world. And there is just a *little* of that on the mono. Plus, a touch of home-made compressor in Gold Star's cutting room. I swoon when I hear the sound. The words, which aging senators have called "drug oriented," are about a jealous man with exceptionally good eyesight. Honest.

Two of the tracks here are produced by The Who, not Kit Lambert. One is "Substitute." We made this straight after "Generation" and Kit wasn't really in a position to steam in and produce, that honor being set aside as a future bunce for Robert Stigwood. God forbid. A blonde chap called Chris at Olympic Studios got the sound, set up a kinky echo, did the mix, etc. I looked on and have taken the credit whenever the opportunity has presented itself ever since. Keith can't even remember doing the session, incidentally, a clue to his condition around this period. The other Who-produced cut was "The Seeker." "The Seeker" is just one of those odd Who records. I suppose I like this least of all the stuff. It suffered from being the first thing we did after *Tommy*, and also from being recorded a few too many times. We did it once at my home studio, then at IBC where we normally worked then with Kit Lambert producing. Then Kit had a tooth pulled, breaking his jaw, and we did it ourselves. The results are impressive. It sounded great in the mosquito-ridden swamp I made it up in, Florida at three in the morning drunk out of my brain with Tom Wright and John Wolf. But that's always where the trouble starts, in the swamp. The alligator turned into an elephant and finally stampeded itself to death on stages around England. I don't think we even got to play it in the States.

The only non-Townshend track on the album is also a non-single. Politics or my own shaky vanity might be the reason, but "Boris The Spider" was never released as a single and should have been a hit. It was the most-requested song we ever played on stage, and if this really means anything to you guitar players, it was Hendrix's favorite Who song. Which rubbed me up well the wrong way, I can tell you. John introduced us to "Boris" in much the same way as I introduced us to our "Generation"; through a tape recorder. We assembled in John's three by ten-foot bedroom and listened incredulously as the strange and haunting chords emerged. Laced with words about the slightly gruesome death of a spider, the song had enough charm to send me back to my pad writing hits furiously. It was a winner, as Harry would say. It still is, for the life of me I don't know why we still don't play it, and the other Entwistle masterpiece, "Heaven and Hell," on stage anymore. There is no piece for the wicked, John's writing is wicked, his piece here is "Boris."

Of interest to collectors is "I'm A Boy." This is a longer and more relaxed version of the single which was edited and had fancy voices added. The song, of course, is about a boy whose mother dresses him up as a girl and won't let him enjoy all the normal boyish pranks like slitting lizards' tummies and throwing rocks at passing cars. Real Alice Cooper syndrome. Of course Zappa said it all when he wrote the original Rock Opera. Nobody noticed, so he had to write a satire on the one Rock Opera people *did* notice. "I'm A Boy" was *my* first attempt at a Rock Opera. Of course the subject matter is a little thin, then what of *Tommy?*

We get right down to The Who nitty gritty with "Magic Bus." Decca records really smarmed all over this one. Buses painted like Mickey Mouse's first trip. Album covers featuring an unsuspecting Who endorsing it like it was *our* idea. "Magic Bus" was a bummer. For one thing, we really like it. It was a gas to record and had a mystical quality to the sound. The first time ever I think that you could *hear* the room we were recording in when we made it. The words, however, were garbage, again loaded with heavy drug inference. For example, "thruppence and sixpence every way, trying to get to my baby." Obviously a hint at the ever rising prices of LSD.

When I wrote "Magic Bus," LSD wasn't even invented as far as I knew. Drug songs and veiled references to drugs were not part of The Who image. If you were in The Who and took drugs, you said, "I take drugs," and waited for the fuzz to come. We said it but they never came. We very soon got bored with drugs. No publicity value. Buses, however! Just take another look at Decca's answer to an overdue *Tommy*: "The Who, Magic Bus, On Tour." Great title, swinging presentation. Also a swindle as far as insinuating that the record was live. Bastards. They have lived to regret it, but not delete it. This record is what that record should have been. It's The Who at their early best. Merely nippers with big noses and small genitals trying to make the front page of *The Daily News*. Now Peter Max, there's a guy who knows how to use a bus! They pay him to ride on them.

To wind up, this album is a piece of history that we want you to know about. It's really a cross-section of our English successes, and when in The States, we get compared to come-and-go heavies who, like everyone else, influence us a little, we get paranoid that a lot of American rock fans haven't heard this stuff. They might have heard us churn out a bit on the stage, but not the actual cuts. As groups, Cream, Hendrix and Zeppelin, etc., have gotten bigger than The Who ever did and a lot quicker. But they don't have the solid, rock solid foundation that we have in this album. This album is as much for us as for you, it reminds us who we really are, The Who.

*   *   *

When the following piece was run in *The Observer* magazine— March 20, 1966—Sunday color supplements were still a relatively new addition to English life. Self-consciously "bright" and "dynamic," they quickly became authentic '60's artifacts in their own right, every bit as "swinging" as the scene they portrayed.

John Heilpern's article catches The Who between "My Generation" and "Substitute"—at exactly the moment they were breaking with producer Shel Talmy. The bewilderment of the new breed of English pop manager, coming face to face with a monolithic American music business that still dwelt happily in the Eisenhower years, is vividly depicted.

If the scale of the operation and the sums of money seem outlandishly small to us today, the phrases and attitudes are timeless. There are several instances where Stamp might be talking about the Sex Pistols rather than The Who. And everywhere, the hand of Kit Lambert is apparent. Aristocratic, autocratic, extravagant Kit in his prime, exaggerating wildly, talking up the numbers and generally putting the most favorable construction on events.

Here's the article, reprinted by kind permission of *The Observer*.

THE WHO

by John Heilpern
ORIGINALLY PUBLISHED IN *THE OBSERVER* COLOUR MAGAZINE © (MARCH 20, 1966)

On November 5, 1965, The Who released a stammering song called "My Generation." It sold more than 300,000 records, won a Silver Disc, became an international hit throughout Europe, and assured the group a gross income of over £1000 a week.

Fourteen months ago The Who were unknown. This is the story of how they made their fame. They are managed by two extraordinary young entrepreneurs, Kit Lambert and Chris Stamp. It's an odd combination. Lambert, son of the composer Constant Lambert, was educated at Lancing and Trinity College, Oxford. He talks very fast. Posh: "When I did National Service, I was the worst officer in the British Army."

Stamp, 23 years old, is the son of an East End tugboatman and brother of Terence Stamp, the film-star. Dressed in Carnaby Street, he speaks in a broad Cockney accent. "I like the blatant-ness of pop, the speed, the urgency. There's either success or failure—it's no use bollockin about."

Two years ago Lambert and Stamp were both successful assistant film directors earning £5000 a year. They decided to make a documentary about pop, and most nights of the week they'd go out in their cars looking for pop groups suitable for the film. After several weeks' search, Lambert came across The Railway Tavern, Harrow and Wealdstone. In a crowded back room were a group called The Highnumbers. "As soon as I saw them I felt a total conviction that this was it. It's as simple as that—this was it! They were The Who."

The next day, Lambert was already thinking in terms of taking them over. He persuaded Stamp to come and see the group. They drove together to the Watford Trade Hall—still one of The Who's most popular venues—and caught the last 20 minutes of their act. "I was knocked out" says

Stamp. "But the excitement I felt wasn't coming from the group. I couldn't get near enough. It was coming from the people blocking my way."

For £2 Stamp and Lambert hired the Youth Club in Notting Hill Gate and auditioned the group in the morning. Four days later, Lambert and Stamp were their managers.

The contract guaranteed each member of the group £1000 a year, irrespective of whether they got another booking. "Pop appealed to us" says Lambert, "because it's a field where it's possible to make a great deal of money very quickly. We've subsequently been proved dead wrong." Within three months, personal savings of £6,000 were eaten up, fine apartments made way for digs, and gold watches were pawned (they still are).

They changed the name of the group to The Who. "The Highnumbers was a nothing name" explains Stamp. "It implied the Top Twenty, but The Who seemed so perfect for them. It was impersonal, it couldn't be dated." Lambert: "It's a gimmick name—journalists could write article called THE WHY OF THE WHO, and people had to go through a boring ritual of question and answer. 'Have you heard The Who? The Who? The Who.' It was an invitation to corniness, and we were in a corny world."

The group began to have their hair styled by Gordon at Robert James hairdressers in the Charing Cross Road. Three-hour sessions every two weeks: "Long hair is glamourous, distinctive." They listened to hundreds of records. Pete Townshend, the lead guitarist, experimented with sound, perfecting a deafening system called "feedback" which became The Who's trademark and was later used by The Beatles. In 10 months £6,000 was spent on electronic equipment.

"Appearance is the most immediate association with the kids," says Lambert. "The clothes just had to be right." They had them specially designed. They went to Carnaby Street, spending as much as £150 a week. They searched for military outfits, period costumes, shopping in women's stores where the colours are brighter and the sweaters distinctive. They held countless photo sessions, four hours at a time. "We didn't want any boy-next-door image," says Stamp. "We hated those grinning gits on other pictures." Even now, £1,000 a year is spent on photographs.

Working alternately on films, Lambert and Stamp went out on the road. They wined and dined promoters, worked 17 hours a day, and buttonholed anyone who'd listen. But it was no use.

The pop boom, which began with the Liverpool sound, was on the decline: record sales were falling off, promoters going bankrupt, and groups which had once gone out for £300 a night were lucky to get £50. After three months, The Who were getting nowhere.

"We realized that if the group were to build up any national following, we must take the West End." They chose the Marquee Club in Soho, a famous haven of mod teenagers, putting enormous pressure on the promoter, Ziggy Jackson. For five weeks they nattered him silly until Jackson finally caved in and let them promote their own show on Tuesdays, a dead night.

"Our primary concern was to get an audience. Money didn't matter." They rushed out 1,500 posters for a London-wide campaign, dealing with The Fly Posters' Association. They printed 2,500 handouts, distributing them at dances, clubs, coffee bars, Saturday-morning markets—anywhere. And the campaign was particularly intensive in the group's home town, Shepherd's Bush: The Who had to acquire a clear, geographical tag. Every street was covered, and 30 key fans from the area were given free tickets. More tickets were at half-price, particularly to a club called The 100 Faces, formed for the occasion. The promotion costs were £300.

But on the night it was raining cats and dogs. The Marquee has a capacity of 1,200. 147 turned up. 69 paid. They turned off the lights and Lambert quietly doled out whiskey to the faithful Shepherd's Bush mods. The Who did the rest: Keith Moon attacked his drums with a sound and fury, breaking four drumsticks, until his clothes stuck to him and his jaw sagged with exhaustion. Roger Daltrey, the singer, dripping with sweat, shouted himself hoarse, smashing his mike onto the floor. Pete Townshend, nicknamed "The Birdman," went berserk, ramming the neck of his guitar into the amplifier until it smashed to bits. And John Entwistle, former french horn player in the Middlesex Youth Orchestra, just stood there, all in black, legs apart. "Without him," says Stamp, "they'd fly away." The Who were booked for another 16 weeks.

"To my mind," says Stamp, "their act creates emotions of anger and violence, and a thousand other things I don't really understand myself." Lambert agrees: "Their rootlessness appeals to the kids. They're really a new form of crime—armed against the bourgeois." (Keith Moon's father is an engineer.) "The point is, we're not saying, Here are four nice clean-cut lads come to entertain you. We're saying, Here is something outrageous—go wild!"

But records are the essence of the business. The group had already failed a recording audition with the biggest British record company, E.M.I. They decided to cut their own demonstration disc at Studio 2000 behind the Marquee: the number was to be their first hit, "I Can't Explain," composed by Pete Townshend.

Shel Talmy, an American independent record producer, heard the record, immediately auditioned The Who in the basement of the 2 I's Coffee Bar and moved in with a recording contract. "The kind of success we hope for," explains Lambert, "could only come from America." Talmy leased the contract to American Decca, and through them to Decca in England. Lambert and Stamp signed for five years. Within weeks, they were to have a blazing row with Talmy and beg American Decca to free them.

On January 15, 1965, they released "I Can't Explain" in Britain. At the same time, Lambert and Stamp moved into an apartment in Belgravia, "It was the only slum in Belgravia," says Lambert, "but it got us credit." In the smallest bedroom they set up an office consisting of a two-line switchboard and a kitchen-table, and hired the first of 20 successive secretaries. With Stamp's wages from filming, Lambert threw a champagne party to launch the record. The world's disc jockeys were invited, but only Dave Dennis of Radio London turned up.

The celebration was premature. Decca printed little more than 1,000 copies of the record, giving it minimum plugging time on their own Luxembourg record shows.

Lambert decided to promote the record virtually single-handed. He went all out: jukebox firms, ballrooms, coffee bars, handing out hundreds of posters, talking personally to every D.J. in sight. He went for the pirate radio stations, where Dave Dennis turned up trumps and plugged the disc as a 'climber' on Radio London.

But most of all, he plugged for television—the key to sales promotion. Lambert had an introduction to Bob Bickford, a former *Daily Mail* journalist who was now editor of "Ready Steady Go." Fortunately, Bickford knew of The Who's reputation at The Marquee and booked the group. Lambert could hardly believe his luck.

In the week that The Who were due on the air, "Ready Steady Go" unexpectedly needed 150 extra dancers at four days' notice. Lambert innocently suggested they went down to The Marquee, where The Who were performing: and a TV official handed out 150 free tickets to the Shepherd's Bush mods and members of Lambert's own club, The 100 Faces. The result was a managerial triumph: on the night half the studio was filled with key fans of The Who. The show was a smash.

On the following Monday Decca swung behind Lambert. Lambert succeeded in getting the group on to Southern TV through an Oxford contemporary, Angus Wright. On February 14 the record began to show at number 47 on the *Music Echo,* a newspaper then in its infancy. It went up gradually, reaching number 25 in the *New Musical Express,* a key chart. And then, the following week it dropped out completely.

Then Lambert and Stamp gambled heavily: they directed a film of "The Who," hoping to persuade a TV programme, "That's For Me" to use it. They worked day and night for three days. The cost was £350, but "That's For Me" took the film for their next show—at a price of £25.

Within a week the record was back at number 23 in the *New Musical Express.* And then a lucky break: "Top of The Pops," a programme networked into 5 million homes, was let down at the last minute by a group with managerial difficulties. They gave The Who their "Tip for the Top" spot. One week later, the disc shot into the Top Twenty—selling 10,000 a day—and finally ended up at number 8 with a sale of 104,000. Lambert went wild, running through Belgravia screaming, "We've cracked it! We've cracked it you bastards!"

But the next morning was like a hangover. Record royalties amounted to almost £35,000, but the publicity campaign wiped out any managerial profit. The shops would make £10,000, songwriter Pete Townshend and his publisher David Platz, would make £2,000, and the taxman, £4,700—everyone would make money except Lambert and Stamp. The Who ended up with £250 each. Decca grossed roughly £16,000. For the first time, they made strong objections to the actual terms of the contract. After three weeks of frantic argument, Decca agreed to raise the percentage deal retrospectively to 4 per cent in England and Europe.

"It's known as The Myth of Pop" says Lambert. "We began to realize that the first record was only a start." In debt up to their eyes, they refused to give in, and instead abandoned making films entirely. They were going for the jackpot, for America.

They went all out for a crucial, second hit. "If we didn't make it, we'd had it" says Stamp. "We had to bring through the image of the group on record. After all, they were creating something, they're not just four geezers in a suit." There was one encouraging sign: the press was at last beginning to take an interest. Richard Green wrote a feature called A DISTURBING GROUP in *Record Mirror,* describing Lambert as "a very loquacious young gentleman who takes great pains to put his points across." And

Boyfriend wrote: "love them or loathe them, The Who have made themselves something that other groups have longed for—a new image."

But the image was about to change. Singer Roger Daltrey had a gimmick of sticking black Sellotape onto a white sweater—changing the designs from night to night. The trick spread, almost by accident, to the rest of the group. Entwistle bought up dozens of medals, pinning them onto a diamond-check jacket. Moon wore a white T-shirt with a coloured target, a picture of Elvis, and the word "Pow!" And a Union Jack, until now draped over Townshend's speaker cabinet, became his jacket. Only in the world of pop could the sacred symbol of British royalty come to be identified by thousands of teenagers as the symbol of The Who. But it was the turning point: The Who were first in the field with Pop Art.

Lambert didn't waste a second: "We never intended to go for a quick profit with the group—we wanted a whole new scene going. We knew Pop Art could swing it." Rather dubiously, they claimed The Pop Art *Sound*, rushing out thousands of specially designed handouts, re-taking hundreds of pictures, contacting every journalist they could lay their hands on. On May 21, the release date of the record, The Who had a live appearance on "Ready Steady Go," shambling rather nervously into the studio dressed in Pop Art gear. They were an overnight sensation.

"D.J.s love a new sound" says Stamp. "It gives them something to say, gives them spiel between records." The record itself went out with a Pop Art cover in bright orange and yellow: *"Pow! Don't walk, run to your nearest record player."* The national Press were now doing full-scale features, fashion houses turned to Pop Art, and Carnaby Street began to rake in a fortune. Within a week, "Anyway, Anyhow, Anywhere," composed by Pete Townshend in a day, made the charts. After three more television shows, it went to number 12, selling 88,000.

Suddenly the established figures in the industry began to sit up. A surprise lunch date arrived from Rolling Stones' manager Andrew Oldham. At the Ad Lib discotheque, where the hierarchy of the pop world were seated with all the snobbery of a church wedding, the humblest table became vacant.

With the success of their second record, The Who went out on a gruelling three-month nationwide tour. Either Lambert or Stamp went with them, attending to the thousand and one crises that can arise with four teenagers travelling as much as 750 miles a week. They stuck with them for another reason: to protect themselves and the group from takeover bids.

Touring expenses were high—£150 a week—but, at least, the money was beginning to pour in. At the Astoria Ballroom, Rawtenstall, Lancs., the Dungeon Club, Nottingham, Trentham Gardens Stoke on Trent—£150 a night.

"My Generation" rocketed into the charts:

People try to put us down,
Talkin 'bout my generation
Just because we get around
Talkin 'bout my generation.

The success of "Generation" meant that The Who now averaged £300 a night. But they have to pay for clothes, instruments, travel (£7,000 a year), and two road managers. Lambert and Stamp took 40 per cent and the agent, Robert Stigwood, took 10 per cent of this. It left them with about £300 a week, set off against royalties. But they didn't keep a penny. Promotional films averaged £15 a week, travel costs another £150, office rental £10, picture sessions another £20, American and overseas promotional budget £60 a week, entertainment £20 a week. And more—telephone and cables £30 a week, office stationery and fan club £20, secretary (Anya Butler) and publicist (Patricia Locke) another £45. They even hired a tour manager: £40 a week.

"My Generation" just squeezed into the American charts at number 97. Stamp decided to go over to America for two weeks to whip up the promotional campaign, and to confront Sir Edward Lewis, the head of British Decca, who happened to be over there at the same time. He took to a stifling New York like lean men to a steam bath. "What a scene," he kept on saying, "what an unbelievable scene!"

He went to see his agent in America, Lloyd Greenfield, on the fifteenth floor of the Rockefeller Plaza. Greenfield is 38 years old, wears monogrammed shirts, and smiles mischievously. He is the man who discovered Buddy Holly, who is to pop what James Dean was to films: "I had his teeth capped, changed his glasses—and the rest was history." And then, "Listen schmock, I'm gonna break my neck to get The Who a hit record here," said Greenfield. "I don't just take on anybody—I was the man who made Buddy Holly."

Greenfield reassured Stamp of his faith in The Who: "The only way to sustain yourself in this business is by visual performance. That's where The Who have it. There's only one group so punchy—Cannonball and the

Headhunters. Stamp smiled, and Greenfield grabbed the phone. "Listen baby, twenty thousand dollars and that's it. That's it!"

Greenfield spent $4,000 promoting "My Generation." "And it's not gonna make it," he said, "It's just not gonna go." The money went on mailing more than 500 records to disc jockeys all over America, together with a personal letter to each one. Promotion men—hired to cover the east and west coasts—talked non-stop to D.J.s and programme managers.

The next day, Stamp got down to business. A girl called Gale, who seemed to turn up from nowhere, spent the day typing out 400 letters to D.J.s. Stamp tore round to the producers of "Hullabaloo," America's top pop show, giving them a promotional film of The Who, hoping to secure a booking. And on to WMCA, the biggest pop station in New York, to meet any disc jockey who would see him.

Stamp went to see his publisher, Happy Goday, Vice-President of the Richmond Organization, in an office packed with demonstration records, sheet music, a piano, and a stereogram that played non-stop. "'Generation' is in the charts by hard graft. If it's in the grooves, it'll go. From there we can't control it." On his desk was the sheet music for a song called "God is My Mother." "Everything is chance. I can hear 8 bars of a song and say no."

But, like Greenfield, Goday was confident of The Who's success in America; "It's a matter of time, the right record." He handed Stamp a personal list of 500 D.J.s. "It's a tough business. I'm 48 and work an 18 hour day, every day of the week. I try not to hurt anyone."

Stamp was fixed up with an interview on WNEW, a radio show broadcast from "The Dudes and Dolls" discotheque, where girls in tights dance on tables. The interview was a farce: *"Hi there everybody! And welcome to Dudes and Dolls where tonight we have Chris Stamp all the way from merrie England. Nice to have you on the show, Chris."* "Nice to be here, Tony." *"Chris, I believe you're the brother of film star Terence Stamp?"* "That's right Tony. As a matter of fact, Tony, he's mad on the pop group I manage called The Who." *"Who's this Chris?"* "The Who, a new Pop Art group with a Pop Art sound. Paul McCartney said The Who were the biggest musical influence on the Beatles in '65".

Stamp started to work hard again at the D.J.s and programme managers, perhaps the most powerful men in American pop. Even now nobody asks any questions if a crate of whiskey arrives on a D.J.'s doorstep. Stamp didn't get very far: they only wanted to know about a hit record. "My Generation" was still getting nowhere and Stamp despaired of his record company.

The next day he telephoned Marty Salkin, Vice-President of American Decca, almost crying with anger. He phoned Lambert for advice and they decided, once and for all, to break the contract with American Decca, whatever the cost. Stamp consulted his American solicitor, Joe Vigoda, who thought there was a legal loophole, and immediately arranged a meeting with Sir Edward Lewis of Decca the next morning.

That night, unable to sleep, Stamp went the round of the discotheques. He went to Arthur's with Kay King, a fashion editor of top-selling *Glamour Magazine*. She agreed to arrange a spread on The Who with pictures by David Bailey. Stamp controlled his delight: to swing the feature he had to agree to a separate picture of himself modelling clothes: "They'll think I'm a fairy, a fairy!"

The meeting with Sir Edward Lewis, aged 65, and the most important man in the record industry, went well. Stamp took Greenfield along: the meeting was cordial, friendly. Sir Edward agreed to see American Decca, his former company, that same afternoon, to see if The Who could change their American label. (Stamp had already received an offer from a rival company offering an inducement fee of $10,000 together with an astonishing 10 per cent of the American retail price.) But at 5:30 p.m. the next day, Sir Edward telephoned to say that nothing could be done. Stamp telephoned Lambert, and said "Break the contract."

Stamp came back from America quite hopeful of the next move. His agent, Lloyd Greenfield, said: "In Britain The Who are today—today. Well in America they may be tomorrow."

So, 14 months after they were originally discovered at The Railway Tavern, The Who wait anxiously for the last breakthrough. Their managers have seen a great deal of their first hunch borne out: they have made an unknown group break into the headlines, the hit parades and the hysteria-belt. But they have discovered, too, "the Big Myth of Pop," and have seen big money sliced up into small parcels, and the constant warning of groups who hit the top for a moment, and then disappear.

And they have realized how, in the bigger and bigger business of the pop world, the stakes get constantly higher, and the risks of failure get greater: scarcely 12 groups, it is said, out of the thousands performing all over Britain, are making "real money"—and that's the only kind of money The Who want.

U.K. SINGLE AND
ALBUM DISCOGRAPHY

With thanks to Chris Charlesworth

(U.K. chart placings follow release date; all singles 7" unless otherwise stated)

Singles

I'm The Face/Zoot Suit
(as The High Numbers)
    Fontana 480 3 July 1964
I Can't Explain/Bald Headed Woman
    Brunswick 05926 15 January 1965 #8
Anyway, Anyhow, Anywhere/Daddy Rolling Stone
    Brunswick 05935 21 May 1965 #10
My Generation/Shout and Shimmy
    Brunswick 05944 5 November 1965 #2

MY GENERA-
TION (LP)

Out in the Street/I Don't Mind/The Good's Gone/La La La Lies/Much Too
Much/My Generation/The Kids Are Alright/Please Please Please/It's Not
True/I'm a Man/A Legal Matter/The Ox
    Brunswick LAT 8616 25 December 1965 #5

Singles

Substitute/Circles
    Reaction 591001 4 March 1966 #5
Substitute/Instant Party (aka "Circles")
    Reaction 591001 4 March 1966 #5

Singles	A Legal Matter/Instant Party (alt.. Version)
	Brunswick 05956 11 March 1966 #32
	Substitute/Waltz for A Pig
	Reaction 591001 15 March 1966 #5
	("Substitute" was released with three different B-sides
	due to a legal dispute with producer Shel Talmy.)
	The Kids Are Alright/The Ox
	Brunswick 05965 12 August 1966 #41
	I'm a Boy (edited version)/In the City
	Reaction 591004 26 August 1966 #2
READY STEADY WHO! (EP)	Batman/Bucket T/Barbara Ann/Disguises/Circles
	Reaction 592001 11 November 1966
Singles	La La La Lies/The Good's Gone
	Brunswick 05968 11 November 1966
	Happy Jack/I've Been Away
	Reaction 591010 3 December 1966 #3
A QUICK ONE (LP)	Run Run Run/Boris the Spider/I Need You/Whiskey Man/Heat Wave/Cobwebs and Strange/Don't Look Away/See My Way/So Sad About Us/A Quick One While He's Away
	Reaction 593 002 3 December 1966 #4
Singles	Pictures of Lily/Doctor Doctor
	Track 604 002 22 April 1967 #4
	The Last Time/Under My Thumb
	Track 604 006 30 June 1967 #44
	I Can See for Miles/Someone's Coming
	Track 604 011 14 October 1967 #10
THE WHO SELL OUT (LP)	Armenia City in the Sky/Heinz Baked Beans/Mary Anne with the Shaky Hand(s) (acoustic version)/Odorono/Tattoo/Our Love Was/I Can See for Miles/Can't Reach You/Medac/Relax/Silas Stingy/Sunrise/Rael
	Track 612 002 mono/613 002 stereo 16 December 1967 #13
	(Mono and stereo versions have different guitar tracks)

Dogs/Call Me Lightning
    Track 604 023 15 June 1968 #25
Magic Bus/Dr. Jekyll & Mr. Hyde (first version)
    Track 604 024 18 September 1968 #26

Bucket T/I'm a Boy/Pictures of Lily/Doctor Doctor/I Can See for Miles/Substitute/Happy Jack/The Last Time/In the City/Call Me Lightning/Mary-Anne with the Shaky Hand(s) (acoustic version)/Dogs
    Track 612 (613) 006 12 October 1968

Pinball Wizard/Dogs Part II
    Track 604 027 7 March 1969 #4

Overture/It's a Boy/1921/Amazing Journey/Sparks/Eyesight for the Blind (The Hawker)/Christmas/Cousin Kevin/The Acid Queen/Underture/Do You Think It's Alright?/Fiddle About/Pinball Wizard/There's a Doctor/Go to the Mirror/Tommy Can You Hear Me?/Smash the Mirror/Sensation/Miracle Cure/Sally Simpson/I'm Free/Welcome/Tommy's Holiday Camp/We're Not Gonna Take It (See Me Feel Me)
    Track 613 013/4 23 May 1969 #2

(Various artists including The Who)
Who tracks: Magic Bus/Young Man Blues (studio version)/A Quick One While He's Away (Remix)
    Track 613 016 1969

The Seeker/Here for More
    Track 604 036 21 March 1970 #19

(Recorded live at Leeds University/February 14, 1970)
    Young Man Blues/Substitute/Summertime Blues/Shaking All Over/My Generation/Magic Bus
    Track 2406 001 23 May 1970 #3

Who tracks: Pictures of Lily/I Can See for Miles/Call Me Lightning (Backtrack 1); Under My Thumb/Magic Bus/Pinball Wizard/The Last Time

(Backtrack 2); Substitute/Disguises/Run Run Run/I'm a Boy/Whiskey Man/Happy Back/So Sad About Us (Backtrack 3); Pictures of Lily/Relax/Sunrise/I Can See for Miles/Our Love Was/Call Me Lightning (Backtrack 4); Magic Bus/Boris the Spider/Mary Anne with the Shaky Hand(s) (acoustic version)/Tattoo/I'm Free/Rael (Backtrack 5)
    Track 2407 001/2/3/4/5 23 May 1970
(five sampler LPs with The Who and various artists)

WOODSTOCK (triple LP)

(Various artists including The Who)
    Who track: We're Not Gonna Take It
    Atlantic 2662 001 June 1970 #35
    Summertime Blues/Heaven and Hell
    Track 2094 002 10 July 1970 #38
    See Me Feel Me/Overture from *Tommy*
    Track 2094 004 10 October 1970

TOMMY (EP)

Overture/Christmas/I'm Free/See Me Feel Me
    Track 2252 001 7 November 1970

BACKTRACK 7 MIXED BAG (LP)

(Various artists including The Who)
    Who tracks: The Seeker/Summertime Blues/Here for More
    Track 2407 007 7 November 1970

BACKTRACK 8 A QUICK ONE (LP)

(Budget reissue of the Who's second LP/track listing as above)
    Track 2407 008 7 November 1970

BACKTRACK 9 THE WHO SELL OUT (LP)

(Budget reissue of The Who's third LP/track listing as above)
    Track 2407 009 7 November 1970

BACKTRACK 14 THE OX (LP)

(Who songs by John Entwistle)
Heinz Baked Beans/Heaven and Hell/Dr Jekyll & Mr Hyde/Fiddle About/Cousin Kevin/Doctor Doctor/Medac/I've Been Away/Whisky Man/In the City/Someone's Coming/Silas Stingy
    Track 2407 014 7 November 1970

Won't Get Fooled Again/Don't Know Myself Single
   Track 2094 009 25 June 1971 #9

Baba O'Riley/Bargain/Love Ain't for Keeping/My Wife/The Song Is WHO'S NEXT
Over/Getting in Tune/Going Mobile/Behind Blue Eyes/Won't Get Fooled (LP)
Again
   Track 2408 102 25 August 1971 #1

Let's See Action/When I Was a Boy Single
   Track 2094 012 15 October 1971 #16

I Can't Explain MEATY, BEATY,
   Recording date: December 1964 BIG AND
   U.K. release: January 15, 1965 Brunswick 05926 BOUNCY (LP)
   U.S. release: February 13, 1965 Decca 31725
   B-side: "Bald Headed Woman" (S. Talmy)
   U.K. chart position: 8
   U.S. chart position: 93
   Running Time: 2' 02"
   Demo: N/A

Anyway, Anyhow, Anywhere
   (Townshend/Daltrey)
   Recording date: April 1965
   U.K. release: May 21, 1965 Brunswick 05935
   U.S. release: June 5, 1965 Decca 31801
   U.K. B-side: "Daddy Rolling Stone" (Derek Martin)
   U.S. B-side: "Anytime You Want Me" (Ragavoy, Mimms)
   U.K. chart position: 10
   U.S. chart position: N/A
   Running time: 2' 40"
   Demo: NA

My Generation
   Recording date: October 13, 1965
   U.K. release: November 5, 1965 Brunswick 05944
   U.S. release: November 20, 1965 Decca 31877

U.K. B-side: "Shout and Shimmy" (James Brown)
U.S. B-side: "Out in the Street"
U.K. chart position: 2
U.S. chart position: 74
Running time: 3' 15"
Demo: Flexidisk with *Maximum R&B* book.

Substitute

Recording date: February 1966
U.K. release: March 4, 1966 Reaction 591001
B-side: 1) "Instant Party"
 2) "Circles" (same song)
U.K. release: March 15, 1966 Reaction 591001
B-side: "Waltz for a Pig" (The Who Orchestra)
U.S. releases: April 1966 Atco 45 6409
 August 1967 Atco 45 6509
B-sides: "Waltz for a Pig" (The Who Orchestra)
U.K. chart position: 5
U.S. chart position: N/A
U.K. running time: 3' 46"
U.S. running time: 2' 58"
Demo: *Another Scoop*

Version 1 (the U.K. single) is available on *Direct Hits* (1968), *Meaty, Beaty, Big & Bouncy* (1971), *The Story of the Who* (1976), *The Singles* (1984), and *The Who Collection* (1985).

Thirty Years Of Maximum R&B contains Jon Astley and Andy Macpherson's remix of Bobby Pridden's recording at Leeds University, which appeared on the *Live at Leeds* album.

A Legal Matter

Recording date: October 12, 1965
U.K. release: March 11, 1966 Brunswick 5956
U.K. B-side: "Instant Party"
(Talmy's production as on U.S. *My Generation* LP)
U.K. chart position: 32
Running Time: 2' 45"
Demo: N/A

The Kids Are Alright

Recording date: possibly October 13, 1965
 as part of the "My Generation" single session;
or November 16, 1965
U.K. release: August 12, 1966 Brunswick 5965
U.S. release: July 1966 Decca 31988
U.K. B-side: "The Ox" (Townshend, Moon, Entwistle, Hopkins)
U.S. B-side: "A Legal Matter"
U.K. chart position: 41
U.S. chart position: N/A
Running Time: 2' 44"
Full Version: 3' 05"
Demo: *Another Scoop*

I'm A Boy

Recording date: August 1, 1966
U.K. release: August 26, 1966 Reaction 591004
U.S. release: December 10, 1966 Decca 32058
B-side: "In the City" (Entwistle, Moon)
U.K. chart position: 2
U.S. chart position: N/A
Running Time: 2' 38"
Version 2: 3' 42"
Demo: N/A
Version 1 appears on:
  Direct Hits
  The Singles
  Who's Missing?
  Who's Better, Who's Best
  Thirty Years of Maximum R&B (remixed)
  My Generation—The Very Best of the Who (remixed)
Version 2 appears on:
  Meaty, Beaty, Big & Bouncy
  The Story of the Who
  The Who Collection

Happy Jack

Recording date: November 10, 1966
U.K. release: December 2, 1966 Reaction 591010
U.S. release: March 18, 1967 Decca 32114
U.K. B-side: "I've Been Away" (Entwistle)
U.S. B-side: "Whiskey Man" (Entwistle)
U.K. chart position: 3
U.S. chart position: 24
Running Time: 2' 12"
Demo: *Another Scoop*

Boris the Spider

Recording date: November 1966
U.K. release: *A Quick One* LP December 1966
U.S. release: *Happy Jack* LP May 1967
Chart position: N/A
Running Time: 2' 26"

Pictures of Lily

Recording date: April 5, 1967
U.K. release: April 21, 1967 Track 604 002
U.S. release: June 1967 Decca
B-side: "Doctor, Doctor" (Entwistle)
U.K. chart position: 8
U.S. chart position: 51
Running Time: 2' 41"
Demo: *Another Scoop*

I Can See for Miles

Recording date: April/September 1967
U.K. release: October 14, 1967 Track 604 011
U.S. release: October 14, 1967 Decca 32206
U.K. B-side: "Someone's Coming" (Entwistle)
U.S. B-side: "Mary-Anne with the Shaky Hands"
U.K. chart position: 10
U.S. chart position: 9
Running time: 4' 04"
Demo: N/A

Magic Bus

    Recording date: June 1968

    U.K. release: September 18, 1968 Track 604 024

    U.S. release: July 27, 1968 Decca 32362

    U.K. B-side: "Dr. Jekyll & Mr. Hyde" (Entwistle)

    U.S. B-side: "Someone's Coming" (Entwistle)

    U.K. chart position: 26

    U.S. chart position: 25

    Running Time: 3' 17"

    Long Version: 4' 28"

    Demo: *Scoop*

Short Version appears on:

    Magic Bus—The Who on Tour

    The Kids Are Alright (1979)

    The Singles (1984)

    CD version of *Meaty, Beaty, Big & Bouncy*

    Who's Greatest Hits

    Thirty Years of Maximum R&B

    My Generation—The Very Best of the Who

    Who's Better, Who's Best (1988)

Long Version appears on:

    Meaty, Beaty, Big & Bouncy LP (1971)

    The Story of the Who (1976)

    The Who Collection (1985)

Pinball Wizard

    Recording date: February 7, 1969

    U.K. release: March 7, 1969 Track 604 027

    U.S. release: March 22, 1969 Decca 732465

    B-side: "Dogs Pt. II" (Moon, Towser, Jason)

    U.K. chart position: 4

    U.S. chart position: 19

    Running Time: 2' 56"

    Demo: *Another Scoop*

The Seeker

    Recording date: January 19, 1970

    U.K. release: March 21, 1970 Track 604 036

U.S. release: April 1970 Decca 32670
B-side: "Here for More" (Daltrey)
U.K. chart position: 19
U.S. chart position: 44
Running time: 3´ 09˝
Demo: *Who Came First* CD

TOMMY Part 1 (LP)

(The first half of Tommy *made available as a single LP)*
Overture/It's a Boy/1921/Amazing Journey/Sparks/Eyesight to the Blind/Christmas/Cousin Kevin/The Acid Queen/Underture
Track 2406 007 13 May 1972

Single

Join Together/Baby Don't You Do It *(live from San Francisco)*
Track 2094 102 17 June 1972 #9

TOMMY Part 2 (LP)

(The second half of Tommy *made available as a single LP)*
Do You Think It's Alright?/Fiddle About/Pinball Wizard/There's a Doctor/Go to the Mirror/Tommy Can You Hear Me?/Smash the Mirror /Sensation/Miracle Cure/Sally Simpson/I'm Free/Welcome/Tommy's Holiday Camp/We're Not Gonna Take It (See Me Feel Me)
Track 2406 008 24 June 1972

TOMMY (double LP)

(The London Symphony Orchestra and Chamber Choir/with guest soloists. Not strictly a Who album but featuring Pete Townshend/Roger Daltrey and John Entwistle among others/track listing as above)
ODE SP 88 001 October 1972

Singles

Relay/Waspman
Track 2094 106 23 December 1972 #21
5.15/Water
Track 2094 115 September 1973 #20

QUADROPHE-NIA (double LP)

I Am the Sea/The Real Me/Quadrophenia/Cut My Hair/The Punk and the Godfather/I'm One/The Dirty Jobs/Helpless Dancer/Is It in My Head/I've Had Enough/5.15/Sea and Sand/Drowned/Bell Boy/Doctor Jimmy/The Rock/Love Reign O'er Me
Track 2657 013 16 November 1973 #2

(Track samplers with various Who tracks)	TRACK ALL-SORTS

Who tracks: Whiskey Man/Won't Get Fooled Again/Pinball Wizard Track 2409 205 25 May 1974	ANISEED

Who tracks: Join Together/Substitute/Let's See Action Track 2409 206 25 May 1974	PEPPERMINT

Who tracks: I'm a Boy/Relay/I Can See for Miles Track 2409 207 25 May 1974	COCONUT

(The Who's second and third albums reissued as a double LP/track listing as above) Track 2409 209/10 1 June 1974	A QUICK ONE/THE WHO SELL OUT (double LP)

Postcard/Now I'm a Farmer/Put the Money Down/Little Billy/Too Much of Anything/Glow Girl/Pure and Easy/Faith in Something Bigger/I'm the Face/Naked Eye/Long Live Rock Track 2406 116 28 September 1974 #10	ODDS AND SODS (LP)

(Featuring The Who and various guest artists/track listing as above/plus additional or retitled tracks): Prologue/Captain Walker/Bernie's Holiday Camp/Extra Extra Extra/Champagne/Mother and Son/TV Studio Polydor 2657 014 March 1975 #21	TOMMY Original Soundtrack (double LP)

Slip Kid/However Much I Booze/Squeeze Box/Dreaming from the Waist/Imagine a Man/Success Story/They Are All in Love/Blue Red and Grey/How Many Friends/In a Hand or a Face Polydor 2490 129 18 October 1975 #7	THE WHO BY NUMBERS (LP)

Squeeze Box/Success Story Polydor 2121 275 24 January 1976 #10	Single

THE STORY OF THE WHO (double LP)	Magic Bus/Substitute/Boris the Spider/Run Run Run/I'm a Boy/Heat Wave/My Generation/Pictures of Lily/Happy Jack/The Seeker/I Can See for Miles/Bargain/Squeeze Box/Amazing Journey/The Acid Queen/Do You Think It's Alright?/Fiddle About/Pinball Wizard/I'm Free/Tommy's Holiday Camp/We're Not Gonna Take It/Summertime Blues/Baba O'Riley/Behind Blue Eyes/Slip Kid/Won't Get Fooled Again Polydor 2683 069 September 1976 #2

Singles	Substitute/I'm a Boy/Pictures of Lily
	(7″ and 12″ versions)
	    Polydor 2058 803 30 October 1976 #7
	Who Are You (edited version)/Had Enough
	    Polydor 2121 361 (WHO 1) DJ1, 2 & 3 14 July 1978
	(DJ1 in presentation sleeve/DJ2 in plain sleeve/DJ3 with blue label and blank B-side)

WHO ARE YOU (LP)	New Song/Had Enough/905/Sister Disco/Music Must Change/Trick of the Light/Guitar And Pen/Love Is Coming Down/Who Are You Polydor 2683 084 (WHOD 5004) 18 August 1978
Single	Long Live Rock/I'm the Face/My Wife Polydor 2121 383 (WHO 2) 1 April 1979 #48
THE KIDS ARE ALRIGHT Soundtrack (double LP)	My Generation (from *The Smothers Brothers* TV show)/I Can't Explain (*Shindig* TV show)/Happy Jack (live/not in the film)/I Can See For Miles (*The Smothers Brothers* TV show/not in the film)/Magic Bus (studio version)/Long Live Rock (studio version)/Anyway, Anyhow, Anywhere (*Ready, Steady, Go!*)/Young Man Blues (live from London Coliseum/1969)/My Wife (live from Kilburn State Theatre/London/December 15/1977/not in the film)/Baba O'Riley (live from Shepperton Studios/May 25/1978)/A Quick One (live from *Rolling Stones' Rock 'n' Roll Circus*/Wembley/December 11/1968)/Tommy Can You Hear Me (studio version)/Sparks (live from Woodstock)/Pinball Wizard (live from Woodstock)/See Me Feel Me (live from Woodstock)/Join Together/Road Runner/My Generation Blues (live from Pontiac Silverdome/Michigan/December 6/1975)/Won't Get Fooled Again (live from Shepperton Studios/May 25/1978) Polydor 2675 179 June 1979 #26

5.15/I'm One
Polydor 2001 916 (WHO 3) September 1979

(The Who plus various artists)
Who tracks: I Am the Sea/The Real Me/I'm the One/5.15/Love Reign O'er
Me/Bell Boy/I've Had Enough/Helpless Dancer/Doctor Jimmy/Zoot Suit
(as The High Numbers)/Get Out and Stay Out/Four Faces/Joker
James/The Punk and the Godfather
   Polydor 2625 037 6 October 1979 #23
*(Reissued on CD in 1993 by Polydor [519 999-2] without the "various
artists"/this was sequenced as above with the addition of "I'm the Face"
[as The High Numbers] at the beginning followed by Zoot Suit.)*
   I'm The Face/Zoot Suit (as The High Numbers)
   Backdoor Door 4 March 1980

QUADROPHE-
NIA Soundtrack
(double LP)

(Reissue of The Who's first album/track listing as above)
   Virgin V2179 October 1980 #20

MY GENERA-
TION (LP)

You Better You Bet (edited version)/The Quiet One
   Polydor 2002 044 (WHO 4) 27 February 1981 #9

Single

You Better You Bet/Don't Let Go the Coat/Cache Cache/The Quiet One/Did
You Steal My Money?/How Can You Do It Alone/Daily Records/You
/Another Tricky Day
   Polydor 2302 106 (WHOD 5073) March 1981 #2

FACE DANCES
(LP)

(Various artists including The Who)
   Who tracks: Baba O'Riley/Behind Blue Eyes/Sister Disco/See Me Feel Me
   Atlantic K 60153 March 1981 #39

KAMPUCHEA
(LP)

Don't Let Go The Coat/You
   Polydor WHO 5 1 May 1981 #47

Single

*The first nine U.K. albums in their original sleeves in a presentation slip
case.*
   Polydor 2675 216 23 May 1981

PHASES
(BOXED SET)

IT'S HARD (LP)   Athena/It's Your Turn/Cooks County/It's Hard/Dangerous/Eminence Front/I've Known No War/One Life's Enough/One at a Time/Why Did I Fall for That/A Man Is a Man/Cry If You Want
       Polydor WHOD 5066 4 September 1982 #11

Singles   Athena/A Man Is a Man
       Polydor WHO 6 25 September 1982 #40
Athena/Won't Get Fooled Again (LP version)/A Man Is a Man or Why Did I Fall for That
       Polydor WHOPX 6 October 1982
(12" Picture disc. All discs list "A Man Is a Man"; those with "Why Did I Fall for That" are rare misprints.)

RARITIES VOL I 1966–1969 (LP)   Circles (aka "Instant Party")/Disguises/Bucket T/Barbara Ann/In the City/I've Been Away/Doctor Doctor/The Last Time/Under My Thumb/Someone's Coming/Mary-Anne With the Shaky Hand(s) (electric version)/Dogs/Call Me Lightning/Dr Jekyll & Mr Hyde
       Polydor SPELP-9 August 1983

RARITIES VOL II 1970-1973 (LP)   Join Together/I Don't Even Know Myself/Heaven And Hell/When I Was a Boy/Let's See Action/Relay/Waspman/Here for More/Water/Baby Don't You Do It (live from San Francisco)
       Polydor SPELP-10 1983

WHO'S LAST (LP)   (Recorded live/mostly from Toronto Maple Leaf Gardens/December 17/1982/during The Who's "Farewell Tour" of the USA and Canada)
My Generation/I Can't Explain/Substitute/Behind Blue Eyes/Baba O'Riley/Boris the Spider/Who Are You/Pinball Wizard/See Me Feel Me/Love Reign O'er Me/Long Live Rock/Won't Get Fooled Again/Doctor Jimmy/Magic Bus/Summertime Blues/Twist and Shout
       MCA WHO 1 10 November 1984 #48

Single   Twist and Shout/I Can't Explain
       MCA 927 November 1984

THE SINGLES (LP)   Substitute/I'm a Boy/Happy Jack/Pictures of Lily/I Can See for Miles/Magic Bus/Pinball Wizard/My Generation/Summertime Blues/Won't

Get Fooled Again/Let's See Action/Join Together/Squeeze Box/Who Are You/You Better You Bet
 Polydor WHOD 17 November 1984

LP/CD 1: I Can't Explain/Anyway/Anyhow Anywhere/My Generation/Substitute/A Legal Matter/The Kids Are Alright/I'm a Boy/Happy Jack/Boris the Spider/Pictures of Lily/I Can See for Miles/Won't Get Fooled Again/The Seeker/Let's See Action/Join Together/Relay/Love Reign O'er Me/Squeeze Box
LP/CD 2: Who Are You/Long Live Rock/5.15/You Better You Bet/Magic Bus/Summertime Blues/Shaking All Over/Pinball Wizard/The Acid Queen/I'm Free/We're Not Gonna Take It/Baba O'Riley/Behind Blue Eyes/Bargain
 Impression IM DP4 October 1985 #44

THE WHO COLLECTION (double LP/CD)

My Generation/Anyway Anyhow Anywhere/The Kids Are Alright/Substitute/I'm a Boy/Happy Jack/Pictures of Lily/I Can See for Miles/Who Are You/Won't Get Fooled Again/Magic Bus/I Can't Explain/Pinball Wizard/I'm Free/See Me Feel Me/Squeeze Box/Join Together/You Better You Bet/Baba O'Riley
 Polydor 835 389-1/2 18 March 1988 #10

WHO'S BETTER/WHO'S BEST (LP)

My Generation/Substitute/Baba O'Riley/Behind Blue Eyes
 Polydor 887 352-2/4/1 March 1988
 (CD/12" and 7" vinyl)

THIS IS MY GENERATION BY THE WHO (EP)

Won't Get Fooled Again/Boney Moronie
 Polydor 887 576-7 May 1988

Single

Won't Get Fooled Again/Boney Moronie (live from Young Vic, 6 April 1967)/Dancing in the Street (live from Philadelphia, 13 December 1979)/Mary Anne With the Shaky Hand (live from New York/1967)
 Polydor 887 576-2/4/1 May 1988
 (CD/12" and 7")

WONT GET FOOLED AGAIN (EP)

(Live tracks from The Who's 1989 "25th Anniversary Tour," including the whole of Tommy performed with guest artists)

JOIN TOGETHER (LIVE BOX SET)

Overture/1921/Amazing Journey/Sparks/The Hawker (Eyesight to the Blind)/Christmas/Cousin Kevin/Acid Queen/Pinball Wizard/Do You Think It's Alright/Fiddle About/There's a Doctor/Go to the Mirror/Smash the Mirror/Tommy Can You Hear Me/I'm Free/Miracle Cure/Sally Simpson/Sensation/Tommy's Holiday Camp/We're Not Gonna Take It/Eminence Front/Face the Face/Dig/I Can See for Miles/A Little Is Enough/5.15/Love Reign O'er Me/Trick of the Light/Rough Boys/Join Together/You Better You Bet/Behind Blue Eyes/Won't Get Fooled Again

    Virgin VDT 102 March 1990

    Join Together/I Can See for Miles/Behind Blue Eyes

    (Live tracks from the 1989 tour)

    Virgin VS 1259 March 1990

JOIN TOGETH-ER (live EP)

(Adds "Christmas" to above release)

    Virgin VST/VSCDT 1259 March 1990

IRON MAN (LP)

(Pete Townshend solo album containing two Who tracks)

    Who tracks: Fire/Dig

    Virgin CDV 2592 March 1991

THE WHO: THIRTY YEARS OF MAXIMUM R&B (BOXED SET)

(Boxed set of four CDs/four cassettes/plus full color seventy-two page book)

CD 1: Pete dialogue*+/I'm the Face/Here 'Tis*/Zoot Suit/Leaving Here/I Can't Explain/Anyway, Anyhow, Anywhere/Daddy Rolling Stone/My Generation/The Kids Are Alright/The Ox/A Legal Matter/Pete dialogue*/Substitute+/I'm a Boy/Disguises/Happy Jack Jingle*/Happy Jack/Boris the Spider/So Sad About Us/A Quick One+/Pictures of Lily/Early Morning Cold Taxi*/Coke 2*/(This Could Be) The Last Time/I Can't Reach You/Girl's Eyes*/Bag O'Nails*/Call Me Lightning

CD 2: Rotosound Strings/I Can See for Miles/Mary Anne with the Shaky Hand/ Armenia City in the Sky/Tattoo/Our Love Was/Rael 1/Rael 2*/Track Records*/Premier Drums/Sunrise/Jaguar*/Melancholia*/Fortune Teller*/ Magic Bus/Little Billy/Russell Harty dialogue*+/Dogs/Overture /Acid Queen/Abbie Hoffman Incident*+/Underture+/Pinball Wizard/I'm

---

(* Indicates recording previously unreleased or unavailable in this version; + indicates live recording)

Free/See Me/Feel Me*+/ Heaven and Hell/Pete dialogue*/Young Man Blues+/Summertime Blues+
CD 3: Shaking All Over+/Baba O'Riley/Bargain+/Pure and Easy/The Song Is Over/ Studio dialogue*+/Behind Blue Eyes/Won't Get Fooled Again/The Seeker (edit)/Bony Moronie+/Let's See Action/Join Together/Relay/The Real Me*/5.15 (single mix)/Bell Boy/Love Reign O'er Me
CD 4: Long Live Rock/Life With The Moons*/Naked Eye*+/University Challenge*/ Slip Kid/Poetry Cornered*/Dreaming from the Waist*+/Blue Red And Grey/Life with the Moons 2*/Squeeze Box/My Wife*+/Who Are You/Music Must Change/Sister Disco/Guitar and Pen/You Better You Bet/Eminence Front/Twist and Shout*+/I'm a Man*+/Pete dialogue*+/ Saturday Night's Alright for Fighting
 Polydor 521 751-2 June 1994

(Remastered, remixed reissue with bonus tracks and new sequencing)
New track listing: Heaven and Hell/I Can't Explain/Fortune Teller/Tattoo/Young Man Blues/Substitute/Happy Jack/I'm a Boy/A Quick One/Amazing Journey/Summertime Blues/Shaking All Over/My Generation/Magic Bus
 Polydor 527 169-2 February 1995

LIVE AT LEEDS (CD)

(Remastered, remixed CD/cassette reissue with bonus tracks)
New track listing: existing tracks/see above/+ Batman/Bucket T/Barbara Ann/Disguises/Doctor Doctor/I've Been Away/In the City/Happy Jack (Acoustic Version)/Man with Money/My Generation/Land of Hope and Glory
 Polydor 527 758-2 June 1995

A QUICK ONE (CD)

(Remastered, remixed CD/cassette reissue with bonus tracks; tracks in brackets are "commercials")
New track listing: existing tracks/see above/+ Rael 2/[Top Gear]/Glittering Girl/[Coke 2]/Melancholia/[Bag O'Nails]/Someone's Coming/[John Mason's Cars— rehearsal]/Jaguar/[John Mason's Cars—reprise]/Early Morning Cold Taxi/[Coke 1]/Hall of the Mountain King/[Radio One—Boris Mix]/Girl's Eyes/Odorono (final chorus)/Mary Anne with the Shaky Hand(s) (electric version)/Glow Girl [Track Records]
 Polydor 527 759-2 June 1995

THE WHO SELL OUT (CD)

WHO'S NEXT (CD)	*(Remastered, remixed reissue with bonus tracks)* New track listing: existing tracks/see above/+ Pure and Easy (alt. version)/Baby Don't You Do It (studio version)/Naked Eye (live from Young Vic)/Water (live from Young Vic)/Too Much of Anything/I Don't Even Know Myself/Behind Blue Eyes (alt. version) Polydor 527 760-2 November 1995
TOMMY (CD)	*(Remastered, remixed reissue/track listing as above)* Polydor 531 043-2 February 1996

QUADROPHE-NIA (CD)	*(Remastered, remixed reissue/track listing as above)*
	    Polydor 531 999-2 June 1996
	 My Generation/Pinball Wizard (live from "Leeds")/Boris the Spider/My Generation (Deep Love Remix)
	    Polydor 854 637-2 (CD single) June 1996
	 (A concurrent 12" single/WHO 1/contained four different dance mixes of "My Generation": Regeneration Mix/Aphrodisiac Mix/Deep Love Remix and Deep Love Instrumental)

MY GENERA-TION: THE BEST OF THE WHO (CD/cassette)	I Can't Explain/Anyway, Anyhow, Anywhere/My Generation/Substitute/I'm a Boy/Boris the Spider/Happy Jack/Pictures of Lily/I Can See for Miles/Magic Bus/Pinball Wizard/The Seeker/Baba O'Riley/Won't Get Fooled Again/Let's See Action/5.15/Join Together/Squeeze Box/Who Are You/You Better You Bet Polydor 333 150-2 August 1996
WHO BY NUM-BERS	*(Remastered, remixed CD/cassette reissue with bonus tracks)* New track listing: existing tracks (see above) + Squeeze Box (live)/Behind Blue Eyes (live)/Dreaming from the Waist (live) Polydor 533 844-2 November 1996
WHO ARE YOU	*(Remastered, remixed CD/cassette reissue with bonus tracks)* New track listing: existing tracks (see above) + No Road Romance /Empty Glass/Guitar and Pen (Olympic '78 Mix)/Love Is Coming Down (Work-In-Progress Mix)/Who Are You (Lost Verse Mix) (6'21") Polydor 533 845-2 November 1996

THE WHO

Disc 1: Heaven and Hell/I Can't Explain/Young Man Blues/I Don't Even Know Myself/Water/Overture/It's a Boy/1921/Amazing Journey/Sparks/ Eyesight to the Blind (The Hawker)/Christmas

Disc 2: Acid Queen/Pinball Wizard/Do You Think It's Alright/Fiddle About/Tommy Can You Hear Me/There's a Doctor/Go to the Mirror/Smash The Mirror/Miracle Cure/I'm Free/Tommy's Holiday Camp/We're Not Gonna Take It/Summertime Blues/Shakin' All Over/Substitute/My Generation/Naked Eye/Magic Bus

Castle EDF CD 326 December 1996

(Remastered, remixed CD/cassette reissue with bonus tracks)
New track listing: existing tracks (see above) + I Like Nightmares/It's in You/Somebody Saved Me/ How Can You Do It/The Quiet One (live)
    Polydor 537 695-2 April 1997

(Remastered, remixed CD/cassette reissue with bonus tracks)
New track listing: existing tracks (see above) + It's Hard (live)/Eminence Front (live)/Dangerous (live)/Cry if You Want (live)
    Polydor 537 696-2 April 1997

Notes:

Catalog numbers indicate the original release or repackage. Release dates and chart positions are based on best possible information but are subject to interpretation.

There have been many reissues of Who material in different formats since the '60s, not all of which are included here. Neither are miscellaneous "various artists" compilations containing readily available Who tracks that have appeared over the years, most notably several television-advertised "Hits from the Sixties" or "Classic Rock"–style albums/a Marquee Club compilation, an "Original Britpop Bands" compilation/a "tribute" album to Elton John and others. Likewise, promo records have not been included.

All of The Who's original albums apart from *My Generation* were reissued on compact disc by Polydor during the late eighties with identical track listings to the earlier vinyl releases. Eight of these have now been superseded by the remastered editions on CD and cassette, released in 1995 and

1996. The remainder of The Who's back catalog will receive similar treatment in the near future. For legal reasons, *My Generation* is currently unavailable in the U.K., except as an American import. The two *Rarities* albums are now available on one CD (Polydor 847 670-2).

A recording of *Tommy* by The London Symphony Orchestra and Chamber Choir (U.K.: ODE SP 88 001; U.S.: ODE SP 99 001) was released worldwide toward the end of 1972. This featured Pete Townshend, Roger Daltrey, John Entwistle and others, and has subsequently been released on CD by Castle Communications.

The *Tommy* film soundtrack recording, a double album, featured all four members of The Who alongside several other musicians and actors, and was released in March 1975 (Polydor 9502).

Live recordings by The Who not found within The Who's own catalog appear on the following albums: *Woodstock* (Atlantic 2663 001/released 1969; reissue K60001)—We're Not Gonna Take It; *Concerts for the People of Kampuchia* (Atlantic K60153, released March 1981)—Baba O'Riley/Sister Disco/Behind Blue Eyes/See Me Feel Me; *The Monterey International Pop Festival* (Rhino Records R270596/released 1993)—Substitute/Summertime Blues/Pictures of Lily/A Quick One/Happy Jack/My Generation (their entire twenty-five-minute set).

Two songs credited to The Who, "Fire" and "Dig," with Simon Phillips on drums, can be found on Pete Townshend's *Iron Man* LP (Virgin CDV 2592, released March 1991).

Unique Who cuts are also available on videos such as Woodstock, The Kids Are Alright, The Who Rocks America 1982, Who's Better Who's Best, Live *Tommy*, and *Thirty Years of Maximum R&B Live*.

U.S. SINGLE AND ALBUM DISCOGRAPHY

*(U.S. chart placings follow release date; for full track listings of albums
see original U.K. discography, except where noted)*

I Can't Explain/Bald Headed Woman
    Decca 31725 13 February 1965 #93
Anyway, Anyhow, Anywhere/Anytime You Want Me
    Decca 31801 5 June 1965
My Generation/Out in the Street
    Decca 31877 20 November 1965 #74
Substitute/Waltz for a Pig
(The lyrics are altered for the U.S.)
    Atco 45-6409 2 April 1966

---

*(Side two differs from U.K. album, insofar as "Instant Party" replaces "I'm
a Man," and "The Kids Are Alright" is [badly] edited)*
Decca DL 4664 (mono)/DL 74664 (stereo) April 1966

The Kids Are Alright (edit)/A Legal Matter
    Decca 31988 July 1966
I'm a Boy/In the City
    Decca 32058 10 December 1966

Happy Jack/Whiskey Man
Decca 32114 18 March 1967 #24

HAPPY JACK (LP)

(Side one differs from U.K. album, insofar as "Heat Wave" is replaced with "Happy Jack")
Decca DL 4892 (mono)/DL 74892 (stereo) May 1967 #67

Singles

Pictures of Lily/Doctor/Doctor
Decca 32156 24 June 1967 #51
Substitute/Waltz for A Pig
(reissue)
Atco 45-6509 August 1967
I Can See for Miles/Mary-Anne with the Shaky Hand(s)
(In the U.K., Mary Anne's affliction only affected one hand; in the U.S. she had "Shaky Hands"!)
Decca 32206 14 October 1967 #9

THE WHO SELL OUT (LP)

(As in the U.K., mono/stereo versions have a different guitar track)
Decca DL 4950 (mono)/DL 74950 (stereo) 6 January 1968 #48

Singles

Call Me Lightning/Dr Jekyll & Mr Hyde *(alt. version)*
Decca 32288 16 March 1968 #40
Magic Bus/Someone's Coming
Decca 32362 27 July 1968 #25

MAGIC BUS— THE WHO ON TOUR (LP)

Disguises/Run Run Run/Dr Jekyll & Mr Hyde (alt. version)/I Can't Reach You/Our Love Was (Is)/Call Me Lightning/Magic Bus/Someone's Coming/Doctor Doctor/Bucket T/Pictures of Lily
Decca 5064(m) 75064(s) September 1968 #39

Single

Pinball Wizard/Dogs Part II
Decca 732465 22 March 1969 #19

TOMMY (double LP)

Decca DXSW 7205 31 May 1969 #4

I'm Free/We're Not Gonna Take It Singles
    Decca 732519 5 July 1969 #37
The Seeker/Here for More
    Decca 32670 April 1970 #44

Decca DL 79175 16 May 1970 #4 LIVE AT LEEDS
(LP)

(Various artists including The Who) WOODSTOCK
(triple LP)
    Cotillion SD 3-500 May 1970 #1

Summertime Blues/Heaven and Hell Singles
    Decca 32708 11 July 1970 #27
See Me Feel Me/Overture from *Tommy*
    Decca 732729 August 1970 #12
Won't Get Fooled Again/I Don't Even Know Myself
(B-side is same song as "I Don't Know Myself")
    Decca 32846 17 July 1971 #15

Decca 79182 14 August 1971 #4 WHO'S NEXT
(LP)

Decca DL 79184 30 October 1971 #11 MEATY, BEATY,
BIG AND
BOUNCY (LP)

Behind Blue Eyes/My Wife Singles
    Decca 32888 6 November 1971 #34
Join Together/Baby Don't You Do It
    Decca 32983 8 July 1972 #17

(Orchestral album/see U.K. discography) TOMMY
ODE SP 99 001 November 1972/ODE QU 89001 (Quad) December 1972
#13

The Relay/Waspman Singles
(In the U.K., Relay omitted the definitive article)
    Track Decca 33041 25 November 1972 #39

Love Reign O'er Me (*edited version*)/Water
Track Decca 40152 27 October 1973 #76

QUADROPHE-NIA (double LP)	MCA2 10004 3 November 1973 #2

Single	The Real Me/I'm One Track MCA 40182 12 January 1974 #92

ODDS AND SODS (LP)	MCA 2126 12 October 1974 #15

Single	Postcard/Put the Money Down Track MCA 40330 November 1974

A QUICK ONE (HAPPY JACK)/THE WHO SELL OUT (double LP)	*(The Who's second and third albums reissued as a double LP)* MCA 2-4067 30 November 1974

MY GENERA-TION/MAGIC BUS (double LP)	*(The Who's first album and fourth [U.S. only] album reissued as a double LP)* MCA 2-4068 30 November 1974 #185

TOMMY Original Soundtrack (double LP)	Polydor PD2-9505 22 February 1975 #2

THE WHO BY NUMBERS (LP)	MCA 2161 25 October 1975 #8

Singles	Squeeze Box/Success Story MCA 40475 22 November 1975 #16 Slip Kid/Dreaming from the Waist MCA 40603 7 August 1976

Who Are You (*edited version*)/Had Enough
   MCA 40948 August 1978 #14

MCA 3050 25 August 1978 #2

Trick of the Light/905
   MCA 40978 2 December 1978

MCA2-11005 23 June 1979 #8

Long Live Rock/My Wife
   MCA 41053 June 1979 #54
5.15/I'm One
   Polydor 2022 September 1979 #45

Polydor PD2-6235 6 October 1979 #46

I'm the Face/Zoot Suit (as The High Numbers)
   Mercury DJ 570 March 1980
You Better You Bet (*edited version*)/The Quiet One
   Warner Bros. WBS 49698 March 1981 #18

Warner Bros. WB HS 3516 March 1981 #4

(*Various artists including The Who*)
Atlantic SD-2 7005 March 1981 #36

Don't Let Go the Coat/You
   Warner Bros. WBS 49743 March 1981 #84

HOOLIGANS (double LP)	I Can't Explain/I Can See for Miles/Pinball Wizard/Let's See Action/Summertime Blues (from *Live at Leeds*)/The Relay/Baba O'Riley/Behind Blue Eyes/Bargain/Song Is Over/Join Together/Squeeze Box/Slip Kid/The Real Me/5.15/Drowned/Had Enough/Sister Disco/Who Are You MCA2 12001 11 September 1981 #52
IT'S HARD (LP)	Warner Bros. WB 23731-1/2 4 September 1982 #8

Singles	Athena/It's Your Turn
	    Warner Bros. WBS 7-29905 4 September 1982 #28
	Eminence Front/One at a Time
	    Warner Bros. WB7-29814 December 1982 #68
	It's Hard/Dangerous
	    Warner Bros. WB7-29731 D 1983
	You Better You Bet/Don't Let Go the Coat
	    Warner Bros. GWB 0412 1983

WHO'S GREAT-EST HITS (LP)	Substitute/The Seeker/Magic Bus/My Generation/Pinball Wizard/Happy Jack/Won't Get Fooled Again/My Wife/Squeeze Box/The Relay/5.15/Love Reign O'er Me/Who Are You MCA 5408 March 1983 #94
WHO'S LAST (LP)	MCA2 8018 November 1984 #81
WHO'S MISS-ING (LP)	Leaving Here/Lubie/Shout And Shimmy/Anytime You Want Me/Barbara Ann/I'm a Boy (alt. version)/Mary Anne with the Shaky Hand(s) (electric version)/Heaven and Hell/Here for More/I Don't Even Know Myself/When I Was a Boy/Bargain (live from San Francisco, December 12, 1971) MCA-5641 30 November 1985 #116
TWO'S MISS-ING (LP)	Bald Headed Woman/Under My Thumb/My Wife (live from San Francisco, December 12, 1971)/I'm a Man/Dogs/Dogs Part 2/Circles/The Last Time/Water/Daddy Rolling Stone/Heat Wave (alt. version)/Going Down (live)/Motoring/Waspman MCA-5712 11 April 19 87

THE WHO

Polydor 835 389-1/2 18 March 1988 #10

WHO'S BET-
TER/WHO'S
BEST (LP)

MCA Vintage Gold, 3″ CD Series, CAD-37303 September 1988

WONT GET
FOOLED AGAIN
(EP)

Who track: My Generation
   Rock and Roll L1989 17 January 1990

THE ROCK AND
ROLL HALL OF
FAME (CD/cas-
sette)

MCA3-19501 24 March 1990 #180

JOIN TOGETH-
ER (LIVE
BOXED SET)

(Various artists including The Who)
Who tracks: Substitute/Summertime Blues/Pictures of Lily/A Quick
One/Happy Jack/My Generation
   Rhino R 70596 9 October 1992

THE MON-
TEREY INTER-
NATIONAL POP
FESTIVAL (CD
BOXED SET)

Original sound recording digitally remastered and issued on one CD
   MCAD 10801 March 1993

TOMMY (CD)

MCAD4/C4-11020 June 94

THE WHO:
THIRTY YEARS
OF MAXIMUM
R&B (BOXED
SET)

(Remastered, remixed reissue with bonus tracks and new sequencing)
   MCAC/D-11215 12 February 1995

LIVE AT LEEDS
(CD/cassette)

A QUICK ONE (CD/cassette)	*(Remastered, remixed CD/cassette reissue with bonus tracks)* MCAC/D-11267 June 1995
THE WHO SELL OUT (CD/Cassette)	*(Remastered, remixed CD/cassette reissue with bonus tracks)* MCAC/D-11268 June 1995
WHO'S NEXT (CD/cassette)	*(Remastered, remixed CD/cassette reissue with bonus tracks)* MCAC/D-11269 October 1995
TOMMY (CD/cassette)	*(Remastered, remixed reissue)* MCAC/D-11417 March 1996
QUADROPHE-NIA (double CD/cassette)	*(Remastered, remixed reissue)* MCAC/D2-11463 June 1996
WHO ARE YOU (CD/cassette)	*(Remastered, remixed reissue)* MCAC/D-11492 November 1996)
THE WHO BY NUMBERS (CD/cassette)	*(Remastered, remixed reissue)* MCAC/D-11493 November 1996

Notes:

Mobile Fidelity Sound Labs has issued an Original Master Recordings on CD of *Tommy* (including the 1973 version of "Eyesight to the Blind"), *Quadrophenia* and *Who Are You* (including a different version of "Guitar and Pen").

All of The Who's original albums were reissued in the U.S. on compact disc by MCA during the late eighties with identical track listings to the earlier vinyl releases. Eight of these have now been superseded by the remastered editions on CD and cassette, released in 1995 and 1996. The remainder of The Who's back catalog will receive similar treatment in the near future.

THE WHO

BIBLIOGRAPHY

Annan, Noel. *Our Age*. London: Weidenfeld & Nicolson, 1990.

Barnes, Richard. *Maximum R&B*. London: Eel Pie, 1982.

Booker, Christopher. *The Neophiliacs*. London: Collins, 1969.

Briggs, Asa. *A Social History of England*. London: Weidenfeld & Nicolson, 1984.

Butler, Dougal. *Moon the Loon*. London: Star, 1981.

Charlesworth, Chris. *Complete Guide to the Music of The Who*. London: Omnibus, 1995.

Cohn, Nik. *Pop from the Beginning*. London: Weidenfeld & Nicolson, 1969.

Fletcher, Tony. *Dear Boy: The Life of Keith Moon*. London: Omnibus, 1998.

Garner, Ken. *In Session Tonight—Radio 1*. London: BBC Publications, 1993.

Greenfield, Robert. *Stones Touring Party*. London: Michael Joseph, 1974.

Lambert, Constant. *Music Ho!*. London: Hogarth Press, 1934.

Lewisohn, Mark. *Complete Beatles Recording Sessions*. London: Hamlyn, 1988.

Marsh, Dave. *Before I Get Old*. London: Plexus, 1983.

Melly, George. *Revolt into Style*. London: Allen Lane, 1970.

Motion, Andrew. *The Lamberts—George, Constant & Kit*. London: Chatto & Windus, 1986.

Napier-Bell, Simon. *You Don't Have to Say You Love Me*. London: New English Library, 1982.

Powell, Anthony. *Casanova's Chinese Restaurant*. London: Heinemann, 1960.

Solomon, Pizzy & Watson. *Record Hits: The British top 50 Charts, 1952–1977*. London: Omnibus, 1979.

Townshend, Pete (Notes in). *The Decade of the Who: "My Generation."* London: Wise Publications, 1984.

Tremlett, George. *The Who*. London: Futura, 1975

Williams, Paul. *Rock and Roll: The 100 Best Singles*. New York: Carrol & Graf, 1993.

Bristol Evening Post

Beat Instrumental

Melody Maker

New Musical Express

Record Mirror

Rolling Stone

Sound International

Trouser Press

Magazines and Newspapers

NOTES

Introduction

1 All Pete Townshend quotes are from "Townshend's Revenge," *Rolling Stone* 97, Dec. 9, 1971. See Reviews.

"I Can't Explain"

1 Some sources incorrectly list IBC studios.

2 All the major Who biographies and rock reference books list Keith Moon's date of birth as August 23, 1947. Now, in his excellent new biography, *Dear Boy: The Life of Keith Moon*, Tony Fletcher has uncovered one more of Keith's many self-inventions. The actual date of birth is August 23, 1946. Tony's discovery should be born in mind throughout this book, wherever Keith's age is mentioned.

"Anyway, Anyhow, Anywhere"

1 "Anyway, Anyhow, Anywhere" was recorded at IBC Studios in Portland Place. Situated opposite the Chinese Embassy, *genuine* morse-code sometimes appeared on tape, as diplomatic signals traffic was (inadvertently) intercepted by the recording equipment.

2 Polydor 527 758-2; in the U.S. UNI/MCA 7674 11267 4.

3 Found on *Scoop* and *Another Scoop,* Townshend's own selection of his demos.

"My Generation"

1 In the event that you're trying to play along, it's worth noting that Pete is conflating the two versions. The single goes from G / A / B flat / C where it ends; it's the *live* version, transposed to A-running A / B / C / D-which ends in D.

2 This version can be found on the *Maximum BBC* bootleg, though the session is wrongly dated as April 22.

3 The Who's BBC recordings are *essential* listening. Currently found only on the *Maximum BBC* bootleg, there are very strong reasons to suppose that an official release is not too far off. Chris Charlesworth's notes in the *30 Years of Maximum R&B* box-set, speak of BBC intransigence; without naming names, there is certainly an *individual* at BBC transcriptions who merits such a description, but there are also people at the BBC who've been making annual attempts to get the material released, for over a decade. We'll see. (The Led Zeppelin sessions did finally appear on Atlantic.)

"A Legal Matter"

1 A friend whose band was signed to Talmy during this era told me, "I'd guess Talmy would have been receiving about 7.5 percent from Decca."
2 The *My Generation* LP version, with its powerful guitar solo, was edited for the U.S. and U.K. singles; *MBBB* uses the shorter version.

"I'm a Boy"

1 American readers can just substitute a deep catcher to get the picture.

"Happy Jack"

1 "I Can't Explain," "Anyway, Anyhow, Anywhere," "My Generation," "The Kids Are Alright," and "I'm a Boy"; "Substitute" was released on Atlantic, not Decca.

"I Can See for Miles"

1 If Pete still holds to his 1971 opinion expressed above, he's had many opportunities to issue a mono version—but it's never happened.
2 C.f. The Stones' "Have You Seen Your Mother?", which sounds like something unpleasant happening in a dustbin, though Keith swears the master tape was fine.

"Magic Bus"

1 Bo Diddley's most successful chart single was "Say Man," a jive-talking novelty record, in which Bo and a pal dispute whose friends and relatives are the ugliest. *The Goon Show* was an English radio comedy show from the 1950s, perhaps most easily thought of as a forerunner to Monty Python.
2 There's a lovely, early '80s film clip of Bo Diddley rehearsing somewhere for a charity show with an English rock star rhythm section. Every time the drummer starts up, Bo stops and tells him he's playing too much. The drummer cannot resist the urge to embellish—supplying technique when feeling is required—but the groove

lies in the opposite direction. When it's played right, it's the simplest, most natural thing in the world—like honey dripping off one's fingers, to paraphrase Iggy Pop.

3 A typical setlist, from a February '68 show in San José, runs "Substitute," "Pictures of Lily," "Summertime Blues," "Tattoo," "Relax," "My Way," "Happy Jack," "I'm a Boy," "A Quick One While He's Away," "Boris the Spider," "Shakin' All Over," "My Generation."

GENERAL INDEX

management philosophy of,
138–39
The Observer article on,
158–66
as producer, 35, 151,
155–56
quits as Who producer, 138,
143, 145
relationship with
Townshend, 33–36, 66,
71, 76, 106, 108, 154
role in *Tommy* project,
128–29
takes over management of
The High Numbers, 7
talents of, 108
Lane, Ronnie (Plonk), 56
Leary, Timothy, 142
Led Zeppelin, xviii, 145
Lennon, John, 152
feedback and, 23, 24
interests of, 55
as songwriter, 83, 86
Lewis, Sir Edward, 164, 166
Lewisohn, Mark, 24
Lifehouse (project), 143, 145
Lindsay-Hogg, Michael, 11
Locke, Patricia, 164
Loss, Joe, 13
LSD, 131
Lulu, 24, 52
Lynx Club (Borehamwood), 13

M ────────────────

Macpherson, Andy, 149
Malcolm Rose Agency, 13
Malo, Ron, 110
Manne, Shelly, 87
Mansfield, Mike, 11
Marcus, Greil, xx
Marine Offences Broadcasting Act,
xvi
Marquee Club (Soho), 7, 12, 14,
160, 161
Marriott, Stevie, 56
Marsh, Dave, 41, 62, 89, 148

Marshall, Jim, 22
Martha and The Vandellas, 96
Martin, George, 8
Mathew, Brian, 39
Max, Peter, 157
Mayer, Roger, 9
McCartney, Paul, 165
interests of, 55
as songwriter, 85
McGowan, Cathy, 52
McGowan, Frankie, 52
McGuinn, Roger, 9–10
McLaren, Malcolm, 54
McManus, Ross, 13
Meaden, Pete, 2, 6–7, 116, 151
Melly, George, 52–53
Melody Maker (magazine)
article on Who/Talmy legal
"Blind Date" feature, 17–18,
41, 44, 56–57, 154
dispute, 58
editorial policies of, 56
"Pop Think-In" feature, 55
review of "A Legal Matter,"
54–55
review of "Pictures of Lily,"
103
Townshend interview, 46
on Who breakup, 28
Merseybeat, 1
Milligan, Spike, 52
Mingus, Charles, 120
Miracles, The, 82, 120
Miss Pamela, 141
Moby Grape, 125
"Mod" style, 6–7, 13, 56, 124, 151,
163
Monkees, The, 85
Monterey Pop (film), 40
Monterey Pop Festival, 40, 110
Montgomery, Wes, 25, 120
Moody Blues, The, 1
Moon, Keith, 16, 50, 104
age of, 3, 197
appearance of, 4
beaten by Daltrey, 27

rock tours, 138, 139, 145
survival tactics in, 42, 44
Pridden, Bobby, 82–83
Private Eye (magazine), 54
Proby, P. J., 24
Purcell, Henry, 76
Pye Studios, 3

Q

Quads (planned Who opera), 70
Quicksilver Messenger Service, The, 125

R

radio. *See* pirate radio; *specific stations and programs*
Radio Atlanta, 116
Radio Caroline, 63, 116
Radio London, xvii, 63, 117, 161
Radio Luxembourg, 78, 115, 161
Radio Sutch, 116
Railway Tavern
(Harrow/Wealdstone), 4, 6, 158
Reaction label, 42, 57, 58, 61–62, 98, 100
Ready, Steady, Go! (TV show), 5, 11–12, 14, 17, 29, 57, 161, 163
record industry, 60–62, 98, 100
American *vs.* English, xiv–xv
release schedules, 83
Record Mirror (newspaper)
feature article on The Who, 162
recording studios, 110
Reed, Jimmy, 78, 120
Reeves, Jim, 1
reggae, 48
Reid, Jamie, 54
rhythm and blues, 11, 26, 86, 120.
See also blues
Rich, Buddy, 87
Richards, Keith, 26–27, 71, 129
bass playing of, 93
drug use of, 18, 130
guitar playing of, 77, 88, 127, 132

on importance of singles, xiv
prison sentence of, 93
showmanship of, 47
singing of, 77
as songwriter, 85, 112, 120
Richmond Organization, 165
RKO Theater (New York), 82
Robinson, Smokey, 44, 82
Roe, Tommy, 38
Rolling Stone (magazine), xx, 90
Townshend interview, 105
Townshend review of *Meaty, Beaty, Big & Bouncy,* xiv, 50–57
Townshend review of "Pictures of Lily," 101
Rolling Stones, The, 1, 2, 11, 83, 93, 127, 139
age of, 3
albums of, xv, xvii
American reception of, xviii
country and western influences on, 77
drug use of, 130
fallow period of, 129–30
image of, xvi, 123, 146
Jones memorial tribute concert, 124
leadership struggle of, 26–28
relationship with The Who, 44, 46, 47
U.S. recording sessions of, 110
working methods of, 132
Rolling Stones Rock 'n' Roll Circus, The (video), 127
Rosen, Steve, 10, 132, 141
Royal Air Force bands, 88–89
Rudge, Peter, 139, 145
Russell Harty Show, The (TV show), 138
Ryder, Mitch, 82

appearance of, 4
aspirations of, 13
avoidance of minor keys, 64, 102, 114, 132
banjo playing of, 10
bass playing of, 93
beliefs of, xvi–xvii
blues influences on, 120
cars of, 95
classical music influences on, 66, 76
on Cohn, 128
creative projects of, 147
on Daltrey, 28
Decade of The Who, The, 48
drug use of, 7, 27, 29, 46, 54, 130–31
on drug use, 7
equipment destruction of, 24–25, 82–83, 160
family background of, 88–89
on feedback, 22–23
flat of, 53
on Gold Star studios, 110
guitar playing of, xvii, 9–11, 19–25, 47, 64–65, 74–75, 83, 86–87, 88, 92, 102, 112–13, 120–21, 133–34, 141–42, 159, 160
on guitar techniques, 141–42
hearing loss of, 41
home setups of, 34–35, 44, 53, 153
on "I Can See for Miles," 110
on "I Can't Explain," 3, 8
on importance of singles, xiv
interests of, 55
interviews with, 18, 44, 46, 53–54, 55, 70–71, 90, 105, 137

on Lambert, 33
on legal dispute with Talmy, 58
on *Magic Bus,* xx
musical training of, 89, 92
on "My Generation," 34–35, 36, 38
on Parker, 25
personality of, 147
photos of, 57
on "Pictures of Lily," 101, 105
on "Pinball Wizard," 132
as producer on "Substitute," 45, 62
relationship with Lambert, 33–36, 71, 106, 108
review of *Meaty, Beaty, Big & Bouncy,* xiv, 150–57
Rolling Stones' influence on, 46–47
on the Scene Club, 116
showmanship of, 47, 83, 145
singing of, 28, 63–64, 74, 121
on singles, 122–23
on smashing of guitar, 24–25
as songwriter, xv–xvi, 2, 15, 26, 30–32, 34–36, 38, 44–46, 55–56, 65–66, 68, 70–71, 76, 83, 85, 92, 102–3, 106, 113–15, 118, 120–21, 122–23, 128–29, 131–34, 140, 141–42, 143, 151–57, 161, 162. *See also specific songs*
on "Substitute," 48
style trademarks of, 19, 66–67, 113–14, 132
on Talmy, 150–51
on *Tommy,* xviii
Track Records, xix, 98, 103

SONG AND ALBUM INDEX

Names in parentheses refer to performers or songwriters.